D0162166

The Transformation of American Capitalism

From Competitive Market
Structures to Centralized
Private Sector Planning

John R. Munkirs

M.E.Sharpe INC.
Armonk, New York
London

Available in the United Kingdom and Europe from M. E. Sharpe
Publishers, 3 Henrietta Street, London WC2E 8LU.

Library of Congress Cataloging in Publication Data

Munkirs, John R.
    The transformation of American capitalism.

    1. United States—Economic conditions. 2. Corporations—United
States. 3. Central planning—United States. 4. United States—Economic
policy. I. Title. II. Title: Centralized private sector planning.
HC103.M77   1985   338.973   83-27093
ISBN 0-87332-247-9
ISBN 0-87332-270-3 (pbk.)

Printed in the United States of America

Contents

Acknowledgments

In writing this book, I became acutely conscious of my intellectual debt to many scholars both past and present. Adherence to tradition dictates that one graciously acknowledge these debts while simultaneously granting absolution to all, all but oneself of course, for any of the book's shortcomings. I am quite pleased to do the former, since I strongly believe that ideas, as well as the books that flow from them, are primarily evolutionary and social in character, and not a priori individual creations; however, permit me to demur slightly from granting my debtees complete absolution. Although scores of individuals are cited in the body of the text for their contribution to a particular idea or concept, special acknowledgments are in order to several groups to whom I owe an extraordinarily large intellectual debt.

First, my own scholarly development was rooted in America's institutionalist tradition. The founders of the institutional school of economics were Professors Thorstein Bunde Veblen, John R. Commons, and Wesley Claire Mitchell. Veblen provided the school with both its philosophical frame of reference and its theoretical approach; Wesley Claire Mitchell (one of Veblen's students), who founded the National Bureau of Economic Research in 1920 and remained its director until 1945, provided the school with a tool kit of descriptive statistical techniques while constantly nourishing the school's empirical bent; John R. Commons, ever the reformer and public practitioner, stressed and nourished the school's activist stand toward public policy, and in concert with many of his students actually drafted much of the nation's original labor legislation.

All three of these intellectual giants were committed to studying the economy as an evolutionary process and at any particular point in time to base their actions and public policy prescriptions on the economy as it existed in reality. In short, they eschewed with great vigor *all* ideological prattlings, whether from the left or the right wing of the political spectrum. To these three my debt is immeasurable. In addition, acknowledgment is due the institutional economists under whom I studied directly—Joe Brown, John Hodges, and Robert Brazelton at the University of Missouri-Kansas City, and Jim Reese and Nelson Peach at the University of Oklahoma.

During the actual writing of the manuscript, many parts of the analyses were tested on numerous graduate and undergraduate students in my Industrial Organization courses at Sangamon State University. Concepts were enthusiastically and at times heatedly debated, clarified, and refined. The final product benefited greatly from these interactions. Of particular note are: Marcia M. Houk, Jean Rosales, Robert D. Brock, Jim Stark, M. Fred Ellis, Larry Chandler, Charles A. Burbridge, and Doug Kamholz. Special thanks must also be given to Professors Alfred Eichner—Rutgers University, Bill Feipel—Illinois Central College, Jim Sturgeon—University of Missouri-Kansas City, and Ed Stuart—Illinois State University, who read the entire manuscript and offered many helpful suggestions. Michael Ayers, my colleague at Sangamon State University for the past decade, was a constant critic, an energetic and wise supporter, and my intellectual companion in developing the Centralized Private Sector Planning theory.

And, as many authors would undoubtedly concur, those who provide logistical support—typing, phoning, editing, copying, proofing, adding columns of data, etc.—while performing vital technical necessities, are also in many ways an emotional crutch whose sustenance often turns utter frustration and exasperation into—we'll probably get done after all. Pat Burtle-McCredie, Nancy Ayers, Ruth Ann Ayers, and Diane M. Munkirs literally performed miracles in the book's preparation. Their common sense, intelligence, technical competence, and enthusiastic encouragement are appreciated beyond my ability to describe.

Penultimately, I wish to acknowledge the staff at M. E. Sharpe, Inc., especially Arnold Tovell and Ann Kearns, who evidently believe, as I do, that the public not only deserves to know, but will invest both time and money to master what is admittedly a difficult subject—the structural and functional characteristics of the U.S. economy, that is, how the economy actually works.

I dedicate this book to three individuals—my wife, Diane, and my two daughters, Desiree and Dimitri.

The Transformation
of American
Capitalism

Chapter One

Introduction

. . . a common belief, a linking idea, to which men may devote themselves, and by which they can co-operate together in a universal enterprise.[1]

H. G. Wells, 1920

One of the great lessons learned from history is that a social system is the most creative and dynamic—and performs best—when its members believe in themselves, believe in what they are doing, and have confidence in the ability of their institutions to perform efficiently and ethically. Events seem to indicate that many Americans are precariously close to losing confidence in themselves and in what they are doing, and that many have already lost confidence in the ability of our economic and political institutions to perform in an efficient and ethical manner. Under these circumstances, cooperation between disparate self-interest groups for the common good of all is quite often unattainable. Most would agree, for example, that controlling stagflation (high levels of unemployment and inflation occurring simultaneously) would benefit all Americans. However, our business elite place the blame for stagflation on labor; labor blames business; and, when they are not busy blaming each other, they join in blaming big government.

The simple fact is, though, that, given the dichotomy between our current beliefs and ideas about economics and power, and the realities of economics and power in our society, there is no viable solution to stagflation. Existing economic theories (neoclassical, Keynesian, Marxist, or the so-called and currently fashionable supply-side economics) concerning the causes of inflation, unemployment, pollution, a carcinogenic food supply, maldistribution of income, inadequate health care for the poor, retarded economic growth, and so on are woefully devoid of adequate insight or understanding of the economy's dominant structural and functional characteristics. Of course, theories based on false assumptions, however rational and/or logical, cannot provide a foundation for effective and responsible private or public policy decision making. Let there be no mistake. Orthodox economic theories and beliefs, whether of the left or of the right, have become part of the problem, rather than helping organize our thoughts and discussions so as to provide realistic and workable solutions to our problems.

An alternative description and explanation of the economy's dominant structural and functional characteristics is set forth in this study. The format of the analysis is as follows. In Chapter 2, the major evolutionary changes that have taken place in the American economy since the 1860s are examined. The *interrelationships* between and among (a) the types of structural and functional changes that have occurred in the economy, (b) the ensuing types of adaptations and modifications that have occurred in our economic ideas and theories, and (c) the ensuing adaptations and modifications that have occurred in governmental policies are illustrated in this chapter. In addition, the ever-increasing dichotomy between economic theory and economic reality—a dichotomy that has developed despite attempts to modify economic theory in light of changing economic conditions—is highlighted.

In Chapters 3, 4, and 5 an alternative explanation (Centralized Private Sector Planning) of the economy's dominant structural and functional characteristics is developed. In Chapter 3 the various planning instruments (formal and/or legally binding planning instruments and informal and/or influential planning instruments) are analyzed. Attention is focused on how these planning instruments are used (a) to coordinate and organize the planning efforts between and among firms within a specific industry (Intraindustry Planning), and (b) to coordinate and organize the planning efforts among firms in several different industries (Interindustry Planning). In Chapter 4, using the concepts developed in Chapter 3, the **Central Planning Core (CPC)** is presented. The CPC may be viewed as the hub or the nerve center wherein many of the country's most important economic and political public policy goals originate. In Chapter 5, the concepts and ideas developed in Chapters 3 and 4 are brought together in order to set forth the Centralized Private Sector Planning theory in its entirety. A descriptive tableau (Central Planning Tableau) consisting of 138 corporations provides the statistical base for the analysis. These corporations account for 11,043,818 employees; $992 billion in sales; and $1.1 trillion in assets as of 1 January 1978. The corporations are segregated into 32 industries within five major market areas—financial, industrial, transportation, public utility, and retailing. The tableau conclusively demonstrates:

- how firms in a given industry, from both a structural and functional perspective, are technologically, financially, and administratively interdependent;
- how each of the several industries, from both a structural and a functional perspective, are technologically, financially, and administratively interdependent; and,
- how over the years a series of planning instruments have *evolved* that both allow and indeed, to some extent, necessitate regional, national and, international Centralized Private Sector Planning.

Currently, in the typical economics textbook, four types of market structures are usually examined—competitive market structures, monopolistically competitive market structures, oligopolistically competitive market structures, and pure monopoly. While these economic theories are still useful in describing and explaining the structure, conduct, and performance of some markets, the position advanced in Chapters 3, 4, and 5 is that the theory of Centralized Private Sector Planning is a more accurate description and explanation of extant economic institutions. In other words, these four traditional economic theories are *special* cases, with the *general* case being centralized planning. The centralized planning proposition is a formidable one, namely, that the cumulative effect of changes in our economic institutions over the last half century or so has created a fundamentally different type of economic system. Indeed, it may well be that upon examining the Central Planning Tableau many will conclude as I have concluded, that the term *capitalism* itself is no longer an appropriate label for describing the American economy.

Careful attention is given to illustrating the differences between Centralized *Public* Sector Planning, as practiced in the Soviet Union and Eastern bloc countries; Decentralized *Public* Sector Planning, as practiced in Japan and many Western European countries; Decentralized *Private* Sector Planning, as set forth in Galbraith's planning technocracy thesis; and the theory of Centralized Private Sector Planning. It is clearly noted that the Soviet system of Centralized *Public* Sector Planning and the American system of Centralized *Private* Sector Planning are *not* in any way similar or, for that matter, converging.

Suggestions to the contrary display a remarkable ignorance of how the two systems function, if not outright addleheadedness or duplicity.

A few brief comments concerning the concept of the anational corporation are presented in Chapter 6. In one sense the anational corporation may be viewed as a futuristic concept: no such organization now exists. Many prominent corporate and intellectual elite, however, are seriously suggesting that the anational corporation is fast becoming, and ought to become, an institutional reality. More importantly though, one cannot understand the rationale for many of the actions and policies of our corporate and political leaders unless one views these actions and policies as strategies to facilitate the creation of anational economic institutions. Neither can one appreciate the full extent of the dichotomy that now exists between our professed economic beliefs and economic reality, without some understanding of the anational corporation as an institution in the very process of being created. Specific emphasis is given to—

• the corporate institutions' historical development from international corporations to multinational corporations to transnational corporations to supranational corporations, leading finally to the emergence of anational corporations;

• the relationship between anational corporations and nation states;

• the relationship between anational corporations and less developed countries—often referred to as the North-South problem; and

• the relationship between anational corporations and socialism—often referred to as the East-West ideological conflict.

In the Epilogue, the primary conclusion to be drawn from the study is set forth.

Before the conclusion of these introductory remarks, a few comments concerning the timeliness of the data in the Central Planning Tableau are in order. First, the data are current as of January 1978. The tableau itself is a third-generation mock-up, the first two having been constructed in January 1972 and January 1976. There were no significant differences between the three tableaux from a statistical perspective. This, of course, is to be expected since the *basic structural characteristics* of an industrial economy do not normally undergo rapid change.

Second, all of the data in the tableau are readily available at any university library. In addition, once the tableau's structural characteristics are understood, updating the statistics—while tedious and time-consuming—requires only patience and effort.

Finally, to the extent that change is always occurring, albeit incrementally, the changes taking place in today's economy, for the most part, lend even greater statistical support to the theory of Centralized Private Sector Planning.

Note

1. H. G. Wells, *The Outline of History*, 4 vols. (New York: The Macmillan Company, 1920; reprint ed., New York: The Review of Reviews Company, 1924), p. 753.

Chapter Two

The Evolution of American Capitalism: From Adam Smith to John Kenneth Galbraith

> *. . . the cruellest of our revenue laws, I will venture to affirm, are mild and gentle in comparison to some of those which the clamour of our merchants and manufacturers have extorted from the legislature, for the support of their own absurd and oppressive monopolies. Like the laws of Draco, these laws may be said to be all written in blood.*[1]
>
> Adam Smith, 1776

> *Our thesis is that the idea of a self-adjusting market implied a stark utopia. Such an institution could not exist for any length of time without annihilating the human and natural substance of society; it would have physically destroyed man and transformed his surroundings into a wilderness. Inevitably, society took measures [governmental regulatory reform] to protect itself, but whatever measures it took impaired the self-regulation of the market . . .*[2]
>
> Karl Polanyi, 1944

In the words of one of this century's most influential economists, John Maynard Keynes:

> . . . the ideas of economists and political philosophers, both when they are right and when they are wrong, are more powerful than is commonly understood. Indeed, the world is ruled by little else. Practical men, who believe themselves to be quite exempt from any intellectual influences, are usually the slaves of some defunct economist.[3]

The fundamental economic ideas to which many of our society's business and political leaders—as well as the general public—are currently enslaved were first assembled into a comprehensive economic doctrine some 200 years ago. In 1776 Adam Smith presented the world with its first encyclopedic analysis of a market system economy. Three major themes formed the core of Adam Smith's analysis of capitalism:

• the self-adjusting nature of market forces in a competitive market structure environment;

• the self-defeating nature of government intervention (laissez-faire), given the existence of competitive market forces; and

• the social, political, and economic evils of monopoly market power.

Adam Smith—competition versus monopoly

From Smith's perspective, if a market

> . . . were divided among twenty, their competition would be just so much the greater, and the chance of their combining together, in order to raise the price, just so much the less. Their competition . . . can never hurt . . . the consumer . . . on the contrary, it must tend to make the retailers both sell cheaper and buy dearer, than if the whole trade was monopolized by one or two persons.[4]

Continuing in this vein, Smith also asserted:

> The interest of the dealers, however, in any particular branch of trade or manufacture, is always in some respect different from, and even opposite to, that of the public. To widen the market and to narrow the competition, is always in the interest of the dealers. To widen the market may frequently be agreeable enough to the interest of the public; but to narrow the competition must always be against it, and can serve only to enable the dealers, by raising their profits above what they naturally would be, to levy, for their own benefit, an absurd tax upon the rest of their fellow citizens.[5]

And Smith left absolutely no doubt about his beliefs concerning the natural propensity of business leaders, if possible, to conspire against the common good concerning both prices and wages. Concerning prices:

> . . . people of the same trade seldom meet together, even for merriment and diversion, but the conversation ends in a conspiracy against the public, or in some contrivance to raise prices.[6]

And, concerning wages:

We rarely hear, it has been said, of the combination of masters, though, frequently of those of workmen. But whoever imagines, upon this account, that masters rarely combine, is as ignorant of the world as of the subject. Masters are always and everywhere in a sort of tacit, but constant and uniform combination, not to raise the wages of labor. . . . To violate this combination is everywhere a most unpopular action, and a sort of reproach to a master among his neighbors and equals.[7]

In terms of technical economic analysis, Smith set forth four basic arguments against allowing firms with monopoly market power to exist: (1) they tend to reduce output below that which would occur under competitive market structure circumstances; (2) they tend to sell their products much above their natural price, reaping abnormally high monopoly profits; (3) they tend to freeze out potential competitors, thus denying some citizens freedom of choice concerning occupation; and (4) they tend to be technically inefficient and to not practice good management:

Monopoly, besides, is a great enemy to good management, which can never be universally established but in consequence of that free and universal competition which forces everybody to have recourse to it for the sake of self-defense.[8]

Smith continues:

By a perpetual monopoly, all the other subjects of the state are taxed very absurdly in two different ways: first, by the high price of goods, which, in the case of free trade, they could buy much cheaper; and, secondly, by their total exclusion from a branch of business, which it might be both convenient and profitable for many of them to carry on.[9]

And, finally:

The monopolists, by keeping the market constantly under-stocked, by never fully supplying the effectual demand, sell their commodities much above the natural price, and raise their emoluments, whether they consist in wages or profit, greatly above their natural rate.

The price of monopoly is upon every occasion the highest which can be got. The natural price, or the price of free competition, on the contrary, is the lowest which can be taken, not upon every occasion indeed, but for any considerable time together. The one is upon every occasion the highest which can be squeezed out of the buyers, or which, it is supposed, they will consent to give; the other is the lowest which the sellers can commonly afford to take, and at the same time continue in their business.[10]

Notwithstanding these rather severe criticisms, however, it is *extremely important* to note that the integrity and honesty of those individuals who operated in markets that possessed considerable market power were never called into question by Smith. In criticizing one of the greatest monopolies of all time, Smith declared:

I mean not, however, by anything which I have here said, to throw any odious imputation upon the general character of the servants of the East India Company, and much less upon that of any particular persons. It is the system . . . the situation in which they are placed, that I mean to censure; not the character of those who have acted in it. They have acted as their situation naturally directed, and they who have clamoured the loudest against them would, probably, not have acted better themselves.[11]

In essence, market power, in Smith's view, was not an individual, personal, or behavioral problem; market power was a structural problem. Thus, criticizing the individual monopolists from Smith's perspective, besides being unfair, would simply not help in solving the economic problems associated with market power.* Since Smith's *Wealth of Nations*, most economists have assumed a linear cause and effect relationship between market structure (the absolute size and number of firms in a given industry) and economic performance. At one end of the spectrum one finds pure competition or a competitive market structure (many, many firms), wherein each individual firm is subject to the impersonal market forces of supply and demand, while at the opposite end lies pure monopoly (one firm), wherein the monopolist possesses excessive market power. In Smith's world of competitive capitalism, market power increases as the number of competitors declines and diminishes as the number of competitors increases.

---

*Absolving those individuals who exercise monopoly market power from any personal responsibility for their economic actions may be properly designated as the *people neutrality concept.*

The genesis of monopoly capitalism

The industrial trusts

Until the latter half of the nineteeenth century, the great bulk of the nation's economic activity was conducted in small scale enterprises owned by a single proprietor or by several individuals joined together through a partnership. During a forty-year period from around 1865 to 1905, however, numerous individual organizations were combined or consolidated into a single *trust* or a *holding company*. These two new business organizational devices were simply legal mechanisms created to eliminate competitive market structures.* As remarked above, Adam Smith contended that it would always be in the interest of producers "to narrow the competition." John Moody, writing in 1904, noted in his book *The Truth About the Trusts* that of the 92 important trusts " . . . 78 control 50 percent or more of their product, and 57 control 60 percent or more. Twenty-six control 80 percent or over."[12]

From an evolutionary point of view, the business community, in attempting to narrow the competition, began by using the partnership form of enterprise, which eventually gave way to the trust, which in turn gave way to the holding company. For example, the Standard Oil Alliance was created in 1867 as a partnership known as Rockefeller, Andrews, and Flager. This partnership was succeeded by the Standard Oil Trust in 1882, which was then succeeded by the Standard Oil Company of New Jersey (a holding company) in 1899. During this thirty-two year period (1867–1899), John D. Rockefeller, Sr., and his associates had combined approximately 400 individual organizations, culminating in Standard's control of around 84 percent of the petroleum market. In commenting on Standard's triumphs, Rockefeller, Sr., adopted a natural law disputation, stating that:

> The growth of the large business is merely a survival of the fittest. . . . The American beauty rose can be produced in the splendor and fragrance which bring cheer to its beholder only by sacrificing the early buds which grow up around it. This is not an evil tendency in

---

*To create a trust the stockholders of several individual companies assigned their stock, without revocation, to a single board of trustees. The trustees, by controlling the majority of the voting stocks of each individual company, could elect the directors of the various companies participating in the trust. Holding companies operated in much the same maner, except that a holding company would *own* outright all the stock of the various operating companies instead of being a *trustee* for their stock.

business. It is merely the working out of a law of nature and a law of God.[13]

John Moody was himself a great admirer of the trust form of business enterprise, and, as did Mr. Rockefeller, he based his beliefs squarely on a natural law philosophy:

> The modern Trust is the natural outcome of evolution of societary conditions and ethical standards which are recognized and established among men today as being necessary elements in the development of civilization. . . . The natural law which engenders monopoly is fundamental.[14]

Table 1 lists the seven holding companies which John Moody labeled "The Greater Industrial Trusts." This table also includes: (1) the cumulative number of organizations combined (over a period of several decades), culminating in the creating of the Trusts, (2) the approximate percentage of the various markets controlled, and (3) the dominant families involved in each of the several industries.* In these seven important industries (petroleum, steel, smelting, copper, sugar, tobacco, and ocean shipping), competitive market structures had been virtually eliminated.†

*By 1890 the dominant legal form of business enterprise had shifted from the trust type of arrangement to that of the holding company. John Moody in his book *The Truth About the Trusts* used the terms (trust/holding company) synonymously; as already noted in regard to economic concentration, there was little difference between the two arrangements. Charles R. Van Hise in his book *Concentration and Control* commented that ". . . the Standard Oil Company of New Jersey, a holding concern, was a direct successor to the trust, the only difference being that the holding company owned all of the stock of the subsidiary companies, instead of being a trustee for this stock; each alike controlled the business of the subsidiary companies, and received and distributed all dividends. The officers of the constituent companies in one case had their orders from the trustees, in the other from the officers of the corporation composed of substantially the same men." Eliot Jones in his book *The Trust Problem in the United States*, published in 1926, commenting on Standard Oil's transfer from a trust to a holding company arrangement said that "the trust had simply hung out a new sign." Most of these holding companies were incorporated in the State of New Jersey. The State of New Jersey changed its incorporation laws in the late 1880s in such a manner as to allow one corporation to *own* another corporation. Since the trusts were coming under increasing criticism at this time, many enterprises simply changed their names and adopted the holding company format.

†For an excellent and exhaustive study of the interrelationships between and among the technological changes, business organizational structures, and business administrative strategies that preceded and succeeded the trust movement in America, see Alfred Chandler's *The Visible Hand* (Cambridge, Massachusetts, Harvard University Press, 1977).

Table 1

Selected Industrial Trusts and/or Holding Companies Formed at the Turn of the Century

Trust/holding company	Approximate percentage of domestic production accounted for	Approximate number of organizations combined*	Dominant family(ies)
1. *Petroleum*			
Standard Oil Alliance, 1867 Standard Oil Trust, 1882 Standard Oil Company of New Jersey, 1899 (New Jersey)	84	400	Rockefeller
2. *Smelting*			
American Smelting & Refining, 1899 (New Jersey)	85	121	Guggenheim Rockefeller
3. *Sugar*			
American Sugar Refining Company, 1891 (New Jersey)	85	55	Havemeyer
4. *Copper*			
Amalgamated Copper Company, 1901 (New Jersey)	35	11	Rockefeller Stillman
5. *Tobacco*			
Consolidated Tobacco Company, 1901 (New Jersey)	90	150	Ryan, Duke, Rockefeller
6. *Steel*			
United States Steel Corporation 1901 (New Jersey)	70	785	Morgan Rockefeller
7. *Atlantic shipping*			
International Mercantile Marine Company, 1902 (New Jersey)	40	6	Morgan

Source: John Moody, *The Truth About the Trusts*, reprinted ed. (New York: Greenwood Press Publisher, 1968), pp. 453, 476. First published by John Moody, 1904.

Note: See footnote on page 13 for a discussion of the relationship between trusts and holding companies.

*J. P. Morgan created the United States Steel Corporation in 1901 after initially purchasing the Carnegie Company of New Jersey for $300,000,000 from Andrew Carnegie. This particular consolidation involved only 11 companies in addition to the Carnegie Company, the Federal Steel Company, the American Steel and Wire Company, the National Tube Company, the National Steel Company, the American Tin and Plate Company, the American Steel Hoop Company, the American Sheet Steel Company, the American Bridge Company, the Lake Superior Consolidated Iron Mines, the Bessemer Steamship Company, and the Shelby Steel Tube Company. But these 12 companies had themselves been created by combining some 785 companies. Thus, these holding companies were the end result of numerous combinations that had occurred over a period of several decades.

The actual concentration of economic power, however, was much greater than indicated by the monopolistic structure in these industries since a large number of the new commercial devices were dominated or greatly influenced by the same families.* As John Moody pointed out:

> . . . these groups themselves are in many important ways, linked one to the other, and the various interests which control them overlap, as it were, into each other's group or circle. . . . It is both interesting and important to note that these able and influential capitalists who control this Railroad Trust are also the men who dictate the policies of and control the Steel Trust, the Oil Trust, the Copper Trust, the Tobacco Trust . . . and many other enterprises of the same kind, great and small.[16]

Antitrust laws and regulatory commissions

The consolidation movement was making competitive structures a myth in an ever-increasing number of markets. Led by groups such as the Farmers' Alliance and the Grange in the West and the Southwest, and by the Noble Order of the Knights of Labor in the East, a populist-style political movement succeeded in obtaining legislative and regulatory reform. The popular cry of the reformist was simply to: (1) where feasible, create competitive market structures, i.e., break up the trusts; or (2) where competitive markets were not economically feasible, such as in railroad transportation, create regulatory agencies. In Table 2 are

---

*One mechanism used by these "influential capitalists" in forming alliances between the various trusts was to interlock the boards of directors. For instance, John D. Rockefeller was the president of Standard of New Jersey and, along with John D. Rockefeller, Jr., was also a director for U.S. Steel. William Rockefeller was a director for both Standard Oil and Amalgamated Copper, while William G. Rockefeller was also a director for Amalgamated Copper. Thus, two members of the Rockefeller family were on the boards of U.S. Steel, Standard Oil, and Amalgamated Copper. Henry H. Rogers, president of Amalgamated Copper, was also on the board of directors of Standard Oil and U.S. Steel. P. A. B. Widener was a director for International Mercantile Marine, Consolidated Tobacco, and U.S. Steel. Grant B. Schley was a director for both American Smelting and Consolidated Tobacco. Clement A. Griscom was International Mercantile Marine's president and a director for U.S. Steel. George W. Perkins was a director for both International Mercantile Marine and U.S. Steel. Lastly, Robert Bacon served as director for both Amalgamated Copper and U.S. Steel.[15] In summary, the companies mentioned in Table 1 had not only combined some 1,528 organizations into just 7 Brobdingnagian enterprises; they had also effected 20 directorship interlocks among the remaining 7 institutions.

Table 2

The Major Antitrust Laws and Regulatory Commissions of the United States Enacted and/or Created between 1887 and 1920

I. Laws to promote competition*

A. The Sherman Act of 1890 (15 U.S.C. 1-7)
B. The Clayton Act of 1914 (15 U.S.C. 12FF.)
C. The Federal Trade Commission Act of 1914 (15 U.S.C. 41ff.)

II. Regulatory Commissions

Enabling legislation	Commission
The Act to Regulate Commerce of 1887	Interstate Commerce Commission (ICC)
The Food and Drug Act of 1906	Food and Drug Administration FDA
The Federal Trade Commission Act of 1914	Federal Trade Commission (FTC)
The Federal Reserve Act of 1913	Federal Reserve Board (FRB)
The Water Power Act of 1920	Federal Power Commission (FPC)

*This legislation was ostensibly designed primarily to promote competitive market structures and thereby restrain monopolistic behavior.

listed the major pieces of antitrust legislation passed, as well as the regulatory commissions created, at the turn of the century. In short, it appeared on the surface that the intention of Congress was to move the country substantially away from its laissez-faire posture. But, to assume that the passage of antitrust laws or the creation of regulatory agencies indicated a major shift in the government's attitude toward laissez-faire, while undoubtedly logical, is, nonetheless, just as undoubtedly disingenous. For instance, Thurman Arnold (Assistant Attorney General of the United States, in charge of the Anti-Trust Division of the Justice Department during the 1930s) has an insightful chapter in his book *The Folklore of Capitalism* entitled "The Effect of the Anti-Trust Laws in Encouraging Large Combinations":

> . . . the anti-trust laws enabled men to look at a highly organized and centralized industrial organization and still believe that it was composed of individuals engaged in buying and selling in a free market.[17]

He goes on to state:

> . . . the growth of great organizations in America occurred in the face of
> a religion which officially was dedicated to the preservation of the eco-
> nomic independence of individuals. In such a situation it was inevitable
> that a ceremony should be evolved which reconciled current mental pic-
> tures of what men thought society ought to be with reality. The learned
> mythology of the time insisted that American industry was made up of
> small competing concerns which, if they were not individuals, neverthe-
> less approached that ideal. Bigness was regarded as a curse because it led
> to monopoly and interfered with the operation of the laws of supply and
> demand. At the same time specialized techniques made bigness essential
> to producing goods in large enough quantities and at a price low enough so
> that they could be made part of the American standard of living. In order
> to reconcile the ideal with the practical necessity, it became necessary to
> develop a procedure which constantly attacked bigness on rational, legal
> and economic grounds, and at the same time never really interfered with
> combinations. Such pressures gave rise to the anti-trust laws which ap-
> peared to be a complete prohibition of large combinations. The same
> pressures made the enforcement of the anti-trust laws a pure ritual. The
> effect of this statement of the ideal and its lack of actual enforcement was
> to convince reformers either that large combinations did not actually
> exist, or else that if they did exist, they were about to be done away with
> just as soon as right-thinking men were elected to office. Trust busting
> therefore became one of the great moral issues of the day, while at the
> same time great combinations thrived and escaped regulation.[18]

This is a rather remarkable statement coming from a man whose job
it was to enforce the antitrust laws. Arnold defined folklore as those
ideas that were thought to be ''basic principles of law and economics''
but which, in fact, were nothing more than reified dogma. Arnold
argued that populist political agitation against the trusts made it necessary for society's leaders to create the framework wherein a ritual
could, whenever necessary, be performed which: (1) at the highest
level of authority, reaffirmed society's belief in competitive market
structures; (2) provided for the obligatory condemnation of trust and
economic combinations; and (3) in essence, never culminated in the
actual creation of a real world with any semblance to the competitive
market structure norm.

Matthew Josephson (in his book *The Robber Barons*), after examining both the reformist campaign rhetoric of President Theodore

Roosevelt and his actions once in office, essentially reached conclusions quite similar to those of Assistant Attorney General Arnold:

> . . . at last the greatly feared, the awaited and the inevitable happened. The reformist ''Rough Rider'' soon placed himself at the head of the extraordinary mass movement of protest which after 1901 swept the country in a great wave, a wave that had swept it before, like cyclones of Kansas, the grasshopper pests of the Northwest, or the droughts, quite native of the climate, but leaving it afterward fundamentally unchanged and as much like itself as before.[19]

Josephson added:

> The sound and the fury were soon over. . . . In 1904, the largest contributors to the election campaign chest—from which Roosevelt pruriently turned his eyes away—would be Frick, Harriman, Morgan, Stillman, George J. Gould, H. H. Rogers. . . . They had all learned . . . that after furiously advocating reform measures designed to stem radicalism, Roosevelt bestirred himself to conciliate the great industrialists.[20]

Roosevelt's reform efforts did, however, receive two important favorable judgments from the Supreme Court. First, J. P. Morgan—in league with E. H. Harriman and J. J. Hill—created a holding company known as the Northern Securities Company which combined the nation's two largest transcontinental railroads, the Northern Pacific and the Great Northern. At Roosevelt's behest, the U.S. Attorney General, W. H. Moody, prosecuted Northern Securities for being in violation of Section 1 of the Sherman Act and won a dissolution decree from the Supreme Court in 1904. Second, in 1905, the Supreme Court enjoined Swift, Armour, Morris, and Hammon—the nation's ''Big Four'' meat packers—from conspiring to fix prices. The Justice Department argued before the Supreme Court that the meat packers had illegally conspired to depress prices paid to livestock producers and to increase prices paid for processed meats. The Supreme Court ruled in favor of the Justice Department and enjoined the meat packers to stop their illegal pricing practices. In commenting on Roosevelt's ''two major victories,'' Harvard professors Merle Fainsod and Lincoln Gordon noted that:

> [t]he direct effects of his two major victories were almost nil. Community of interest within the controlling Hill-Morgan group continued to direct the policy of both Northwestern railroads, while the meat packers simply disregarded the injunction in the Swift case.[21]

Nonetheless, the Northern Securities antitrust ritual enshrined Theodore Roosevelt in the minds of his public as well as in the history books as the Great Trustbuster. But, as many have noted, Roosevelt's reformist attempts left the industrial landscape "fundamentally unchanged." In essence, the antitrust rituals performed during this period worked much in the manner that Assistant Attorney General Arnold described.

The regulatory commissions also operated in a mode that seemed to run counter to the legislative intent stated in their enabling legislation. For instance, in 1892, Charles E. Perkins (president of the Chicago, Burlington, and Quincy railroads) wrote a letter to his friend Richard Olney (Attorney General of the United States) recommending that Olney attempt to have the ICC disbanded. Olney replied to Perkins that:

> . . . looking at the matter from a railroad point of view exclusively, it would not be a wise thing to undertake. . . . The attempt would not be likely to succeed; if it did not succeed, and were made on the grounds of the inefficiency and uselessness of the Commission, the result would very probably be giving it the power it now lacks. The Commission, as its functions have now been limited by the courts, is, or can be made of great use to the railroads. It satisfies the popular clamor for a government supervision of railroads, at the same time that the supervision is almost entirely nominal. Further, the older such a commission gets to be, the more inclined it will be found to take the business and railroad view of things. It thus becomes a sort of barrier between the railroad corporations and the people and a sort of protection against hasty and crude legislation hostile to railroad interests. . . . *The part of wisdom is not to destroy the commission but to utilize it.*[22] (emphasis added)

Here again, we have another U.S. Attorney General stating that the antitrust legislation would operate primarily as a mechanism to provide a framework for an almost entirely ritualistic exercise. Simply stated, the passing of laws and the creation of regulatory commissions are not to be viewed as valid criteria in judging the actual legislative commitment to and/or power to effect reform in the economic sphere. First, legislation may be declared unconstitutional by the courts. The Supreme Court, its members appointed for life by the president, is not as subject to democratic pressures as legislatures. The courts have traditionally been exceedingly conservative regarding economic reform. Second, legislation viewed negatively by business is usually subject to strong contrivances and manipulation by clever and resourceful people.

On the one hand, legislation can be written so as to insure a negative interpretation in the courts. On the other hand, legislation can be stated in such vague and ambiguous terminology as to render its supposed intent meaningless. Third, the enforcement and regulatory apparatuses of the law can simply be left so understaffed as to render them impotent. Fourth, the people who are in charge of running the enforcement and regulatory apparatuses are political appointees. Most often people are appointed who sincerely believe in a laissez-faire philosophy, who find it difficult in principle to effectively regulate the private sector, and who will usually do so only under extreme and sustained pressure. Further, quite often the people found running the regulatory agencies have worked in and intend to return to the very businesses they are supposed to be regulating. Fifth, career government employees who, like everyone, have a natural desire for personal security and who may believe that the government should actively enforce various regulatory statutes must, nonetheless, constantly be concerned as to whether their actions might arouse an industry campaign against their continued employment. Finally, regulatory agencies may be created by politicians, but quite consciously given no real power. This is achieved by using one or more of the devices mentioned above in order to accomplish two purposes: (1) a new regulatory agency or law may be created to appease a populist, grassroots political movement—the new law or agency can be hailed as significant legislative reform, indicating a get-tough or no-nonsense attitude on the part of the legislature; and, (2) by not giving sufficient or effective support to the implementation and enforcement aspects of the law or agency, politicians can maintain their support from business.*

In conclusion, the genesis of monopoly capitalism (1860s to 1920s) created a stark dichotomy between society's professed belief in Adam Smith's competitive market structure capitalism and economic reality. Society's response to the expanding dichotomy between cherished economic beliefs concerning what economic reality ought to be and actual economic conditions was to create a series of judicial and legislative rituals. The primary function of these rituals was to enhance our ability to maintain intellectual and psychological equilibrium while (1) steadfastly professing a commitment to competitive markets and (2) continuing unimpeded in turning our economic landscape into a panorama of monopolized enterprises.

---

*This may properly be designated the *legislative status quo concept*.

The great theoretical schism

Changing market structures and new economic theories

During the 1930s the Western world witnessed the greatest economic depression since the inception of the capitalist order. Not only was the Depression so comprehensive as to touch the lives of almost everyone; it was also long-lived. It was during this time that fascist regimes came to power in Europe, while in the United States populist-inspired political agitation once again became widespread. Many viewed the rise of fascism in Europe and the often violent political agitation in America as being caused by, or as a direct result of, the breakdown of the economic system.

The Depression lasted so long (almost twelve years) that even the most faithful began to have doubts. Under these circumstances, it became increasingly difficult to successfully argue for adherence to a laissez-faire philosophy. Thus, it was quite natural that market structures (the size and number of firms in a given industry) once again became a focal point for debate. The debate that occurred centered around the theoretical economic models created by Edward Hastings Chamberlin and Joan Robinson.

Both Chamberlin and Robinson argued that the models of pure competition and pure monopoly were woefully inadequate as tools to describe real world market forces. Robinson stipulated that:

> [i]t is customary, in setting out the principles of economic theory, to open with the analysis of a perfectly competitive world, and to treat monopoly as a special case. It has been the purpose of the foregoing argument to show that this process can with advantage be reversed and that it is more proper to set out the analysis of monopoly, treating perfect competition as a special case. . . . We see on every side a drift towards monopolization under the names of restriction schemes, quota systems, rationalization, and the growth of giant companies,[23]

while Chamberlin stated that:

> . . . the idea of a purely competitive *system* is inadmissable; for not only does it ignore the fact that the monopoly influence is felt in varying degrees throughout the system, but it sweeps it aside altogether. . . . In fact, as will be shown later, if either element is to be omitted from the picture, the assumption of ubiquitous monopoly has much more in its favor.[24]

It is quite clear then that Chamberlin and Robinson were not merely saying that pure competition in all its precise theoretical trappings did not exist in the real world, but rather that monopolistic behavior was in fact all pervasive. The central point in both Chamberlin's and Robinson's analyses was that, while pure monopoly did not exist, when an industry or market was dominated by a "few firms," monopoly market power did exist; and, thus, many negative aspects associated with pure monopoly would be present.

Chamberlin and Robinson both believed that the monopolistic behavior exhibited by producers in industries dominated by only a few firms was not due to overt collusion. Robinson stated:

> There is no collusion between monopolists. Each tries to maximize his own profits without regard to the interest of the others.[25]

As illustration, in an industry dominated by four or five large firms, if one firm reduced its prices, each of the other firms—being aware of their competitor's price reduction—would undoubtedly be forced to reduce its prices also. If, due to these price reductions, the additional quantity of items sold was on a percentage basis less than the price reduction, the net outcome would be less total revenue for the entire industry. In effect, once the number of firms in a particular market becomes small enough so that each may expect its actions to be counteracted by its competitors, price competition may become irrational if the goal of each competitor is to maximize profits. Further, simple logic allows each firm to understand (without any consultation with its competitors) that price competition would decrease each firm's profits. Thus, price competition is eliminated, not via overt collusion, but simply by producers' realizing their economic interdependence, and, in turn, acting in their own economic self-interest. In addition, excess capacity, or the underutilization of productive capabilities, may also come about for similar reasons. For instance, if an industry dominated by a few firms finds the demand for its product, at given prices, to be falling, the industry may reduce prices or reduce output. If each individual firm believes that a reduction in prices will not significantly increase sales, each firm may choose to stabilize its total revenue and maintain profits and/or minimize losses by reducing supply as opposed to reducing prices. No collusion need occur. Each firm is confronted with the same problem—falling demand. Given the existence of market power in industry, quite often the rational business decision may be to curtail production. But, this may cause both idle machines and unemployment to exist, i.e., excess capacity. Indeed, Chamberlin emphasized that *the most common result* of monopolistic competition was, in fact,

> . . . excess productive capacity, for which there is no automatic corrective. Such excess capacity may develop, of course, under pure competition, owing to miscalculation on the part of producers, or to sudden fluctuations in demand or cost conditions. But it is the peculiarity of monopolistic competition that it may develop over long periods "with impunity,.''..and may, in fact, become permanent and normal through a failure of price competition to function. The surplus capacity is never cast off, and the result is high prices and waste.[26]

Chamberlin placed great importance on the fact that monopoly prices could exist even when monopoly profits were not present:

> . . . there is a blending of competition and monopoly. The only essential difference between them is in the matter of profits: . . . monopoly profits disappear, but all the other phenomena which arise from monopoly elements in the situation remain. Among them are monopoly prices and outputs, selling expenditures, and possibly discrimination. Perhaps the matter is most easily cleared up by the realization that the whole theory of monopoly as familiarly conceived is part and parcel of the theory of monopolistic competition, at least as I have sought to describe it.
>
> Parenthetically, there might be mentioned an argument frequently encountered, especially in the field of public utilities and railroads: that a field is competitive if profits are not excessive. Thus it has been held that railroads need no longer be regulated, since their profits are held in check by the competition of other forms of transportation; and similar propositions have been made with respect to other utilities. The answer is, of course, that profits are only one element in the situation; rates, discriminatory practices, service in all its aspects, investment, and other policies may be strikingly influenced by monopoly elements, even though profits are not excessive.[27]

Clearly, one of Chamberlin's major creative insights was to show that, while it was possible to eliminate monopoly profits, especially in the long run, monopoly prices as well as economic waste in the form of idle plant capacity and high unemployment would be a chronic problem for economies dominated by monopolistically competitive industries.

On the other hand, Robinson believed that her major insight was to have shown that in imperfectly and/or monopolistically competitive industries workers would *not* receive a wage equal to their contribution to the productive process. Robinson stated,

> . . . what for me was the main point, I succeeded in proving within the framework of the orthodox theory, that it is not true that wages are normally equal to the value of the marginal product of labour.[28]

Robinson concluded that, when workers received a wage less than the actual value of their contribution to the productive process, eventually this would result in increasing the maldistribution of both income and wealth, saying:

> [t]he change in the composition of the national dividend brought about by the monopolists would then enhance and not mitigate the maldistribution of wealth.[29]

Of course, Chamberlin and Robinson used very technical and abstract theoretical arguments in elaborating their positions. But, for our purposes, we simply need to note and to summarize their central conclusions, which were:

• that the models of pure competition and pure monopoly did not explain the dominant real world market forces;

• that while pure monopoly did not exist, monopoly market power did exist in monopolistically competitive and/or imperfectly competitive markets;

• that the existence of market power led to idle capacity, high unemployment, monopoly prices, wage exploitation, and increases in wealth and income maldistribution; and, finally,

• that the negative effects of market power came about not through collusion, but simply because businesses were being run in an "economically rational" manner, given existing *structural* market conditions.

The potency of Chamberlin's and Robinson's arguments was twofold. First, the Western world was presented with an elaborate and technically sophisticated economic explanation as to why habitual idle capacity and unemployment existed in the industrial economies. And the Depression's foremost characteristics were, after all, high levels of unemployment and idled plants. Second, their explanation was "people neutral" since no ill motives were attributed to any group or economic class.

Table 3

The Major Antitrust Laws and Regulatory Commissions of the United States Enacted and/or Created in the 1930s)

I. Laws to protect competitors*

   A. The Robinson-Patman Act of 1936 (Public Law 692, 74th Cong.), amended the Clayton Act, Section 2.
   B. Miller-Tydings Act of 1937 (Public Law 314, 75th Cong.), amended the Sherman Act, Section 1.
   C. Wheeler-Lea Act of 1938 (Public Law 445, 75th Cong.), amended the Federal Trade Commission Act, Section 5.

II. Regulatory Commissions

Enabling legislation	Commission
The Securities Exchange Act of 1934	Securities and Exchange Commission (SEC)
The Federal Communication Act of 1934	Federal Communication Commission (FCC)
National Labor Relations Act of 1935	National Labor Relations Board (NLRB)
Civil Aeronautics Act of 1938	Civil Aeronautics Board (CAB)

*This legislation was designed primarily to provide limitations on "unfair competitive practices" among existing competitors and was not designed for the purpose of re-creating competitive market structures.

Finally, it is extremely important to keep in mind that neither Chamberlin nor Robinson was saying that *competition* no longer existed among producers. The crucial point was that *competition among competitors in competitive market structures* led to different economic results from those of *competition among competitors in monopolistically or imperfectly competitive market structures.*

Antitrust laws and regulatory commissions—revisited

Table 3 lists the major antitrust legislation passed and the regulatory commissions created in the 1930s. The three major antitrust laws passed during this period were in the form of amendments to existing legislation. The Robinson-Patman Act of 1936 amended Section 2 of the Clayton Act while the Miller-Tydings Act of 1937 amended Section 1 of the Sherman Act. Finally, the Wheeler-Lea Act of 1938 amended Section 5 of the Federal Trade Commission Act.

It is important to note that the original antitrust laws (Sherman, Clayton, and Federal Trade acts) were designed primarily to prevent monopolistic behavior by promoting or creating competitive market structures, whereas the Robinson-Patman, Miller-Tydings, and Wheeler-Lea amendments were designed primarily to maintain the status quo by limiting "unfair competitive practices" among competitors in monopolistically competitive market structures. From a pragmatic point of view, the latter approach could be viewed as an attempt to slow down or stop the continual drift toward even greater monopolization. Nonetheless, there was not even a hint in these amendments that Congress was seriously considering moving toward the creation of truly competitive market structures.

Notwithstanding governmental attempts to combat the Depression through amending the antitrust laws and creating a new series of regulatory agencies, in the last quarter of 1937 the economy suffered a severe downturn with unemployment rising to 17 percent of the labor force. A frustrated President Franklin D. Roosevelt sent a lengthy message to Congress in part stating:

> • To the Congress of the United States:
> Unhappy events abroad have retaught us two simple truths about the liberty of a democratic people.
> The first truth is that the liberty of a democracy is not safe if the people tolerate the growth of private power to a point where it becomes stronger than their democratic state itself.
> The second truth is that the liberty of a democracy is not safe if its business system does not provide employment and produce and distribute goods in such a way as to sustain an acceptable standard of living.
> Both lessons hit home.
> • One of the primary causes of our present difficulties lies in the disappearance of price competition in many industrial fields. . . .
> • We have witnessed the merging out of effective competition in many fields of enterprise. *We have learned that the so-called competitive system works differently in an industry where there are many independent units, from the way it works in an industry where a few large producers dominate the market.* (emphasis added)
> • Managed industrial prices mean fewer jobs. It is no accident that in industries like cement and steel where prices have remained firm in the face of a falling demand pay rolls have shrunk as much as 40 to 50 percent in recent months. Nor is it mere chance that in most competitive industries where prices adjust themselves quickly to falling demand, pay rolls and employment have been far better maintained.

• Among us today a concentration of private power without equal in history is growing . . . of all corporations . . . less than 5 percent of them [own] 87 percent of all the assets of all of them.

• The power of a few to manage the economic life of the Nation must be diffused among the many or be transferred to the public and its democratically responsible government. If prices are to be managed and administered, if the Nation's business is to be allotted by plan and not by competition, that power should not be vested in any private group or cartel, however benevolent. . . .

• To meet the situation I have described, there should be a thorough study of the concentration of economic power in American industry and the effect of that concentration upon the decline of competition.[30]

It is instructive to note that President Roosevelt, while perhaps using the rhetoric of a political crusader, nonetheless stated the economic arguments of Chamberlin and Robinson—a few large producers dominating individual markets, the disappearance of price competition, and the reduction of output rather than prices in the face of falling demand—in a clear and precise manner.

President Roosevelt asked Congress to appropriate $500,000 for the purpose of funding a comprehensive study to examine the existence and the effects of concentration of economic power in American industry. Responding to the President's message, Congress established the Temporary National Economic Committee (TNEC) in June 1938. Besides Congressional testimony consisting of 37 volumes (approximately 17,000 pages), the Committee printed 43 monographs, each dealing with a specific economic problem. The study lasted 33 months and cost approximately $1,000,000. The TNEC issued its final report 26 March 1941. In substance the report clearly documented the monopolization of many American industries (see Table 4). Indeed, as shown in Table 4, many of America's industries were dominated by as few as four firms. Within the taxonomy of economics such industries are labeled oligopolistically *competitive* market structures.* Further, the economic consequences that flowed from the theoretical analyses of

---

*Industrial organization economists, for pedagogical purposes, use four basic structural models—pure competition, pure monopoly, monopolistic competition and/or imperfect competition, and oligopoly. Pure monopoly exists when there is only one producer in the industry, while oligopoly is usually defined as 4 firms accounting for 50 percent or more of an industry's total sales. Industries where 25 to 40 firms (each accounting for only a small percentage of total sales) account for over 50 percent of total sales are labeled monopolistically and/or imperfectly competitive markets.

Table 4

Four-Firm Concentration Ratios for Selected Products

Product	Number of producers	Percentage produced by four largest producers
Inlaid linoleum	4	100.0
Watt-hour meters, alternating current	4	100.0
Snuff	11	99.2
Refrigerator cabinets, domestic	11	98.6
Asbestos shingles	8	97.4
Machine-finished paper containing ground wood	11	96.4
Coal tar products; crudes	14	95.6
Refrigerating systems, complete without cabinets	15	95.4
Power transformers; 501 kw. and over	14	95.0
Lithopone	10	94.6
Hydrocarbon; acetylene	23	92.7
Tractors, "all purpose," wheel type, belt HP [horsepower] under 30, steel tires	10	92.0
Plug chewing tobacco	18	91.7
Oxygen	26	91.4
Typewriters, standard	8	91.2
Radio receiving tubes for replacement, AC, glass and metal	12	91.2
White lead in oil, pure	106	90.6
Tractors, "all purpose," wheel type, belt HP 30 and over, rubber tires	11	90.6
Aluminum ware, cast	14	90.5
Copper plates and sheets	17	90.5
Passenger cars and chassis	15	90.4
Corn starch	10	89.2
Milk bottles	12	89.2
Metal working files and rasps	14	89.2
Tin cans, vent-hole top	8	88.8
Cultivators; 2, 3, and 4, 5, and 6 tractor drawn or mounted	14	88.6
Aluminum ware, stamped	25	87.8
Distributor transformers, 1/2 to 500 kilowatts	24	87.8
Zinc oxides, Chinese white and zinc white	18	87.3
Scrap chewing tobacco	64	87.3
Steam turbines, other than marine	9	87.0
Carburetor engines, motor vehicle, other types	16	86.0
Steel strips and flats, hot rolled for cold rolling	14	86.0
Tractors, other than "all purpose," 30 HP and up, steel and rubber tires	11	85.4
Window glass	9	85.0
Cigarettes	32	84.8
Gypsum, neat plaster	23	84.7

Product	Number of producers	Percentage produced by four largest producers
Nickel alloys, plates, sheets	13	84.3
AC synchronous timing motors, 1/20 HP and up; under 1 HP, capacitor type	26	84.1
Steel, rolled blooms and billets for forging	15	83.8
Adding machines	9	83.1
Rubber arctics and gaiters	12	82.9
Refined sugar, soft or brown	12	82.6
Steel skelp	10	82.2
Rubber-soled canvas shoes	11	82.1
Wallboard except gypsum, rigid, cellular fiber	15	82.1
Aluminum ingots	24	81.7
Matches, strike anywhere	9	81.5
Wire and cable, paper insulated	12	81.3
Cotton woven chambrays and cheviots	19	81.0
Rubber and footholds	16	80.7
Machine-made tumblers, goblets, and barware	8	80.0
Batteries, dry, other than 6 inch, 1½ volt	14	80.0
Rayon yarns by denier, 100 (88-112)	13	79.4
Motors, direct current, 1 HP to 200 HP	40	79.4
Partially refined oil sold for rerunning	36	79.2
Combines, harvester-thresher, 6 foot cut and wider	12	79.1
Steel, plates, universal	14	79.0
Brass and bronze tubing and pipe, seamless	18	78.9
Heating and cooking apparatus, kerosene	12	78.8
Truck and bus tires	25	78.8
Coal tar resins derived from phenol and/or cresol	19	78.7
Rayon yarns by denier, 300 (250-374)	15	78.4
Radio receiving sets, beyond standard broadcast, socket power, $45-$65	24	78.0
Turkish and terry-woven towels	26	77.7
Smoking tobacco	119	77.5
Tobacco and cheese cloth	21	77.2
Machine-glazed Kraft wrapping paper, other	23	76.9
Domestic refrigerators, 6 foot, under 10 foot	25	76.8
Canned meats	24	76.5
Passenger car tires	26	76.5
Steel, semifinished rolled blooms, billets and slag	37	76.5
Narrow-neck packers' ware	25	76.3
Steel, black for trimming	12	76.0
Granulated sugar	21	75.8
Woolen woven goods, other	24	75.6
AC synchronous timing motors, 1/20 HP and up, under 1 HP, split phase	29	75.5
Passenger car, truck, and bus inner tubes	26	75.3

(Table 4 continued on p. 30)

Product	Number of producers	Percentage produced by four largest producers
Commercial cars, trucks, and busses	82	75.3
Thermostats	54	75.3
Steel rails	5	(1)
Car and locomotive wheels, rolled and forged	5	(1)
Lead oxides; litharge	5	(1)
Beer cans	5	(1)
Corn and other syrups	6	(1)
Axles, rolled and forged	6	(1)
Corn sugar	7	(1)
Oxides, other	7	(1)
Steel, pierced billets, rounds, and blanks for seamless pipes and tubes	8	(1)
Electric household ranges, 2½ kilowatts and over	8	(1)
Steel, sheet and tin plate	9	(1)
Ignition cable sets or wire assemblies for internal combustion engines	9	(1)
Stainless steel plates and sheets	10	(1)
Films, except X-ray	10	(1)
Sensitized photographic paper	11	(1)
Paper, ground wood, printing	11	(1)
Beer bottles	11	(1)
Lighting glassware, including electric light bulbs	12	(1)
Cameras, including motion picture	13	(1)
Packing rings, electrodes; miscellaneous graphite and metal graphited specialties	13	(1)
Ferro-alloys, electric furnace	14	(1)
Steel, heavy web, 3 inch and over	14	(1)
Carburetor engines, motor vehcile, industrial	16	(1)
Wool, meat packing	18	(1)
Flat glass, other	18	(1)
Sanitary cans, including condensed milk cans	18	(1)
Carburetor engines, aircraft	19	(1)
Wallboard, except gypsum	25	(1)
Cash registers, etc.	27	(1)
Storage batteries, other	28	(1)
Spark plugs	30	(1)
Power switchboards and parts	31	(1)
Telephone and telegraph apparatus	31	(1)
Men's work shoes, wood or metal fastened	33	(1)
Canned soups	44	(1)
Aluminum products, other	61	(1)
Motor vehicle hardware, including locks	62	(1)

Source: Clair Wilcox, "Competition and Monopoly in American Industry," Temporary National Economic Committee (TNEC), Monograph 21, 1940, pp. 117-118.

(1) Information withheld in order to avoid the approximate disclosure of data for individual enterprises.

Chamberlin and Robinson, given monopolistic and/or oligopolistic conditions, were also substantiated. Nonetheless, soon after the report's completion, the country became engaged in a world war, and the possibility of a dramatic confrontation between our public and private sector institutions was averted. Due to the war's insatiable demand for goods, unemployment dropped steadily from 1939 on, so that by 1944 the unemployment rate stood at only 1 percent. The same entrepreneurs who had been unable to organize and run the economic system satisfactorily in the 1930s literally performed miracles in the 1940s when offered "cost plus" government contracts. (One must hasten to add that, historically, cost plus government contracts and deficit spending were not typically thought of as being the motor force of a capitalist's economic system, at least, that is, before World War II.)

Finally, it must be noted—notwithstanding the efforts of Chamberlin and Robinson—that the central message that continued to be received in most economics classrooms, as well as to be taken from the rhetoric of the vast majority of businessmen and politicians, was that the economy, while *significant* exceptions did exist, still, by and large, resembled Adam Smith's conception of competitive market structure capitalism. Joan Robinson, for example, in referring to the impact of her work on the economics profession, made the following comments in the second edition of her book, *The Economics of Imperfect Competition*, published in 1969:

> All this had no effect. Perfect competition, supply and demand, consumer's sovereignty and marginal products still reign supreme in orthodox teaching. Let us hope that a new generation of students, after forty years, will find in this book what I intended to mean by it.[31]

In terms of classroom instruction, it was not so much that the new models were ignored or not considered, but rather that they were taught as representing exceptions to the general case—the general case being that competitive market structures (as opposed to monopolistically competitive market structures) still reigned supreme.

The laissez-faire monopoly doctrines—1940s

Several concepts advanced in the literature during the 1940s and 1950s set forth a justification for the government's continuing a laissez-faire policy toward even the most monopolized industries. These may be appropriately categorized as the *laissez-faire monopoly doctrines*. They will be so called hereafter, and it is on these doctrines that attention will now be focused.

Workable or effective competition

Economists who did not believe it wise to attempt to create competitive market structures were confronted with a very subtle and age-old problem. The concepts of competitive markets and laissez-faire were not only inextricably interdependent, but both terms also had become religious articles of faith, deeply imbedded in America's psychological makeup. In the vernacular, competitive markets were what it was all about, and the government which governed least, governed best. As pointed out by John Maurice Clark:

> Competition is an indispensable mainstay of a system in which the character of products and their development, the amount and evolving efficiency of production, and the prices and profit margins charged are left to the operation of private enterprise. In our conception of a tenable system of private enterprise, it is a crucial feature that the customer should be in a position (as Adam Smith put it) "to exert effective discipline over the producers in these respects." Otherwise government would feel constrained to undertake discipline over these matters—as it does in the field of public-service industries.[32]

How could a defense be made simultaneously for competitive markets, for laissez-faire, and for the status quo economic reality of monopolistically competitive market structures? As all good students of history can attest, the world's social philosophers have traditionally looked for answers to such problems by carefully reexamining the meaning of key concepts. Clark, in his seminal work "Toward a Concept of Workable Competition," published in the *American Economic Review* in 1940, said that a competitive market structure economy "does not and cannot exist and has presumably never existed." In place of a competitive market structure economy, Clark substituted the concept of a "workable competitive economy." He stated his "generic definition" of workable competition as follows:

> Competition is rivalry in selling goods in which each selling unit normally seeks maximum net revenue, under conditions such that the price or prices each seller can charge are effectively limited by the free option of the buyer to buy from a rival seller or sellers of what we think of as "the same" product necessitating an effort by each seller to equal or exceed the

attractiveness of the others' offerings to a sufficient number of sellers to accomplish the end in view.[33]

Presumably, accepting Clark's definition of workable competition, an industry consisting of only two firms could be considered workably competitive. Clark never gave any concrete meaning to the terms "effectively limited" or "sufficient number of sellers," which prompted the University of Michigan's Professor William Shepherd to comment:

> Workability was an imprecise, elastic and variable criterion . . . it was capable of rendering acceptable nearly any industry situation.[34]

In a somewhat more caustic vein, the University of Chicago's Professor George J. Stigler reasoned that:

> [t]o determine whether any industry is workably competitive, therefore, simply have a good graduate student write his dissertation on the industry and render a verdict. It is crucial to this test, of course, that no second graduate student be allowed to study the industry.[35]

These rather severe and unequivocal criticisms notwithstanding, it is certainly not an overstatement to note that the vast majority of businessmen and politicians, as well as most members of the economics profession, embraced and/or accepted the idea that the country's monopolistically and/or imperfectly competitive market structures were indeed "workably competitive."

Gales of creative destruction

Joseph A. Schumpeter also attempted to rationalize government's continuation of a laissez-faire policy by redefining the meaning of competition. In his book *Capitalism, Socialism and Democracy*, published in 1942, Schumpeter argued:

• that the U.S. economy was and had been dominated by large monopolies since the 1890s;

• that technological economies of scale made large monopolies inevitable and desirable;* and, finally,

---

*Economists say that a firm which can simultaneously increase its output and lower its per unit production cost is experiencing "economies of scale." The economies of scale concept has been reified in economic analysis and is used in almost litany fashion by professional economists and businessmen to justify our industrial monopolies.

- that large monopolies constituted the lifeblood of *competitive* capitalism.

It is important to note that Schumpeter was not eschewing *competition* itself; rather, he was arguing (1) that *competitive market structures* were undesirable, and (2) that the real meaning of competition had been misunderstood by laymen, politicians, and professional economists. In Schumpeter's words:

> Economists are at long last emerging from the state in which price competition was all they saw. . . . However, it is still competition within a rigid pattern of invariant conditions, methods of production and forms of industrial organization in particular, that practicaly monopolizes attention. But in capitalist reality as distinct from its textbook picture, it is not that kind of competition which counts but the competition from the new commodity, the new technology, the new source of supply, the new type of organization (the largest-scale unit of control for instance)—competition which commands a decisive cost or quality advantage and which strikes not at the margins of the profits and the outputs of the existing firms but at their foundations and their lives. . . . The businessman feels himself to be in a competitive situation even if he is alone in his field or if, though not alone, he holds a position such that investigating government experts fail to see any effective competition between him and any other firm in the same or a neighborhood field and in consequence conclude that his talk, under examination, about his competitive sorrows is all make believe.[36]

It is also important to note that Schumpeter viewed profit maximization as the motor force behind all economic activity and, further, that most capitalists believed—and according to Schumpeter rightly so—that profits arose from innovation such as the creation of a new product, a new technology, or a new form of business organizational structure.

> . . . I include this with wages of management in order to single out and emphasize what I believe to be the fundamental source of industrial gain, the profits that the capitalist order attaches to successful introduction of new goods or new methods of production or new forms of organization. I do not see how it could be denied that industrial history testifies convincingly to the importance of this element of capitalist returns.[37]

In essence, the innovator of a new product or a new technology gains temporary monopoly profits while destroying its outdated competition. Innovation is essentially a "creative-destruction" process, however, since it results in higher levels of productivity concomitant with reduced prices. As illustration, the flat bottom river boat gave way to the steamship just as overland horse-drawn stages and freight wagons gave way to the railroads. In turn, the railroads underwent painful readjustments and bankruptcies due to the competitive pressures from the air transport and the trucking industries. In Schumpeterian terms:

> This process of Creative Destruction is the essential fact about capitalism. It is what capitalism consists in and what every capitalist concern has got to live in.[38]

Within the business community and the economics profession, Clark's concept of "workable competition" and Schumpeter's "gales of creative destruction" were christened "the new competition." Simply by assigning a new meaning to the term competition, the ill effects of monopolistically competitive market structures were defined out of existence. Yet the real world does exist. If competition among competitors in monopolistically or imperfectly competitive market structures automatically leads to idle plant capacity, high unemployment, monopoly prices, a maldistribution of income, and other ills, as suggested by the logic of Chamberlin's and Robinson's *theoretical models*, why didn't the U.S. economy relapse into a depression after World War II when wartime production subsided? The answer, of course, is to be found in the economic views of John Maynard Keynes.

Aggregate demand creates its own supply

Sir Roy F. Harrod in his book *The Life of John Maynard Keynes* noted that Keynes* was:

> . . . an individualist to the finger-tips. For him those concerned with government were a lesser breed of men, whose role was essentially a

---

*Keynes presented his theory of macro-economics in 1936 in his book *The General Theory of Employment, Interest and Money*. General acceptance of his ideas, however, did not occur in the United States, for the most part, until the late 1940s or early 1950s. During the war years, though, the government essentially followed a Keynesian fiscal policy approach with its deficit spending related to wartime production. In short, government spending during the war and the consumer's pent-up demand for goods and services unleashed immediately after the war had precisely the effects on the economy that Keynes said fiscal policy would have. Many economists have observed that the country's wartime experience with deficit spending actually helped to prove or validate Keynes's approach to the government's use of monetary and fiscal policy.

subordinate one. The idea that a government, however popularly elected, should be entrusted to make certain value judgments on behalf of the community was anathema to him.[39]

But Harrod also noted that Keynes was ". . . violently opposed to laissez-faire. . . ."[40] Keynes himself voiced his opposition to laissez-faire, explaining that one must:

> . . . clear from the ground the metaphysical or general principles upon which, from time to time, *laissez-faire* has been founded. . . . The world is *not* so governed from above that private and social interest always coincide. It is *not* so managed here below that in practice they coincide. It is *not* a correct deduction from the Principles of Economics that enlightened self-interest always operates in the public interest. Nor is it true that self-interest generally *is* enlightened; more often individuals acting separately to promote their own ends are too ignorant or too weak to attain even these. Experience does *not* show that individuals, when they make up a social unit, are always less clear-sighted than when they act separately.[41]

Keynes explained what appears at first blush to be a clear contradiction—the support for both individualism and collectivism—in the following manner:

> . . . the enlargement of the functions of government, . . . would seem to a nineteenth-century publicist or to a contemporary American financier to be a terrific encroachment on individualism. *I defend it, on the contrary, both as the only practical means of avoiding the destruction of existing economic forms in their entirety* and as the condition of the successful functioning of individual initiative.
>
> For if effective demand is deficient, not only is the public scandal of wasted resources intolerable, but the individual enterpriser who seeks to bring these resources into action is operating with the odds loaded against him. The game of hazard which he plays is furnished with many zeros, so that the players as a whole will lose if they have the energy and hope to deal all the cards.
>
> . . . The authoritarian state systems of today seemed to solve the problem of unemployment at the expense of efficiency and of freedom. *It is certain that the world will not much longer tolerate the unemployment which, apart from brief intervals of excitement, is associated—and, in my*

opinion, inevitably associated—with present day capitalistic individualism. But it may be possible by a right analysis of the problem to cure the disease whilst preserving efficiency and freedom . . . if effective demand is adequate, average skill and average good fortune will be enough.[42] (emphasis added)

Keynes's starting point rested on four fundamental propositions. First, he reaffirmed his belief in Adam Smith's proposition that the profit maximizing ethic provided the crucial link between the present and the future. As long as entrepreneurs were reasonably assured of making future profits on current investments, the necessary capital to sustain adequate growth and full employment would be forthcoming. Second, he concurred with those who argued that entrepreneurial behavior in modern industrial societies was not regulated by "impersonal market forces," but instead that entrepreneurs possessed substantial monopoly market power. Third, he also concurred that rational economic behavior on the part of those possessing market power dictated that entrepreneurs (when confronted with falling consumer demand, caused for whatever reason) would reduce output and lay off workers. Such reductions in the work force, in turn, created even less consumer buying power, setting off a chain reaction between work force reductions and reductions in the aggregate "effective demand" for goods and services. Last, Keynes also accepted the "people neutrality" concept. Given a decline in the aggregate effective demand for goods and services, an entrepreneur would be, in Keynes's words, "operating with the odds loaded against him," and further that " . . . the game of hazard which he plays is furnished with many zeros." Based primarily on these four concepts, Keynes reasoned that severe depressions could not be avoided (given the existence of monopolistically and/or imperfectly competitive market structures) unless the government (through monetary and fiscal policies) could bring about and/or sustain a suitable level of aggregate demand.

Notwithstanding the fact that the proper implementation and use of Keynesian monetary and fiscal policies would necessitate the federal government's taking a more active role in economic affairs, Keynes viewed his theories as being more conservative than radical. He concluded his book *The General Theory of Interest, Employment and Money* saying:

. . . The foregoing theory is moderately conservative in its implications. For whilst it indicates the vital importance of establishing certain central controls in matters which are now left in the main to individual initiative, there are wide fields of activity which are unaffected.

. . . If our central controls succeed in establishing an aggregate volume of output corresponding to full employment as nearly as is practicable, the classical theory comes into its own again from this point onwards. If we suppose the volume of output to be given, i.e., to be determined by forces outside the classical scheme of thought, then there is no objection to be raised against the classical analysis of the manner in which private self-interest will determine what in particular is produced, in what proportions the factors of production will be combined to produce it, and how the value of the final production will be distributed between them. . . .[43]

In essence, if the government, through the use of Keynesian monetary and fiscal policy, could eliminate the more visible adverse effects of monopoly market power (idle plant capacity and high levels of unemployment), from Keynes's point of view, it would *not* be necessary for the government to modify its laissez-faire policy in terms of antitrust enforcement, government ownership, and/or the implementation of more forceful regulatory measures. As stated earlier, Keynes defended government's use of monetary and fiscal policy as stabilizing tools, saying, "I defend it . . . as the only practical means of avoiding the destruction of existing economic forms in their entirety." Keynes' views on this point proved to be very presentient. Primarily due to government's acceptance and application of Keynesian economics, during the 1950s and up until the mid 1960s the country experienced relatively low levels of unemployment and inflation, coupled with steady economic growth.* The federal legislation which empowered the executive branch of government to actively pursue a full employment policy was entitled the "Employment Act of 1946." This legislation established a Council of Economic Advisers (composed of three members appointed by the president) to assist the president. The Act also established a Joint Economics Committee (composed of ten senators and ten House members) to act as a legislative liaison between the executive and legislative branches of government. It said in part:

*The theory of Centralized Private Sector Planning presented in Chapters 3, 4, and 5 will clearly show why Keynesian macro-economics has itself been outdated by the structural and functional changes that have evolved in the economy since World War II.

An act to declare a national policy on employment, production, and purchasing power . . .

. . . The Congress hereby declares that it is the continuing policy and responsibility of the federal government to use all practical means . . . to promote maximum employment, production and purchasing power . . . [44]

The Employment Act of 1946 can be viewed as the legislative codification of Keynesian economics.

It is important to note, however, that America's economic successes during the postwar period were usually credited to competitive capitalism. The few economic adversities that were experienced, on the other hand, were usually blamed on the monetary and fiscal policies of an unwise and bureaucratic federal government. In short, once the government began to employ monetary and fiscal tools as part of a conscious effort " . . . to promote maximum employment, production and purchasing power . . . " the government automatically became the focal point for criticism whenever the country experienced any economic problems. As illustration, the small economic recessions which occurred from time to time during this period (small in terms of depth and duration) were characterized as "rolling readjustments," which could themselves be eliminated only if the "scoundrels" in power were voted out of office and replaced by those who understood government's proper role in a "free private enterprise" economy.

It is absolutely crucial to keep in mind that Chamberlin, Robinson, Schumpeter, Clark, and Keynes all agreed that most of the key industries which formed the foundation of the modern industrial economies were, although technically efficient, nonetheless, monopolistically competitive industries characterized by:

- producers having considerable market power; and
- a high degree of personal rivalry between and among producers, that is, robust competition.

But, robust competition, under *monopolisticaly competitive market structure* conditions, does an economy little good if entrepreneurs find it in their pecuniary self-interest to operate at less than 50 percent of actual plant capacity. Two important conclusions can be drawn from all this:

- technically efficient plants and robust competition, given

monopolistically competitive market structures, are insufficient criteria for sustaining a viable standard of living; and
  • Keynesian economics did, in fact, literally save the capitalistic economies.

The laissez-faire monopoly doctrines—1950s

Countervailing power

Harvard economics professor John Kenneth Galbraith, viewing America's industrial landscape in the early 1950s, concluded that:
  • most industries were dominated by a few giant firms; and
  • where competitive market strucures did not exist, a laissez-faire policy could be defended *in certain circumstances* since new restraints on the exercise of monopoly market power had been developed. Galbraith christened these new restraints "countervailing power."

> In fact, new restraints on private power did appear to replace competition. They were nurtured by the same process of concentration which impaired or destroyed competition. But they appear not on the same side of the market but on the opposite side, not with competitors but with customers or suppliers. It will be convenient to have a name for this counterpart of competition and I shall call it *Countervailing Power*.

> To begin with a broad and somewhat too dogmatically stated proposition, private economic power is held in check by the countervailing power of those who are subject to it. The first begets the second. The long trend toward concentration of industrial enterprise in the hands of a relatively few firms has brought into existence not only strong sellers as economists have supposed but also strong buyers as they have failed to see. The two develop together, not in precise step but in such manner that there can be no doubt that the one is the response to the other.[45]

Hence, in the Galbraithian world of countervailing power, giant corporations negotiate with giant unions, and highly concentrated manufacturing industries sell their products to equally concentrated retail chains. Further, the existence of countervailing power provided at least a *partial defense* for laissez-faire.

Since the development of countervailing power is irregular and incomplete, it does not provide a blanket case for the exclusion of state interference with private decision. . . . Nonetheless, it is countervailing power which, in the typical modern industrial market, regulates the power of private decision. As such it provides the negative justification for leaving decisions in private hands, for it prevents those decisions from working harm on others.[46]

Galbraith stated explicitly in his book *American Capitalism* that neither the liberals nor the conservatives would appreciate the countervailing power concept. On the one hand, conservatives would not like the concept because it provided a justification for the existence of market power for "unions, farmers, mass buyers and others." On the other hand, liberals would be annoyed with the concept since it provided a justification for leaving economic decisions in private hands. Galbraith mused that "this is often the case with reality" and further added, "There is nothing an economist should fear so much as applause, and I believe I am reasonably secure."[47]

Galbraith concluded the countervailing power argument with the following propositions:

• that a defense for laissez-faire was untenable unless monopoly market power was offset by some countervailing power;

• that the development of countervailing power in some areas had proven beneficial to both consumers and workers and had in fact worked to counteract the exercise of monopoly market power by corporations;

• that there was a need to develop additional countervailing power groups on behalf of consumers and workers; and, finally,

• that the government should take a constructive attitude toward assisting consumers and others in creating countervailing power groups.

Many in the academic community (especially in the areas of political science, public administration, business, and management) completely ignored points three and four of Galbraith's argument. In short, the conventional wisdom continued to be that the economy was basically a competitive market structure economy and that, where monopoly power did exist, a countervailing power had already been developed. The countervailing power concept, then, was used—or perhaps misused— by many to support the position that the government should continue to follow a laissez-faire monopoly doctrine.

Social responsibility

Adolph A. Berle, Jr., in his book *The 20th Century Capitalist Revolution*, argued that corporations had undergone a metamorphosis, and, instead of being primarily economic institutions, they were "quasi-political institutions." Berle advanced essentially the same type of disputation that Clark, Schumpeter, and Galbraith used in pointing out the *causal* forces behind the growth and concentration of power in corporate America:

> Concentration of economic power occurred, driven by the deepest force of the time. Demand for a high standard of living required mass production and mass distribution. Technological advance made this production possible in many of the goods and services considered most essential to the life of a modern population. But, in the quantity and prices desired, it had to be accomplished by mass organizations. Factually that organization was achieved by great corporate units.[48]

Berle too, then, appealed to the trilogy of technology, mass production and distribution, and corporate concentration of power.

Nonetheless, Berle argued that the potentially negative aspects of corporate power were circumscribed or "severely limited," since corporate officers of necessity were bound by a "higher law" which forced them, at least in the long run, to act in a "socially responsible" manner:

> Deep in human consciousness is embedded the assumption that somewhere, somehow, there is a higher law which imposes itself in time on princes and powers and institutions of this terrestrial earth. . . . Keepers of the tradition of this higher law—medicine men in primitive times, magicians or sybils in the ancient world or divines today—are regularly listened to with respect. . . . Throughout western history a priest could commonly intimidate a policeman; the cross could quite frequently stop the king. . . . It is here suggested that a somewhat similar phenomenon is slowly looming up in the corporate field through the mist that hides from us the history of the next generation. There is beginning to be apparent a realization of a counter force which checks, and remotely acts on and in time may modify in certain areas the absolute power of business discretion.[49]

The question as to whether or not corporations are socially responsible or are bound by a higher law is, of course, a red herring. The crucial issue is always: Who actually has power, and is their power legitimate in the eyes of the people? President Franklin Roosevelt gave the appropriate democratic response clearly, concisely, and accurately when he told Congress and the American people:

> . . . if the Nation's business is to be allotted by plan and not by competition, that power should not be vested in any private group or cartel, however benevolent. . . . The liberty of a democracy is not safe if the people tolerate the growth of private power to a point where it becomes stronger than their democratic state itself. [50]

As a matter of historical fact, though, yet another concept had been created that—rightly or wrongly—would be used by many with great success to defend laissez-faire even under the most monopolized conditions.

Antitrust and regulatory commissions—re-revisited

During the 1940s and 1950s, only two major pieces of antitrust legislation were passed—the Cellar-Kefauver Act of 1950 and the McGuire-Keogh Act of 1952. No major regulatory agencies were created. The basic intent behind these two antitrust laws was to provide yet another legal mechanism for slowing down the monopolization process—especially in the manufacturing and retail trades. As illustration, the Cellar-Kefauver Act prohibited the acquisition of " . . . the whole or any part of the assets . . . " by a corporation of another corporation if such acquisition would tend " . . . to lessen competition . . . " and/or " . . . tend to create a monopoly. . . ."

In fact, though, neither the Cellar-Kefauver Act nor the McGuire-Keogh Act was even mildly successful in slowing down the economy's steady drift toward ever increasingly monopolized markets. As one example, between 1953 and 1969 there were approximately 16,570 mergers in the manufacturing sector alone. In short, during this period the political and economic communities, by and large, simply turned their attention away from the study of market structures (micro-economics). Instead, attention was focused almost exclusively on building ever more intricate and sophisticated macro-economics models, and *monetary* and *fiscal* policy became the key economic buzzwords. Indeed, the deemphasizing of micro-economic analysis and antitrust reform reached such a nadir during the postwar decades, and as yet has showed no signs of recovery, that in 1970 University of Michigan economics professor William Shepherd could say, without concern for substantial dissent:

> . . . the dissolution of existing firms (however dominant their position) has now virtually disappeared from the anti-trust arsenal . . .[51]

He further added:

> Though it would be unduly harsh to call it a "charade" anti-trust policy has now largely acquiesced in and therefore ratified, existing market structures.[52]

In conclusion, during the 1940s and 1950s, with the advent of economic prosperity, especially relative to the country's depression experiences of the 1930s, and with the creation of the laissez-faire monopoly doctrines, the country's monopolitically and oligopolistically competitive industries were essentially freed from even minimal governmental supervision.

Private sector planning, decentralized—1960s

The technology connection

From a structural perspective, during and after World War II, economic concentration in manufacturing in terms of both (1) the aggregate amount of economic activity accounted for by the largest firms and (2) economic concentration within individual industries had proceeded unchecked. On the one hand, between 1950 and 1970, the 200 largest manufacturing corporations had increased their share of all manufacturing assets from 48 to 61 percent. By 1972, the 200 largest manufacturers controlled as large a percentage of all manufacturing assets as were controlled by the 1,000 largest manufacturers in 1940. On the other hand, in many of the core industries (steel, copper, aluminum, industrial chemicals, automobiles, computers, etc.) which form the industrial heartland of modern economies, as few as 2 or 3 firms had achieved overwhelming dominance (see Table 5).

As stated above, many economists rationalize the demise of competitive market structures and the creation of monopolized industries by ritualizing the supposed increases in efficiency that accompany monopolization. Simply stated, the argument is that in many industries

Table 5

Assets and Concentration Ratios for Selected Manufacturing Industries (1968)

Industries	Number of firms	Assets (in millions of dollars)	Concentration ratios* (approximate)
Motor vehicles	(3)	27,361	90-100
Computers	(1)	6,743	70-80
Heavy electrical equipment	(2)	8,015	70-80
Iron and steel	(4)	12,692	50-60
Industrial chemicals	(4)	10,705	60-70
Telephone equipment	(1)	2,721	80-90
Tires and tubes	(3)	5,381	70-80
Copper	(3)	3,880	60-70
Aluminum	(3)	4,760	80-90
Commercial aircraft	(3)	4,387	80-90
Metal containers	(2)	2,410	80-90
Drugs	(4)	2,360	70-80

Source: Adapted from William G. Shepherd, *Market Power and Economic Welfare* (New York: Random House, 1970), pp. 152-53.

*A concentration ratio is simply the percentage of an industry's assets, sales, or employees that is accounted for by a designated number of producers. For example, in the above table, the three firms' concentration ratio, for assets, in the automobile industry is approximately 95 percent. The above concentration ratios differ from those published by the U.S. Bureau of the Census because they have been adjusted to more accurately reflect relevant markets in terms of both product definition and geographical area.

one or two firms, by using the most efficient technology available (the lowest per unit production cost technology), could produce quantities sufficient to adequately supply the economic demands of the entire community. The thesis that the organizational structure of economic institutions is largely determined by industrial technology may be appropriately referred to as the *technology connection*. In the 1960s, a small yet influential group of scholars extended the technology connection thesis to include the notion of decentralized private sector planning. A more detailed analysis of the Decentralized Private Sector Planning (DPSP) thesis is presented in Chapter 3. The concept is being sketchily introduced here primarily to provide continuity in the evolution-of-American-capitalism argument. The following is a basic outline of the DPSP thesis:

• Economic institutions are organized and operated so as to conform to the existing technological imperatives—the technology connection.

• The use of modern technology demands long-range planning.

• The existence of DPSP reduces the traditional image of our economy (a free enterprise market system regulated by competitive forces) to the level of an absurd ideological abstraction.

• Continuing to insist that our economy is still effectively regulated by competitive market forces makes rational discussion of economic problems impossible, leaving the planning technocracy unconstrained and free to pursue its own interest, which quite often does not coincide with the general public's interest.

• Thus, DPSP raises serious political questions, such as—

    a. Who are the planners?

    b. What are their values?

    c. How much power do they have vis-à-vis the government?

These latter questions will be addressed explicitly in later chapters, but for now attention will be turned once again to the regulation and legislation question.

Consumer protection and environmental legislation

During the 1960s and 1970s, little attention was paid to creating additional antitrust legislation or to enforcing existing laws. The 1960s must be viewed as a watershed period, however, in terms of enacting legislation with both a consumer protection and environmental orientation. In any modern industrial society, this type of legislation would be needed—even under competitive market structure conditions—in order to protect and maintain the *delicate* balance that exists between *homo sapiens* and our physical environment. As illustration, the Water Quality Act of 1965 and the National Air Quality Act of 1970 were legislative attempts on the government's part to protect the physical environment on which man's very existence is dependent. As important as these types of laws are for the country's general welfare, they do not deal directly with the issue of the economic concentration of market power and thus will not be analyzed. One point should be mentioned, however, regarding the economic impact of these laws on industrial concentration. Many of these laws were quite detrimental to the country's smaller and middle-sized businesses, causing many of them to fail. Specifically, many smaller businesses simply could not meet the cost associated with implementing the air, water, and land waste disposal standards contained in these laws. On the other hand, the economy's monopolized sector, for the most part, adapted quite well when and where it believed itself compelled to do so. Such being the case, in a very limited sense, the consumer and environmental legislation passed during this period probably contributed to furthering the concentration of economic power in the economy.

Summary

Figure 1 is a flowchart summarization depicting the principal authors and concepts discussed in this chapter. In addition, the chart illustrates the growing dichotomy between the community's *dominant* theoretical economic belief and economic reality. Time is on the horizontal axis, and change is on the vertical axis. Line ER (economic reality) represents the increasing concentration of economic power as growing numbers of competitive market structures have been transformed into monopolistically and/or oligopolistically competitive market structures. Line ET (economic theory) represents Adam Smith's conception of competitive market structure capitalism. The series of step functions, lines ET_1 through ET_6 represent some of the more important attempts to modify Smith's central ideas. These modifications have been only marginally successful. This is indicated graphically by the increasingly larger gaps between ET and ER, represented by line segments A through G.

As one illustration, by the 1920s, monopolized markets had become an accomplished fact in many key industries. The political community's reaction to the populist agitation which accompanied these structural market changes was the creation of several standing regulatory commissions and the enactment of three major antitrust laws. Initially, the creation of these laws and commissions appeared to indicate that the government had reached a new consensus concerning its laissez-faire public policy posture. The movement from ET_0 to ET_1 depicts this *apparent* shift in attitude that accompanied the Genesis of Monopoly Capitalism. Nonetheless, the dichotomy between ET_1 and ER is larger (line B is longer than line A) since, for all practical purposes, the government continued to follow a laissez-faire policy. In other words, from a public policy perspective, Adam Smith's conception of competitive market structure capitalism maintained its dominant position in the eyes of policymakers as being the most accurate portrayal of economic reality.

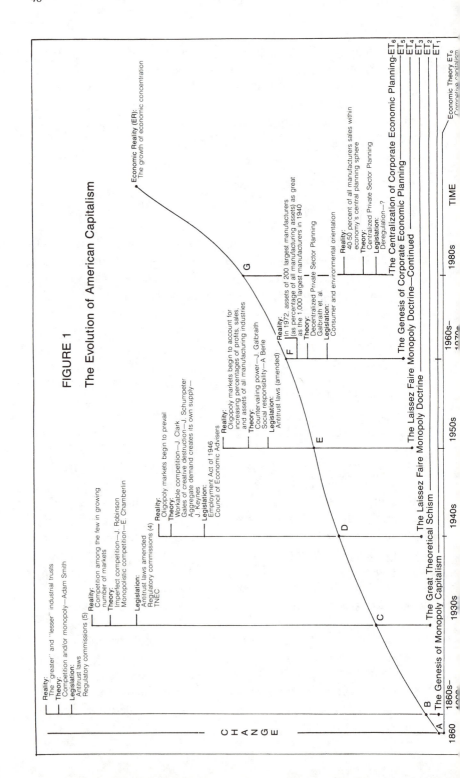

FIGURE 1

The Evolution of American Capitalism

The community's enduring belief in the existence of competitive market structure capitalism is partially explained by the fact that basic economic beliefs are religious in nature and, being so, are difficult to modify, even under the most trying circumstances. Also, with the government's implementation of Keynesian monetary and fiscal policies, the more devastating characteristics of monopolized markets—high levels of unemployment and idle plant capacity—were, in a relative sense, eliminated. Simultaneous with economic prosperity, a major shift occurred within the economics and business professions away from the study of micro-economics (the study of economic market structures) toward an almost total emphasis on the study of Keynesian macro-economics. This brought about a nearly complete eclipse in scholarly studies and/or criticism being directed toward the existence of monopolized markets. In addition, in those few cases where criticism and political pressures were directed toward markets where there were only one or two firms—that is, toward markets where even the most vivid imaginations and adept statistical transformations could not render a competitive market structure verdict—the ideas of Clark, Schumpeter, Berle, and Galbraith were often called upon to rationalize the government's belief in and adherence to the laissez-faire monopoly doctrine. Stated more specifically, by accepting Keynes's monetary and fiscal policy prescriptions, coupled with the ideas of Schumpeter et al., the government could rationally continue to pursue a laissez-faire monopoly doctrine in terms of the actual enforcement of the antitrust laws and/or the adoption of effective regulatory measures.

In conclusion, the central message depicted in Figure 1* is that, while repeated attempts have been made to displace the economic orthodoxy of Smith's competitive capitalism, none have been successful. The dichotomy between economic theory and economic reality has continued to grow throughout this century. Further, Chapters 3, 4, and 5 provide additional graphic evidence that this process is indeed continuing, if not actually accelerating, as the century draws to a close. Indeed, the question as to how much farther the dichotomy can grow before our basic economic belief in competitive capitalism becomes completely

---

*This figure is (1) merely a pedagogical device for giving a composite view of the ideas and concepts discussed in this chapter and is (2) *not* to indicate that (a) the step functions, (b) the growth of economic concentration, or (c) the dichotomy between economic reality and orthodox economic theory is subject to mathematical precision.

dysfunctional (for example, as happened in the 1930s) is assuming ever greater significance.

Notes

1. Adam Smith, *An Inquiry into the Nature and Causes of the Wealth of Nations* (New York: The Modern Library, 1937), p. 612.

2. Karl Polanyi, *The Great Transformation* (Boston: Beacon Press, 1957), p. 3.

3. John Maynard Keynes, *The General Theory of Employment, Interest, and Money* (New York: Harcourt, Brace and Company, 1936), p. 383.

4. Smith, *Wealth of Nations*, pp. 342–343.

5. Ibid., p. 250.

6. Ibid., p. 128.

7. Ibid., pp. 66–67.

8. Ibid., p. 147.

9. Ibid., p. 712.

10. Ibid., p. 61.

11. Ibid., pp. 605-606.

12. John Moody, *The Truth About the Trusts*, reprinted ed. (New York: Greenwood Press Publishers, 1968), pp. 486–487.

13. John D. Rockefeller, Sr., quoted in Rebecca Gruver, *An American History*, 2nd ed. (New York: Addison-Wesley Publishing Company, 1976), p. 607.

14. Moody, *The Truth About the Trusts*, pp. 494–495.

15. Ibid., pp. 4, 46–47, 62, 70, 97–98, 111, 152.

16. Ibid., pp. 441–442.

17. Thurman Arnold, *The Folklore of Capitalism* (New Haven: Yale University Press, 1937), p. 207.

18. Ibid., pp. 207–208.

19. Matthew Josephson, *The Robber Barons* (New York: Harcourt, Brace and World, Inc., 1934), p. 445.

20. Ibid., pp. 450–451.

21. Merle Fainsod and Lincoln Gordon, *Government and the American Economy* (New York: W. W. Norton and Company, Inc., 1941), p. 458.

22. Quoted in Robert C. Fellmeth, *The Interstate Commerce Omission* (New York: Grossman Publishers, 1970), pp. xiv-xv.

23. Joan Robinson, *The Economics of Imperfect Competition* (London: Macmillan and Company, Ltd., 1969), p. 307.

24. Edward Hastings Chamberlin, *The Theory of Monopolistic Competition*, 8th ed. (Cambridge, Mass.: Harvard University Press, 1965), p. 11.

25. Robinson, *The Economics of Imperfect Competition*, p. 309.

26. Chamberlin, *The Theory of Monopolistic Competition*, p. 109.

27. Ibid., pp. 195–196.

28. Robinson, *The Economics of Imperfect Competition*, p. xii.

29. Ibid., p. 319.

30. U.S. Congress, Temporary National Economic Committee, *Investigation of Concentration of Economic Power*, Part I, Economic Prologue (Washington, D.C.: Government Printing Office, 1939), pp. 185–190.

31. Robinson, *The Economics of Imperfect Competition*, p. xii.

32. John Maurice Clark, *Competition as a Dynamic Process* (Washington, D.C.: The Brookings Institute, 1961), p. 9.

33. John Maurice Clark, "Toward a Concept of Workable Competition," *The American Economic Review*, Vol. 30 (June 1940), p. 243.

34. William G. Shepherd, *Market Power and Economic Welfare* (New York: Random House, 1970), p. 16.

35. George J. Stigler, "Comment," *The American Economic Review* (May 1956), p. 505.

36. Joseph A. Schumpeter, *Capitalism, Socialism and Democracy*, 3rd ed. (New York: Harper and Row, 1950), pp. 84–85.

37. Ibid., p. ix.

38. Ibid., p. 83.

39. Roy F. Harrod, *The Life of John Maynard Keynes* (New York: Orion Books, 1951), p. 233.

40. Ibid.

41. John Maynard Keynes, *The End of Laissez-Faire* (London: The Hogarth Press, 1927), pp. 39–40.

42. Keynes, *The General Theory*, pp. 380–381.

43. Ibid., pp. 377–379.

44. U.S. Joint Economic Committee, Employment Act of 1946, as Amended, with Related Laws (Washington: Government Printing Office, 1977).

45. John Kenneth Galbraith, *American Capitalism* (Boston: Houghton Mifflin Company, 1952), p. 111.

46. Ibid., pp. 167–68.

47. Ibid., pp. 168–69.

48. Adolf A. Berle, Jr., *The 20th Century Capitalist Revolution* (New York: Harcourt, Brace and Company, 1954), pp. 164–165.

49. Ibid., pp. 69–70.

50. U.S. Congress, Temporary National Economy Committee, *Investigation of Concentration of Economic Power*, Part I, pp. 185–190.

51. Shepherd, *Market Power and Economic Welfare*, p. 101.

52. Ibid., p. 166.

Chapter Three

Centralized Private Sector Planning: The Basic Building Blocks and Interstitial Elements

The purpose of studying economics is not to acquire a set of ready-made answers to economic questions, but to learn how to avoid being deceived by economists.[1]

Joan Robinson

The contribution of economics to the exercise of power may be called its instrumental function—instrumental in that it serves not the understanding or improvement of the economic system, but the goals of those who have power in the system.[2]

John Kenneth Galbraith

In this chapter, as well as in Chapters 4 and 5, the theory of **Centralized Private Sector Planning** (**CPSP**) will be developed. In the present chapter, some of the building blocks and interstitial elements which, when taken together, help to make up "the whole" are presented. In the context of the CPSP, the term "building blocks" refers to those corporations and industries that are part of the economy's CPSP group. The term "interstitial elements" signifies the several planning instruments which, when used coincidentally, bind these corporations and industries together to form a structurally and functionally integrated production and distribution system.

In addition, the **Central Planning Tableau** (**CPT**) that accompanies this study is divided into two parts: (a) the **Central Planning Core** (**CPC**), and (b) those industries that actually engage in the production and distribution of goods and services. In Chapter 4, using the ideas developed in this chapter, the CPC's structural and functional characteristics will be examined. In actuality, the CPC consists of seven banks

(Citicorp, the Chase Manhattan Corporation, Manufacturers Hanover, J. P. Morgan and Company, Chemical New York Corporation, Continental Illinois Corporation, and First Chicago Corporation), four insurance companies (Prudential Insurance Company, Metropolitian Life, Equitable Life Assurance, and New York Life), and one diversified financial institution (Continental Corporation). In the context of CPSP, the CPC—as its name suggests— is the focal point of the planning process. More specifically, the CPC is a tightly bonded and cohesive group of institutions that functions as a vehicle for organizing and coordinating the production and distribution activities between and among various industries. Finally, in Chapter 5 the ideas discussed in Chapters 3 and 4 will be both integrated and expanded upon so as to provide a more complete and/or composite perspective of the CPSP theory.

In a very real sense, the meaning, importance, and functional nature of the planning instruments developed in this chapter (as well as the CPC introduced in Chapter 4) *cannot* be correctly grasped without first having a nascent idea or understanding of the fundamental nature of the CPSP theory itself. Simply put: It is often difficult, if not impossible, to form a correct idea of a *part* without some understanding of the *whole* to which it belongs. To gain such an understanding, let us begin by delineating the various approaches to economic planning currently in practice. This will provide a topography or relief within which the theory of CPSP can be placed.

Generic approaches to economic planning

Basically, economic planning may occur in either public or private sector institutions. In turn, both public sector and private sector economic planning may be either highly centralized or decentralized. These various planning approaches are depicted in Table 6.

Centralized Public Sector Planning

Economies that are usually portrayed as typifying centralized public sector planning include those of Russia, China, and Eastern European Soviet bloc nations. As illustration, in Russia a comprehensive and detailed ''Five-Year Economic Plan'' for the entire nation is drawn up by the Gosplan (a Council of Ministers) in Moscow. The Five-Year Economic Plan explicitly outlines the authority vested in and the

---

Table 6

Generic Approaches to Economic Planning

Public sector planning	Private sector planning
Centralized[a]	Decentralized[c]
Decentralized[b]	Centralized[d]

[a]Countries that have adopted a Centralized Public Sector Planning approach would include Russia and China, as well as the Eastern European Soviet bloc nations.

[b]Countries that have adopted a Decentralized Public Sector Planning approach would include Japan, Germany, France, and Sweden.

[c]Decentralized Private Sector Planning refers to the type of economic planning that takes place in many of America's largest corporations as envisioned by Galbraith, Bazelon, Myrdal, et al.

[d]Centralized Private Sector Planning refers to the theory being developed later in this chapter and in Chapters 4 and 5 and is primarily an American institutional arrangement.

---

responsibilities of each of several regional economic councils, each individual industry within each region, and each of the individual factories or plants within each industry. Membership on Gosplan, however, is limited to Communist Party members (as is true of virtually all other government positions). Also, the leadership positions within the country's economic institutions are almost without exception reserved for members of the Communist Party. Finally, nearly all the country's manufacturing and service industries are nationalized, trade unions are controlled by the state, and the vast bulk of agricultural production is done through state-controlled "agricultural collectives or state farms." In essence, then, a centrally controlled and monolithic party—the Communist Party—creates a comprehensive and very detailed economic plan which is used to administer, or direct, the nation's economic activities. This approach may be viewed as the archetypical model for centralized public sector planning.*

Decentralized Public Sector Planning

Economies that are usually portrayed as typifying decentralized public sector planning would include such countries as Japan, Germany,

---

*For an excellent discussion concerning how the five-year economic plan is created and administered, see Allan G. Gruchy's *Comparative Economic Systems* (New York: Houghton Mifflin Company, 1966). Also, see Paul R. Gregory and Robert C. Stuart's *Soviet Economic Structure and Performance* (New York: Harper and Row, Publishers, 1974).

France, and Sweden. While the governments in these countries do not engage in all-encompassing economic planning as does the Gosplan, they do engage in an extensive amount of national economic planning which, to varying degrees, is closely coordinated with the private sector. For instance, in France the government creates a very elaborate economic plan wherein the country's long-range national goals are specified. In addition, the output from each industry that must be forthcoming if the goals stated in the national plan are to be met is explicitly stated. In developing *Le Plan* for the nation's economy, various committees made up of representatives from industry (both management and labor), agriculture, and government are involved. After receiving recommendations from the various planning committees, the government finalizes and then publishes its *Le Plan*. While industries are not compelled by law to be part of the national planning process, the government may use its taxing powers, as well as government regulation, to encourage cooperation. The government, for example, may attempt to regulate both access to capital markets as well as the actual price a specific industry must pay for borrowing money, in order to elicit a cooperative attitude. Also, an industry's tax obligations may be adjusted upward or downward. Lastly, in France many businesses are state-owned. Thus, through a combination of taxation, regulation, and state ownership the French government has considerable leverage in executing *Le Plan*. Nonetheless, the methods employed by the French government in eliciting cooperation from the private sector are essentially "indirect" in nature; i.e., unlike Russia's five-year economic plan wherein economic institutions receive direct orders from the government to produce a certain type and quantity of good or service, the French use an indirect carrot and stick approach. Since private sector institutions are free to choose whether or not to be part of the planning process, and since the government uses basically indirect methods in seeking private sector cooperation, the French planning system may be appropriately referred to as decentralized public sector planning, in order to differentiate it from the centralized public sector planning approach used by the Soviet Union. The French system of economic planning, primarily due to its indirect approach, is often referred to as "indicative planning."*

*The election of François Mitterrand's socialist government has not altered in any fundamental sense France's indicative planning approach. Notwithstanding the pre-election nationalization rhetoric, in terms of sales and/or assets the French government still owns less than one-third of France's economy. Futhermore, in terms of monetary and fiscal policy, the government still uses the indicative approach in its planning efforts.

Other countries that engage in decentralized public sector planning may have more or less government ownership, more or less government regulation, and more or less cooperation between government and business in creating and executing their national economic plans than exists in France. The essential point, however, is that these countries consider cooperation between public and private institutions an essential ingredient in the creation and execution of national economic policy.

Decentralized Private Sector Planning

In the 1960s, as noted in Chapter 2, several influential economists argued that the "imperatives of technology" demanded and/or necessitated that modern corporations engage in high-level and long-range economic planning—and further, that economic planning within the modern corporation had already advanced to the point where the market system itself had undergone a major metamorphosis.

In the words of John Kenneth Galbraith:

> . . . in this larger context of change, the forces inducing human effort have changed. This assaults the most majestic of all economic assumptions, namely that man in his economic activities is subject to the authority of the market. Instead, we have an economic system which, whatever its formal ideological billing, is in substantial part a planned economy. . . . The imperative of technology and organization, not the images of ideology, are what determines the shape of economic society.[3]

Briefly summarized, Galbraith's argument, stated substantially in his own words, is as follows:

• The imperatives of technology and organization and not the images of ideology are what determine the nature of economic institutions.

• It is not to individuals but to organizations that power in the economic world and power in society at large has passed.

• The process of modern industrial decision making entails drawing on and appraising the specialized knowledge and information of numerous individuals because of:

    a. the massive technological and investment requirements of large-scale modern industry,

    b. the detailed and long-range planning that both investment

requirements and the application of modern technology make necessary, and

 c. the need for *group decisions* which long-range planning makes
necessary.

 • A decision that requires the specialized knowledge of a group is
subject to safe review only by another such group which possesses
similar knowledge and expertise.

 • Group decisions, unless acted upon by another similar technically
competent group, tend to be absolute.

 • The absolute characteristic of group decision making within corporate America gives the corporation almost complete autonomy.

 • The traditional owner capitalist or entrepreneur is a dying species
since the crucial and "absolute decisions" are in substantial measure
made by a planning technocracy.

 • Finally, the goals and methods of the planning technocracy:

 a. are not subject to effective public or democratic scrutiny, and

 b. are very often not in the best interest of the vast majority of the
working and consuming public.

Thus, the technology connection begets planning; planning begets
group decision making; group decision making begets absolute decisions; and the absolute nature of group decisions begets corporate
autonomy; and corporate autonomy negates or renders inoperative the
basic principles of democratic pluralism, substituting in its place decentralized private sector planning.

 Gunnar Myrdal (Professor of International Economics, University
of Stockholm, and Swedish Minister of Trade and Commerce) also
viewed technology as an active and basic force in shaping both institutional structures and social relationships:

> Technological and organizational developments have in many fields been
> increasing the size of the units in relation to the markets. At the same
> time, in all other fields the individual units have found the means by which
> to combine.

> They have thereby come into a position where they can influence the
> markets and manipulate the prices. The markets and the prices have more
> and more lost their character of being given and objective conditions,
> outside the influence of the individual units. . . . The markets have be-
> come consciously regulated by the participants.

> When this happens on a large enough scale, a fundamental institutional

change has occurred in the position of the human beings in relation to each other and to the community.[4]

And, concerning the "fundamental institutional change" that had occurred:

> . . . our national economies have become increasingly regulated, organized and coordinated, i.e., planned. . . .[5]

David T. Bazelon, in his witty and profound book *The Paper Economy*, actually predated both Galbraith and Myrdal in analyzing the relationship between the imperatives of modern technology and decentralized private sector planning:

> . . . as centers of industrial and financial power, market organizers, and general governing bodies,big corporations are necessarily planning agencies. . . . It is intelligence and knowledge applied in the administration of our complex social technology: planning and technology go together; they are common imperatives. You can, then, easily see that: (1) planning is indispensable; (2) it is in glaring contradiction to our free enterprise ideology; (3) it is something that takes both superior intelligence and training, which signifies the heightened importance of intellectual experts; and finally, (4) the problem of power in the modern setting cannot be dissociated from it.[6]

Professor Bazelon placed great importance on the role that ideology (classical and neoclassical economic ideology) played in preventing rational discussion concerning both the location and exercise of power in American society:

> The idea of Competition is one of the most mindless notions ever to dominate the supposed thinking of a society of grown men. It is a religious tenet of faith, because: (1) it requires that the evidence of one's senses be denied; and (2) it forbids non-ritualistic thinking. . . . It is in essence a theology of militant mindlessness. With this idea as the keystone of The System, it becomes impossible to discuss anything rationally—What are we doing? Why are we doing it? Does it work? What are the alternatives? and so on.[7]

Whether a rational discussion of economic problems is possible, given the overwhelming dominance of classical and neoclassical economic ideology, is indeed an extremely crucial question. Consider the following two statements: (1) We should deregulate the price of natural gas and let the *market system* set the price; as opposed to: (2) We should deregulate the price of natural gas and let the *petroleum industry* set the price. Of course, the market system usually brings to mind Adam Smith's *impersonal market forces of supply and demand* while the *petroleum industry—or more precisely the energy industry—for an increasing number of observers connotes a group of private sector monopoly planners.* Presumably, a rational discussion of the world's energy problems must be predicated on some empirical knowledge concerning whether the energy industry actively plans and regulates supply and demand or whether the industry is primarily regulated, itself, by impersonal market forces. In his book *The Managed Economy*, Michael D. Reagan points out clearly and concisely the political questions that decentralized private sector planning raises:

> The automatic economy is dead. The managed economy is the phrase that applies to both the public and private sectors. . . .
>
> Once we begin to look at our system as one that is consciously planned rather than impersonally directed by market forces, some essentially political questions come to the fore. Who will do the managing? For whose benefit? What will be the goals? Who will set them? How? Are the institutional arrangements of our society, designed as they were for a quite different situation, adequate to the managerial task? If not, what needs to be changed?[8]

If the technology connection in conjunction with rational thought dictates the necessity for economic planning, Reagan's questions certainly deserve more attention from a much wider audience than they have yet received. And, of course, it is obviously true that many American corporations engage in long-range economic planning. For instance, General Motors has an elaborate planning technocracy devoted to developing very intricate and detailed short-run (5 to 10 years) economic plans, as well as more expansive or broadly gauged (10 to 20 years) economic plans. Simply put: The decentralized private sector planning thesis can be denied only by those with a singular immunity to common sense and real world experience. Nonetheless, one purpose in writing this book is to demonstrate how economic planning has become much more centralized than heretofore realized. In short, economic planning between and among the corporations and industries that make up the base or foundation of America's economy (automobiles, energy, steel, computers, food, etc.) has evolved to the point where:

• from a structural and functional perspective, these corporations and industries have become technologically, financially, and administratively interdependent; and

• over the years a series of planning instruments has evolved that both allow and, indeed, to some extent, necessitate cooperation and coordination between and among these key industries in their production and distribution activities.

In terms of a definition, then, CPSP may be viewed *as a process whereby the production and distribution activities of the economy's key corporation and industries are organized and coordinated so as to bind these corporations and industries together into a functionally integrated production and distribution system.*

The remainder of this chapter will be devoted to an examination of the various planning instruments in the CPSP process. These planning instruments are divided into two basic categories: (1) formal and/or legally binding planning instruments, and (2) informal and/or influential planning instruments. Within these two major groupings, there are several subcategories, each of which will be discussed briefly. An abbreviated Central Planning Tableau will then be constructed to illustrate the basic characteristics of the various planning instruments from both a *structural* and *functional* perspective.

Formal and/or legally binding planning instruments

The three primary planning instruments classified as formal and/or legally binding are: (1) corporate stock, (2) corporate boards of directors, and (3) corporate debt.

Corporate stock

Ownership and control

A vote for each share renders a combination between a few principal stockholders, to monopolize the power and benefits of the bank, too easy. An equal vote to each stockholder, however great or small his interest in the institution, allows not that degree of weight to large stockholders which it is reasonable they should have, and which, perhaps, their security and that of the bank require. A prudent mean is to be preferred.[9]

Legally, the owners of a corporation are its stockholders. Being the corporation's legal owners, stockholders are entitled to elect those who are legally responsible for running the corporation—the board of directors. In essence, then, the members of a corporation's board of directors are the elected representatives of the corporation's legal owners—its stockholders. This seems straightforward enough, but, as with many other seemingly straightforward ideas, in actual practice it becomes somewhat more complicated. In fact, there are three basic approaches to electing a corporation's directors—the English Common Law method, the majority share method, and the proportional or limited share method.

On the one hand, under the English Common law method, each stockholder may cast only one vote for each directorship position, regardless of the number of shares owned. Thus, under this system, one stockholder who owns 90 percent of a corporation's stock can be outvoted by two stockholders each of whom owns 5 percent. If such were to happen, the shareholder who contributed nearly all the corporation's equity capital would be effectively disenfranchised. On the other hand, under the majority share voting method, each stockholder is permitted one vote for each share of stock owned for each directorship position. Given this method, any one individual or group controlling 51 percent of a corporation's stock can be assured of filling each seat on the board of directors with a representative of its choice. In effect, if two people combine voting rights equalling 51 percent, they can effectively disenfranchise a stockholder who controls the other 49 percent. It would seem much more equitable and just for a person who contributed 49 percent of a corporation's equity capital to have some representation on the corporation's board of directors.

In considering these two extreme approaches (English Common Law versus majority share), Alexander Hamilton, in a report concerning the creation of a National Bank, submitted to the House of Representatives on 14 December 1790, said that "a prudent mean is to be preferred." Specifically, for the National Bank, Hamilton suggested the following proportional or limited share voting method:

> The number of votes to which each stockholder shall be entitled shall be according to the number of shares he shall hold, in the proportions following—that is to say: For one share, and not more than two shares, one vote; for every two shares above two, and not exceeding ten, one vote;

for every four shares above ten, and not exceeding thirty, one vote; for every six shares above thirty, and not exceeding sixty, one vote; for every eight shares above sixty, and not exceeding one hundred, one vote; and for every ten shares above one hundred, one vote; but no person, co-partnership, or body politic shall be entitled to a greater number than thirty votes.[10]

Given Hamilton's formula, stockholders who owned a large share of stock as well as those who owned only a few shares would usually be capable of electing some representative to the Bank's board of directors. The proportional or limited share voting method, then, is a safeguard against disenfranchisement and tends to provide more proportionate representation. Numerous formulas can be created, similar to Hamilton's, to allow for proportional representation. A minority—yet a significant number—of large corporations in the United States, either in their articles of incorporation or in their bylaws, have a provision which allows for a method of proportional or limited share voting called *cumulative voting.**

Cumulative voting is a very simple and straightforward method. Each stockholder determines the number of votes he may cast in an election by multiplying the shares of stock owned by the number of directors to be elected. In addition, all of a stockholder's votes may be cast for one candidate, or spread among several candidates. To illustrate, assume a corporation has 100,000 shares of voting stock outstanding and 15 members on its board of directors. Also, assume only two stockholders—Stockholder A owning 93,740 shares and Stockholder B with 6,260 shares. In order to determine the number of

*The English Common Law method of voting has been almost universally abandoned. Twenty states (Alabama, Colorado, Connecticut, Delaware, Florida, Iowa, Louisiana, Maryland, Minnesota, Nevada, New Jersey, New Mexico, New York, Oklahoma, Oregon, Rhode Island, Tennessee, Utah, Vermont, and Virginia) adhere to the majority share method, unless a corporation specifically states in its bylaws or in its articles of confederation that it allows cumulative voting. In these twenty states, then, cumulative voting is permitted but not required. Also, twenty states (Alaska, Arizona, Arkansas, California, Idaho, Illinois, Indiana, Kansas, Kentucky, Michigan, Mississippi, Missouri, Montana, Nebraska, North Dakota, Pennsylvania, South Dakota, Washington, West Virginia, and Wyoming) require by law that the cumulative voting procedure be used. In addition, five states (Hawaii, Ohio, Texas, North Carolina, and South Carolina) require that cumulative voting be allowed if any stockholder or proxy holder so requests. Usually such a request must be in the form of a written notice delivered to the corporation's secretary 48 hours before the scheduled meeting. Finally, five states (Georgia, Maine, New Hampshire, Wisconsin, and Massachusetts) have no legal provisions regarding the cumulative voting procedures.

votes each stockholder has, the number of shares owned is multiplied times the number of directors to be elected. In this case, Stockholder A would have 1,406,100 votes and Stockholder B would have 93,900 votes. Now, how could Stockholder A divide his votes in order to assure the election of his candidates to all 15 positions? It cannot be done! That is, 1,406,100 divided by 15 equals 93,740 votes; and, if Stockholder B casts all his 93,900 votes for *one* individual, that individual would automatically be one of the 15 top vote getters.* Stockholder B, then, is automatically assured of representation by owning only 6.26 percent of the corporation's voting stock. In effect, under the cumulative voting method, any stockholder who owns a bare majority (50 percent + 1 share) of a corporation's stock can be assured of electing a majority of the corporation's directors, but will be unable to stop anyone with significant minority shareholder interest from obtaining representation proportionate to his or her holdings.

In summary, the theoretical components in the overall argument that stockholders should have a right to determine whom a corporation's leadership team will consist of, including the narrower argument for proportional representation, are as follows:

• All stockholders as the providers of a corporation's equity capital will: (a) given wise and effecive management decisions, reap rewards in the form of profits, and (b) given unwise and ineffective management decisions, possibly lose their capital investments.

• All stockholders, as a group, generally possess enough knowledge and information to make rational decisions concerning the competence and/or effectiveness of a corporation's leadership team.

• All stockholders, then, as providers of the corporation's equity capital, should legally be defined as owners, and, as owners, should have the right to choose the corporation's leaders, that is, choose those to whom they have entrusted their money.

---

*The following formula can be used to determine how many shares of stock a person must own in order to elect a given number of people to a corporation's board of directors, given the existence of cumulative voting.

$$\frac{\left[\begin{array}{c}\text{Shares outstanding} \\ \text{of voting stock}\end{array} \times \begin{array}{c}\text{Number of} \\ \text{directors wanted}\end{array}\right]}{\left[\begin{array}{c}\text{Total number of directors} \\ \text{on the board}\end{array}\right] + 1} + 1 = \begin{array}{c}\text{Number of shares} \\ \text{needed to} \\ \text{elect the number} \\ \text{of directors} \\ \text{stipulated}\end{array}$$

For an excellent discussion of the cumulative voting procedure, see Harvey G. Guthmann's and Herbert E. Dougall's Corporate Financial Policy, 3rd ed. (Englewood Cliffs, N. J.: Prentice-Hall, Inc., 1955).

• Finally, *no* owner (whether majority or minority) should be totally disenfranchised, but, instead, all owners should share *proportionately* (proportionate to the amount of stock owned) in the right to choose the corporation's leaders.

The separation of ownership and control. As logical as the above argument may seem, the crucial question still remains; that is, in the real world, what is the relationship between the modern corporation's board of directors and its owners, the stockholders? Several quotes will provide examples of the conventional wisdom that currently exists among the vast majority of scholars interested in this question. William H. Husband and James C. Dockeray note that:

> the dispersion of ownership necessarily means that financial interest in the form of stock investments is not required to effectuate control. Instead, power of direction is achieved through techniques of organization whereby the votes of stockholders are marshaled into the hands of a small group. . . . Under the circumstances, there is a reversal of the normal, statutory flow of power so that the management directs and controls the stockholder instead of being selected by the stockholders.[11]

Harry G. Guthmann and Herbert E. Dougall state:

> When the number of stockholders is small, their interest is likely to be considerable and their participation in meetings active. As the number grows, the weight of the individual's voting power diminishes and he tends to become inert. Among our larger American corporations, the average individual's voting power is negligible, his acquaintance with the problems of the business small, and his ability to judge individual members of management slight. Under such circumstances a board of directors once placed in the saddle is well-nigh self-perpetuating and permanent. . . .

> A very real problem of control has thus been created by the growth of the corporation and the diffusion of voting power over large scattered groups of stockholders. In theory, the interest of stockholders in profits induces their selection of competent and efficient men. But if self-perpetuating dynasties are created, which like the ancient lines of kings, are overthrown only because of the grossest misbehavior or by the machinations of other rulers, what guarantees of social efficiency are left in the system?[12]

There are two crucial elements common to both of these quotations.

Table 7

Number of Common Stockholders for Selected Years for Selected Corporations

| Corporation | Number of stockholders per selected years | | | |
	Other years	1929	1940	1978
Standard Oil Company of New Jersey (now Exxon)	NA	62,317	136,355	693,176
Du Pont	809 (1900)	9,970	63,467	202,573
General Motors	NA	NA	NA	1,225,384
United States Steel	17,723 (1902)	102,905	163,425	258,239
International Harvester	NA	NA	24,946	132,429
General Electric	NA	51,882	215,556	566,000

Source: Moody's Industrial Manual (New York: Moody's Investors Service, Inc., various years).

Note: NA = Not available.

First, stock ownership has become so widely dispersed (stock ownership *diffusion*) that no individual stockholder or group has control of stock sufficiently large enough in voting power to give the holder control and/or influence over the selection of a corporation's board of directors. And thus, second, the boards of directors of America's largest corporations have become, for all practical purposes, self-perpetuating dynasties; further, stockholders, for all practical purposes, have become effectively disenfranchised.

The degree to which the " . . . diffusion of voting power over large scattered groups of stockholders" has become a reality for many of our large corporations is aptly depicted in Table 7. For example, at the turn of the century, Du Pont (E. I.) de Nemours and Company had 809 stockholders. Du Pont's stockholders increased in number, however, to 9,970 in 1929; 63,467 in 1940; and 202,573 in 1978. Exxon increased its number of stockholders from 62,317 in 1929 to 693,176 in 1978. The number of stockholders owning shares in United States Steel increased from 17,723 in 1902 to 258,239 in 1978.

Consider the following:

• Many corporate decisions are the product of a lengthy planning process involving experts from numerous disciplines that usually takes many months (and very often several years) to formulate and implement—à la the decentralized private sector planning thesis of Galbraith, Myrdal, and others.

• Many corporations' Chief Executive Officers (CEOs)—let alone the average stockholder—could not identify, without looking at a chart, the names of all the corporation's subsidiaries (often numbering in the hundreds), or for that matter all the foreign countries in which the corporation was actually doing business at a given point in time.

• The vast majority of stockholders would spend more money attending the annual stockholders' meetings than they would earn in profit for the year from their stock. And, what if one owned stock in a half-dozen or more different corporations?

In essence, *from a purely logical point of view*, the sheer complexity of the modern corporation, coupled with the diffusion of stockholders in terms of both the amount of stock held and geography, tend to compel in a very ironclad manner indifference on the part of most individual stockholders toward attempting to actively influence corporate decisions and/or to influence corporate decision makers through the process of voting their shares. While substantial participation in the election of a corporation's leadership team for the vast majority of stockholders is nonexistent, a ritual has been created whereby the formal trappings of stockholder participation are maintained. This ritual is known as *proxy voting*.

Figure 2 contains a typical example of a proxy statement sent to shareholders on behalf of a corporation's management and/or board of directors. Stockholders, by signing and returning the proxy to the corporation, are, in effect, legally delegating those individuals specified on the proxy statement to act on their behalf at the stockholders' meeting and to also exercise their voting privileges.

The proxy statement in Figure 2, when signed and returned, would allow three existing members of the corporation's board of directors to exercise the voting privileges of the absent stockholders. This would, in turn, allow the existing directors to control the entry and exit of individuals into and out of their group. In actual fact, then, proxy voting is a mechanism whereby the voting privileges of many of the corporation's legal owners are centralized and controlled by the corporation's existing management team. In the academic literature, this has become known as the separation of "ownership and control."

Several studies have been undertaken over the last several decades with the specific intention of determining, *from an empirical point of view*, the degree to which the separation of ownership and control is an

FRONT

PROXY

XYZ, INC.

Annual Meeting of Shareholders, May 8, 1968

The undersigned holder of Common Stock of XYZ, Inc. (the Company) hereby appoints JANE DOE, JOHN SMITH and WILLIAM BROWN, or any of them acting alone in the absence of the others, the proxies of the undersigned, with full power of substitution, to vote the shares of the undersigned, with all the powers the undersigned would have if personally present, at the Annual Meeting of Shareholders of the Company to be held on May 8, 1968, and at all adjournments thereof:

(1) In the election of eleven directors; and

(2) In the transaction of such other business as may properly come before the meeting.

UNLESS INSTRUCTIONS TO THE CONTRARY ARE SPECIFIED, SAID PROXIES WILL VOTE IN THE ELECTION OF DIRECTORS, AND WILL USE THEIR DISCRETION WITH RESPECT TO ANY MATTERS REFERRED TO IN ITEM 2.

BACK

(Continued from other side)

The undersigned acknowledges receipt of the Notice of Annual Meeting and Proxy Statement dated April 18, 1968.

This proxy is solicited on behalf of the Management of the Company, and may be revoked in the manner set forth in the Proxy Statement.

Dated 1968

. . . .
(Signature)

Please date, and sign exactly as your name appears hereon and return in the enclosed envelope. If shares are held jointly each shareholder named should sign. Executors, administrators, trustees, etc., should so indicate when signing. If signed by an agent, attach the instrument authorizing the agent to execute the proxy, or a photostatic copy thereof. If the signer is a corporation, please sign the full corporate name, by a duly authorized officer.

FIGURE 2

Example of a Typical Proxy Statement Used by America's Large Corporations accomplished fact in corporate life. One of the first, and certainly a seminal, work was that of Adolf A. Berle and Gardiner C. Means, *The Modern Corporation and Private Property*, originally published in 1932. Berle and Means argued:

> As the ownership of corporate wealth has become more widely dispersed, ownership of that wealth and control over it have come to lie less and less in the same hands. Under the corporate system control over individual wealth can be and is being exercised with a minimum of ownership interest. Conceivably it can be exercised without any such interest. Ownership of wealth without appreciable control and control of wealth without appreciable ownership appear to be the logical outcome of corporate development.[13]

In determining which corporations were "management controlled" and which were controlled by "minority ownership," Berle and Means used ownership of 20 percent of a corporation's voting stock as an indicator of minority ownership control:

> The dividing line between minority and management control was drawn roughly at 20 percent, though in a few special instances a smaller holding was credited with the power to control. It is notable that in none of the companies classed under management control was the dominant stock interest known to be greater than 5 percent of the voting stock. Cases falling between 20 and 5 percent were usually classed as joint minority management control.[14]

Their sample consisted of the 200 largest nonfinancial corporations (including 42 railroads, 52 public utilities, and 106 industrials) in existence in 1929. Of the 200 corporations examined, 44 percent were classified as "management controlled."

Robert J. Larner, in the early 1960s, while still a graduate student in economics at the University of Wisconsin, conducted a study to determine if the trend toward management control had increased, decreased, or remained stable since the time of the Berle and Means study. Larner used essentially the same methodology as employed by Berle and Means, except that he reduced the "minority ownership control" threshold to only 10 percent, stating that:

> in view of the greater size of the 200 largest nonfinancial corporations in 1963 and the wider dispersion of their stock, this lower limit to minority

control seems too high. In the present study a firm is classified as immediately controlled by minority stock ownership if 10 percent or more of its voting stock is held by an individual, family, corporation or *group of business associates*.[15] (emphasis added)

Even after reducing the minority ownership control threshold from 20 to 10 percent, Larner determined that, in 1963, 84.5 percent of the country's 200 largest nonfinancial corporations were "management controlled."

The minority ownership control threshold. Clearly, the actual minority ownership control threshold is a judgment call, not subject to a precise mathematical formulation, and differs from corporation to corporation. Scholars interested in this question do differ. For example, in 1968, the House Subcommittee on Domestic Finance, chaired by the late Wright Patman, completed a study (*Commercial Banks and Their Trust Activities: Emerging Influence on the American Economy*) wherein the Committee adopted a 5 percent minority ownership control threshold level:

> The Subcommittee in carrying out this survey, determined that in general a stockholder of 5 percent or more of any class of stock in a single corporation was a significant factor in judging the extent to which a bank might have substantial influence or control over a corporation.[16]

The Committee went on to add:

> In practical terms, it is clear that control of a small percent, even 1 or 2 percent, of stock in a publicly held corporation can gain tremendous influence over a company's policies and operations.[17]

In 1970, Congress amended the Securities Exchange Act of 1934 so as to require any person owning 5 percent of a corporation's stock to report such to the SEC. Previously, only those owning stock totaling 10 percent or more were required to report.* Presumably, Congress changed its stock ownership reporting law to reflect the belief by some of its members that 5 percent was a relevant minority stock ownership control threshold.[18] Lastly, in 1974 Arthur F. Burns (then Chairman of the Board of Governors, Federal Reserve System), in response to a

---

*Corporate officers, as well as members of boards of directors, are required to report their stock holdings regardless of amount.

letter from the late Senator Lee Metcalf, wherein Senator Metcalf had requested that the Federal Reserve System require its member banks to report their ''20 or 30'' largest stockholders, replied that:

> . . . the Board recognizes that stockholdings below 5 percent can in some circumstances constitute control.[19]

In essence, there seems to be a rather broad consensus within the academic community and within government (from those of various ideological persuasions) to the effect that seemingly small amounts of stock ownership in a large corporation may be an effective tool for establishing strong influence, if not outright minority ownership control, over many of the country's public corporations.

The idea that a corporation's board of directors could become a ''self-perpetuating dynasty,'' if the vast majority of stockholders either do not bother to vote their shares at all or do so by proxy, is a rather straightforward proposition. The idea that a group which controlled somewhere between 5 and/or 10 percent of a corporation's voting stock could significantly influence and perhaps even dominate the corporation, however, is not as obvious. The arguments upon which the minority ownership control thesis is usually supported are as follows. First, it would be extremely difficult for an outside group to dismantle a controlling minority. To cite an extreme case, if one had wanted to acquire, say, 10 percent of General Electric's common stock in January 1978 (approximately 22.7 million shares at $50 each), this would have required an investment approaching $1 billion. To say the least, this could present a rather difficult financial operation for even the wealthiest individuals and/or corporate institutions. Thus, a group who already owned 10 percent of General Electric's voting stock would be substantially immune to external pressures.

Second, as is indicated in Table 8, Column 6, it would take the marshaling of votes from tens of thousands of shareholders via proxies to obtain the voting power equal to that already possessed by the minority ownership group. And, once a proxy battle started, the minority control group would also be busy collecting proxies, further increasing its already substantial voting power. In addition, the minority control group, being an inside group, would not itself be hampered by the extremely expensive procedure of printing and mailing duplicate proxies, as would be the case for the outside group which was attempting to gain control.

Table 8

The Approximate Number of Stockholders Necessary to Represent 10 Percent of Selected Corporations' Voting Stock (1 January 1978)

Corporation	Column 1 Voting stock outstanding	Column 2 Voting stock outstanding, less 10 percent (Column 1 × 90 percent)	Column 3 Number of common stockholders	Column 4 Average number of shares per stockholder* (Column 2 ÷ Column 3)	Column 5 10 percent of voting stock	Column 6 Number of stockholders equivalent to 10 percent of the voting stock* (Column 5 ÷ Column 4)
General Electric Company	227,154,000	204,438,600	553,000	369	22,715,400	61,559
IBM	148,574,612	133,717,151	581,513	230	14,857,461	64,598
International Harvester	28,729,000	25,856,100	128,583	201	2,872,900	14,293
United States Steel	84,169,399	75,752,460	248,986	304	8,416,939	27,687
Standard Oil, California	170,390,000	153,351,000	268,000	572	17,039,000	29,788
General Motors	285,568,178	257,011,361	1,225,384	210	28,556,817	135,985

Source: Moody's Industrial Manual, 1978.

*Column 4 is probably 50 to 75 percent higher than the actual average number of shares owned by the vast majority of stockholders. For example, "over three-quarters of GM stockholders own 100 shares or less. More than half own 50 shares or less" (see GM's 1980 *General Motors Public Interest Report*). Thus, Column 6 is probably 2 or 3 times lower than real world circumstances would dictate. Table 8, then, is simply a pedagogical device to help illustrate why the experts contend that the owner of a significant, yet small, minority of voting stock (given otherwise widespread stock ownership diffusion) can very often obtain strong influence, if not outright working control, of a large corporation.

Third, if a majority of the corporation's board (essentially an inside group) decided to resist the takeover efforts of an extremely well-financed third party, a much more serious proxy battle would probably take place. It is important to note, however, that any individual or group who already owned 10 percent or more of a large corporation's voting stock would undoubtedly be a member of the country's corporate elite and, as such, would automatically command a great deal of respect and allegiance from many other corporate leaders as well as other large stockholders. After all, the corporate elite (the Fords, Rockefellers, Du Ponts, Graces, Gettys, etc.) have been guiding our economic system since the turn of the century and are viewed by many as having transcendent business acumen and powers. Further, the ultimate winner of such a contest would be the group that collected the most votes, either directly or by proxy. The commanding lead which a minority owner who already controlled 10 percent of the corporation's voting stock would begin with, coupled with its ability to command the loyalty and allegiance of other large stockholders, would represent a formidable obstacle to its removal from power.

Fourth, and last, Figure 3 contains several illustrations which will also help in understanding how minority stock ownership can be translated into real economic power. To begin, assume that a corporation has 100,000 shares of common stock outstanding, that it has 15 directors on its board, and that cumulative voting is either required or allowed. On the one hand, as is indicated by Example I in Figure 3, if all 100,000 shares were voted in an election, it would take 50 percent plus one share to insure majority representation on the board. On the other hand, Example II, if only 25,000 shares were voted, it would take only 12.5 percent of the voting stock outstanding to insure majority representation. In addition, if one determined that having 5 representatives on the 15-person board would be sufficient, this could be accomplished by controlling 31.2 percent of the outstanding shares if all 100,000 shares were voted, but would require controlling only *7.8 percent* if only 25,000 shares were voted, as is illustrated in Examples III and IV.* One can easily imagine, then, that a director on the board of a corporation who represented 10 percent of the corporation's outstanding stock

---

*Remember that in cumulative voting the number of votes a stockholder is entitled to is determined by multiplying the total number of shares owned or controlled by the number of directors on the board or by the number of directorships actually up for election.

FIGURE 3

Cumulative Voting and Minority Control

In the four examples listed below the assumptions are that the corporation has 100,000 shares of common stock outstanding and a 15-member board of directors.

EXAMPLE I: Assuming all 100,000 shares were voted, stock control amounting to 50 percent + 1 vote would insure the election of eight directors.

$$\frac{100,000 \times 8}{15 + 1} + 1 = 50,001 \text{ shares} \qquad \begin{array}{l} 50 \text{ percent of} \\ \text{stock outstanding} \end{array}$$

EXAMPLE II: Assuming only 25,000 shares were voted, stock control amounting to 12.5 percent would insure the election of eight directors.

$$\frac{25,000 \times 8}{15 + 1} + 1 = 12,501 \text{ shares} \qquad \begin{array}{l} 12.5 \text{ percent of} \\ \text{stock outstanding} \end{array}$$

EXAMPLE III: Assuming all 100,000 shares were voted, stock control amounting to 31.2 percent would insure the election of five directors.

$$\frac{100,000 \times 5}{15 + 1} + 1 = 31,251 \text{ shares} \qquad \begin{array}{l} 31.2 \text{ percent of} \\ \text{stock outstanding} \end{array}$$

EXAMPLE IV: Assuming only 25,000 shares were voted, stock control amounting to 7.8 percent would insure the election of five directors.

$$\frac{25,000 \times 5}{15 + 1} + 1 = 7,813 \text{ shares} \qquad \begin{array}{l} 7.8 \text{ percent of} \\ \text{stock outstanding} \end{array}$$

Note: The basic formula explained in the footnote on page 63 has been modified to take into account the fact that not all stock is voted because of widespread stock diffusion:

$$\frac{\left[\begin{array}{cc} \text{Number of stock} & \times \text{ Number of directors} \\ \text{actually voted} & \text{required/needed} \end{array} \right]}{[\text{Number of directors}] + 1} + 1 = \begin{array}{l} \text{Number of} \\ \text{shares to} \\ \text{elect the} \\ \text{number of} \\ \text{directors} \\ \text{stipulated} \end{array}$$

would be listened to rather attentively by the other directors. In essence, if one's ability to exercise control by coercion, if necessary, is well known, the use of coercion is most often unnecessary.

In any event, in corporations where cumulative voting is required or permitted, the minority ownership control threshold will be significantly lower than would be the case where the majority share voting procedure is used. In the study by the House Subcommittee on Domestic Finance, *Commercial Banks and Their Trust Activities*, previously referred to, members of the subcommittee underscored this point.

> . . . When a corporation has thousands of shareholders almost all holding a small number of shares, a holder of even 1 percent of the shares may be by far one of the largest shareholders.

> . . . Where cumulative voting arrangements exist whereby the number of votes equals the number of shares held times the number of directors up for election . . . 1 or 2 percent stockholders have an excellent chance of electing one or more members to the Board of the corporation in which they hold stock.[20]

From a philosophical perspective, cumulative voting was a mechanism designed specifically to facilitate proportional representation between minority and majority stockholders. In reality, however, due to the evolutionary changes in stock ownership diffusion, the cumulative voting procedure makes it possible for an individual or group with a seemingly small minority ownership position (from 2 to 5 percent of the voting stock) to exercise strong influence over a corporation's management.* In addition, even without cumulative voting, strong influence, if not outright control, may be obtained by controlling as little as 10 percent of a corporation's voting stock.

Summarizing the minority ownership control threshold concept:

• given the nature of the modern corporation in terms of both sheer size and complexity;

• given the existence of massive stockholder diffusion in terms of both geography and the miniscule amount of shares owned per individual stockholder; and

• given that the minority ownership control threshold will vary from corporation to corporation;

*Approximately 20 percent of the corporations which are in the Centralized Private Sector Planning model are required to or permit cumulative voting in their board of director elections.

• the general consensus seems to be that, in most large corporations, the minority ownership control threshold will fall somewhere between 5 and 10 percent of the corporation's voting stock.

Nevertheless, as already noted, the results of Larner's study indicated—notwithstanding the use of a 10 percent threshold level as criterion for determining "management control" versus "ownership cntrol"—that 84.5 percent of the country's 200 largest corporations in 1963 fell within the management controlled classification. Since the existing empirical studies seemed to indicate that no individual or cohesive group of individuals owned as much as 5 or 10 percent of the voting stock in the country's largest corporations, Larner concluded that the separation of ownership and control, first analyzed by Berle and Means in 1932, had become the dominant characteristic of America's industrial landscape.

Minority voting control. From a CPSP perspective, Larner's argument contains two basic propositions. First, in most of the country's largest corporations, ownership of as little as 10 percent of the common stock would constitute strong influence if not outright control. Second, in the vast majority of large corporations no "individual or group of business associates" owns 10 percent of the common stock—empirical proof of the separation of ownership and control thesis. Many, however, further conclude that the separation of ownership and control thesis, for all practical purposes, could be interpreted to mean that the modern corporation's board of directors is free from "outside" influence and/or control from those who voted their shares. For this latter proposition to be valid, one must assume that *only the owners* of a corporation's stock are allowed voting privileges. And, of course, this is not true. The CPC, for example, holds hundreds of billions of dollars worth of stock in trust accounts for tens of millions of individuals—stock over which the CPC exercises both investment and voting privileges. In short, as will be discussed briefly below and in much more detail in Chapters 4 and 5, as stock *ownership* has become more and more widely scattered among tens of million of people, the actual *voting control* over this same stock has, in recent decades, become more and more concentrated. In terms of exercising influence and power through stock, however, it is neither stock ownership nor voting control that is crucial, but, rather, it is a combination of both. The concept of *minority voting control*, then, consists of both the stock that a group of business associates may own individually and/or collectively, as well as the stock over which the group may hold investment and voting privileges even though it does not own the shares.

The statistics on *minority voting control* indicate a far greater concentration of stock investment and voting privileges than has generally been believed to exist. Indeed, the statistics strongly suggest that corporate management in the modern corporation is not as free from "outside" control as *implicitly* suggested by Larner's and Berle and Means's studies. And, in terms of corporate stock, minority voting control is *one* of the key variables in the CPSP process.

Within the context of CPSP, stock (a formal and/or legally binding planning instrument) performs two distinct roles:

• It is *one* of the important interstitial elements in forming an organization *structure* conducive to centralized economic planning.

• It may be used as a *functional* or *implemental* planning instrument conducive to organizing and coordinating the production and distribution activities within, between, and among corporations in various industries.

Stock as a structural planning instrument. In reference to CPSP, the term *structure* refers to both the number of corporations *within a given industry*, as well as the various technological, financial, and administrative *intra*-locking ties that exist between and among these corporations. In addition, though, and perhaps even more important from a CPSP perspective, are the technological, financial, and administrative *inter*-locking ties that also exist between and among the various industries.

The illustration in Table 9 will be quite helpful in developing an understanding of how stock is *one* of the integral interstitial elements within the CPSP *structural* framework. As presented in Table 9:

• Two corporations (General Electric and United Technologies) produce 90 to 95 percent of all commercial aircraft engines.

• They sell their engines to two other corporations (Boeing and McDonnell Douglas) who, in turn, produce 90 to 95 percent of all commercial aircraft.

• McDonnell Douglas and Boeing sell many of their jet aircraft to UAL, Inc., American Airlines, and Eastern Airlines, who, in turn, account for 30 to 40 percent of all commercial air transportation.

• Five corporations (Exxon, Mobil, Standard Oil of California, Standard Oil of Indiana, and Atlantic Richfield) account for 60 to 70 percent of all jet aviation fuel production.

• Of the 12 corporations mentioned, the CPC *controls* more than 10 percent of the common stock in 7 of these corporations and controls, at

Table 9

Stock As an Important Intra-Interlocking Interstitial Element in Forming an Organizational Structure Conducive to Economic Planning, for Selected Industries and Corporations (1 January 1978)

Industries and corporations	Concentration ratios (percent)	Minimum[a] CPC stock holdings (percent)	Cumulative voting required or permitted
I. Commercial aircraft engines	90-95		
General Electric Company		9.3	No
United Technologies Corporation		9.2	Yes
II. Commercial aircraft	90-95		
The Boeing Company		10.4	Yes
McDonnell Douglas Corporation		4.5	Yes
III. Commercial air transportation	30-40		
UAL, Inc.		13.3	Yes
American Airlines		10.5	No
Eastern Airlines		4.7	No
IV. Jet aviation fuel	60-70		
Exxon Corporation		10.4	No
Mobil Corporation		11.2	No
Standard Oil (California)		8.3	No
Standard Oil (Indiana)		16.6	No
Atlantic Richfield Company		13.0	No

Source: See the Appendix.

[a]See Chapter 5, the section on The Planning Instruments, Corporate Stock, for a more detailed examination of the CPC's stockholdings.

a minimum, 9.3, 9.2, 8.3, 4.7, and 4.5 percent of the common stock in the remaining 5 corporations.

• Four of the 12 corporations have cumulative voting procedures.

Upon examining the information in Table 9 and becoming cognizant of the following key structural characteristics—the small number of corporations in each industry, the fact that the four industries are both technologically and financially interdependent since they buy and sell from each other, and the fact that the CPC controls significant amounts of stock in each corporation in each industry—a very explicit set of interdependent structural relationships begins to emerge. In turn, these structural relationships seem to suggest a tremendous interdependency between and among the production activities of each industry. On the one hand, there is a clear *physical and/or technological interdependency*, both from the standpoint of the actual quantities to be produced, as well as the requisite integration requirements in terms of size, weight, metallurgical specifications, etc. Just as one example, engineers and technicians in the commercial aircraft engine industry must work closely with their counterparts in the commercial aircraft industry in developing and producing each new generation of transport aircraft. In turn, the types and amounts of aviation fuel produced depend directly on the various quantities and types of aircraft and aircraft engines that are manufactured. On the other hand, a very definite *financial interdependency* also exists since the prices charged and the profits accumulated by each industry are also interdependent. The commercial aircraft industry's profits, for instance, are partially determined by the *prices* they receive for their aircraft from the commercial air transportation industry. In addition, though, the size of their profits is also dependent on the *cost* which they incur from purchasing aircraft engines.

A conscious recognition of these technological and financial interlocking ties and/or interdependencies would seem sufficient, from a purely logical perspective, to indicate the economic benefits to be derived from, if not the outright necessity of, coordinating the production and distribution activities within, between, and among the corporations in these four industries. In short, what is beginning to emerge is a form of vertical integration (aircraft engines, aircraft, air transportation, and jet aviation fuel) such as already exists, for example, in the petroleum industry, where the major companies own the oil fields, the pipelines, the refineries, and many of the gasoline distribution stations. The structural analysis (depicted in Table 9) as it now stands, however, is certainly not sufficient to indicate how this would work from an operational standpoint. Nevertheless, before expanding the structural analysis, let us briefly examine how common stock may be used as a *functional* planning instrument.

Stock as a functional planning instrument. It is very important to note that under normal circumstances—especially given the obvious interdependencies that exist between and among the corporations and industries in Table 9—a cooperative attitude toward the solution of commonly shared problems would probably be more or less automatically forthcoming. Nonetheless, it is also obvious that the achievement of cooperation and compromise often requires the application of pressure. In turn, any cohesive group (e.g., the CPC) that has the capacity to buy and sell large blocks of a corporation's stock is in a position to strongly influence a corporation's administrative leaders from both a carrot and stick perspective. For instance, in order to persuade a recalcitrant management team to cooperate with a particular plan, the CPC could engage in a sell-off of the corporation's stock. One must keep in mind that "minority stock control" (5 or 10 percent) often means controlling shares of stock numbering in the tens of millions, with dollar values measured in the hundreds of millions—if not billions. Short of all-out economic warfare, a corporation's management is always sensitive to the economic results of even a limited sell-off of the corporation's stock by a large investor, for several very good reasons:

• If a company's stock declines in price, the indication is that the company is not doing well.

• This, in turn, has an overall adverse effect on the public relations of the company which could adversely affect its business.

• A decline in the value of the company's stock destroys the value of stock options held by principal officers because it could cause the price of the corporation's stock to fall below the price at which the stock options were granted.

• An adverse business climate could also make it much more difficult for the corporation to raise capital.[21]

On the other hand, from a carrot perspective, the CPC could engage in the widespread buying of a corporation's stock, which would have exactly the opposite effects of a sell-off; that is, the price of the corporation's stock would begin to rise, stock options would become more valuable, the public would itself begin to buy the corporation's stock, and, as the corporation's image became more positive, the corporation's management would be able to raise even more capital through either borrowing and/or issuing more stock. This brings us to the *most* important aspect of the corporate stock instrument as a functional planning tool, namely, the ability of a cohesive group, such as the CPC, to cause the general stock-buying public to sell and buy stock which, in turn, can cause massive shifts of capital from this corporation to that corporation, from this industry to that industry, through the CPC's ability to cause a corporation's image to be enhanced or depreciated by its own buying and selling maneuvers. In short, while the corporate stock instrument is important functionally as a carrot and stick instrument for achieving cooperation and compromise— given that all the various management teams are in agreement as to a particular planning strategy—the corporate stock instrument is also a vitally important functional mechanism for achieving the necessary capital allocations to effectively implement agreed-upon planning strategies. And, once again, within the context of CPSP, it is this latter function that is by far the most important characteristic of the corporate stock instrument.

In any event, for now let us continue to our elaboration of the formal and/or legally binding planning instruments; specifically, let us turn our attention to the role played by a corporation's board of directors.

Boards of directors

> People of the same trade seldom meet together, even for merriment and diversion, but the conversation ends in a conspiracy against the public, or in some contrivance to raise prices.[22] (Adam Smith, 1776)

> The practice of interlocking directorates is the root of many evils. It offends laws human and divine. Applied to rival corporations, it tends to the suppression of competition and to violation of the Sherman law. Applied to corporations which deal with each other, it tends to disloyalty and to violation of the fundamental law that no man can serve two masters. In either event it leads to inefficiency; for it removes incentive and destroys soundness of judgement. It is undemocratic, for it rejects the platform: "A fair field and no favors,"—substituting the pull of privilege for the push of manhood.[23] (Louis D. Brandeis, 1913)

> Hitherto, to the best of our knowledge, it has never been considered reprehensible for businessmen within a particular business to meet for discussions of mutual interest for the purpose of bringing order in the Market.[24] (executive, Gulf Oil Corporation, 1952)

The "management" or leadership team in American corporations consists of the corporation's board of directors and the corporation's officers. On the one hand, the directors, from a legal standpoint, are elected by the stockholders and, from a practical standpoint, are a self-electing and/or self-perpetuating dynasty.*

*In America's 200 largest manufacturing corporations: (1) the average board size is 15 members, (2) 90 percent of the corporations hold directorship elections annually (for the entire board); i.e., directors are elected for one-year terms, (3) 90 percent of the time a majority of the board's members are "outsiders," (4) approximately 30 percent of the corporations have cumulative voting procedures for directorship elections, (5) board of director meetings are usually held on a monthly basis, and finally (6) a corporation's top 5 or 6 operating officers are almost always board directors.

On the other hand, the officers of a corporation are hired, supervised, and terminated by the board of directors. The Conference Board,* one of America's most influential business institutions, published a report in 1969 in which directors were noted as having the following responsibilities:

• to establish the basic objectives and broad policies of the corporation;

• to elect the corporate officers, advise them, approve their actions, and audit their performance;

• to safeguard and to approve changes in the corporate assets (issuance of securities, pledge of assets for loans, declaration of dividends, and conveyance of property);

• to approve important financial decisions and actions (such as budgets, capital appropriations, officers' compensation, and financial audits) and to see that proper annual and interim reports are given to stockholders;

• to delegate special powers to others to sign contracts, open bank accounts, sign checks, issue stock, make loans, and perform such other activities as may require board approval;

• to maintain, revise, and enforce the corporate charter and bylaws; and,

• to assure maintenance of a sound board through regular elections and the filling of interim vacancies.[25]

More recently, in 1978, the Business Roundtable (which also is one of America's most prestigious and authoritative business organizations)† published a report concerning directorship responsibilities, stating in part the following:

*In 1977, the Conference Board's leadership group consisted of a 32-member board of trustees. These trustees were from the boards of directors of the following corporations: Allied Chemical Corporation, American Telephone and Telegraph Company, Allis-Chalmers Corporation, Consolidated Edison Company of New York, Inc., Amax, Inc., E. I. Du Pont de Nemours and Company, Texas Instruments, Trans World Airlines, B. F. Goodrich, Prudential Insurance Company, United States Steel, The Continental Group, Inc., Gulf Oil Corporation, General Foods Corporation, Krafts Corporation, International Business Machines Corporation, Citicorp, The Chase Manhattan Corporation, Manufacturers Hanover, J. P. Morgan and Company, and Metropolitan Life.

†In 1977, corporations who had directors that were also on the Business Roundtable's 45-member policy committee included—Coca Cola, Owens-Corning, International Business Machines, Allied Chemical, American Telephone and Telegraph, General Foods, Bethlehem Steel, Exxon, Aluminum Company of America, Monsanto, Proctor and Gamble, The Continental Group, Inc., General Electric, Federated Department Stores, Prudential Insurance, Kennecott Copper, General

• It is generally understood that a principal Board function is the selection of the Chief Executive Officer and his principal management associates. A corollary function is to replace managers, including Chief Executive Officers, who have not met their responsibility . . . ;

• . . . The Board does have a major role in, and a major account-ability for, the financial performance of the enterprise;

• . . . The focus should be on a system assuring prior Board consideration of any major commitment of corporate resources over a period of time. Normally these corporate resource allocations decisions will be embodied in corporate "strategic plans" and Board consideration of such plans should be an integral part of the strategic planning process;

• Traditionally established procedures called for Board approval of significant capital investments—including plant and equipment construction or acquisition of land. . . . Moreover these investments budgets or plans must be reviewed in the context of a more comprehensive plan which takes into account projected cash flow and overall corporate financial capability . . . ;

• All of these considerations suggest that the governing notion should be corporate resource allocation (strategic planning); and,

• A Board should plan for its own continuity, succession for the retirement of directors and the designation of new Board members.[26]

In essence, then, the executives and directors of many of America's Brobdingnagian corporations have provided a clear view as to what they consider their most important functions, namely, to select the corporation's management team—its officers—and its directors, and, further, to have responsibility for establishing the corporation's "basic objectives and board policies" (Conference Board report) and to "be an integral part of the strategic planning process" (Business Roundtable report).

After the board has formulated the corporation's strategic plans, the corporation's "operating" management—its officers—is responsible for conducting daily operations during the implementation process. Referring again to the Business Roundtable's report:

Motors, Hewlett-Packard, Goodyear Tire and Rubber, Chrysler, Firestone, J. C. Penney, E. I. Du Pont de Nemours and Company, Union Carbide, U.S. Steel, National Steel, Mobil Oil, Ingersoll-Rand, Eli Lilly, Citicorp, Metropolitan Life, Continental Illinois Corporation, Chemical New York Corporation, J. P. Morgan and Company, Manufacturers Hanover, and the Chase Manhattan Corporation.

The role of the Board cannot be considered except in the context of the indispensable role played by operating management in the conduct of day-to-day corporate affairs . . .

However, despite its crucial role, operating management does not stand in an independent relationship. . . . Operating management derives its authority and legitimacy from the Board of Directors.[27]

Universally, a corporation's five or six highest ranking operating officers are also members of the corporation's board of directors. Having the operating officers actively participate in the corporation's "strategic planning" processes minimizes divisiveness and more nearly assures that the corporation's management will operate as a smoothly functioning team. A corporation's board, then, is usually composed of both "insiders," members of the corporation's operating officer cadre, and "outsiders," who are most often business executives from other large corporations. The trend over the last several decades has been toward an ever-increasing percentage of director positions being held by "outsiders." In turn, as the number of outside directors increases, so do the number of board of director (BOD) interlocks between and among corporations and industries.

Within the context of CPSP, boards of directors perform two distinct, yet interdependent, roles. Just as with common stock:

• they are one of the important interstitial elements in forming an organizational *structure* conducive to CPSP; and,

• they may also be viewed as a *functional* planning tool.

Boards of Directors as a structural planning instrument. As indicated in Table 10, from a *structural* standpoint, General Electric and United Technologies are indirectly *intra*locked, since the corporations are in the same industry and both have directors who are also CPC directors. Specifically, 7 members (35 percent) of General Electric's board and 2 members (including the Chief Executive Officer) of United Technologies' board are also CPC directors. Further, since 2 of Boeing's directors are also CPC directors, the two industries (commercial aircraft engines and commercial aircraft) are indirectly *inter*locked. The term "indirect BOD *intra*lock," then, is used to refer to companies *within* a specific industry that have indirect BOD linkages, while the term "indirect BOD *inter*lock" is used to refer to companies in different industries that have indirect BOD linkages.

Table 10

Common Stocks and Boards of Directors As Interstitial Elements in Forming an Organizational Structure Conducive to Economic Planning, for Selected Industries and Corporations (1 January 1978)

Industries and corporations	Concentration ratios (percent)	Minimum[a] CPC stock holdings (percent)	Number and percentage of direct BOD interlocks with the CPC		Number of indirect directorship (IDI) and indirect institutional (III) interlocks with CPC
			Number[b]	Percent[c]	IDI–III[b]
I. Commercial aircraft engines	90-95				
General Electric Company		9.3	7	35	34–8
United Technologies Corporation		9.2	2*	14	20–4
II. Commercial aircraft	90-95				
The Boeing Company		10.4	2	18	15–3
McDonnell Douglas Corporation		4.5	0	0	3–1

	30-40 / 60-70				
III. Commercial air transportation	30-40				
UAL, Inc.		13.3	3*	18	27-6
American Airlines		10.5	3	18	49-7
Eastern Airlines		4.7	2	12	30-7
IV. Jet aviation fuel	60-70				
Exxon Corporation		10.4	7*	41	24-5
Mobil Corporation		11.2	4*	21	54-11
Standard Oil (California)		8.3	3*	21	21-4
Standard Oil (Indiana)		16.6	4*	22	20-4
Atlantic Richfield Company		13.0	5*	33	44-10

Source: See the Appendix.

[a]See Chapter 5, the section on The Planning Instruments, Corporate Stocks, for a more detailed analysis of the CPC's stockholdings.

[b]These figures do not represent all of the personnel interlocks between the various corporations and the CPC. They represent *only* board of director interlocks.

[c]These figures represent the percentage of a corporation's board of directors that is directly interlocked with the CPC.

*Designates a corporation's Chief Executive Officer (CEO). In almost all cases, a corporation's CEO is also a member of its board of directors and quite often holds the board's chairmanship position. Thus, the CEO's of United Technologies and UAL, Inc., as well as the CEO's for all five energy companies, are members of the CPC.

To illustrate, consider the following:

I

A. commercial aircraft engines
   1. G.E.—"X" is a director on G.E.'s board.
   2. U.T.—"Y" is a director on U.T.'s board.
   3. Citicorp—both "X" and "Y" are directors on Citicorp's board.

Therefore, G.E. and U.T. have an "indirect BOD *intra*lock" via Citicorp.

B. commercial aircraft
   1. Boeing—"N" is a director on Boeing's board.

C. commercial air transportation
   2. UAL, Inc.—"O" is a director on UAL's board.
   3. Citicorp—both "N" and "O" are directors on Citicorp's board.

Therefore, Boeing and UAL have an "indirect BOD *inter*lock" via Citicorp. In other words, industries B and C are indirectly interlocked.

The existence of these types of indirect BOD intra- and interlocking ties is dependent upon *each* of the corporations having *direct* BOD interlocks with the CPC. For example, as indicated in Table 10, 7 members of Exxon's board of directors are also CPC directors. All 12 corporations in Table 10, as a group, have 42 "direct BOD interlocks" with the CPC. In addition to these three types of interlocking ties—
   • direct BOD interlock,
   • indirect BOD intralock, and
   • indirect BOD interlock,
there is a fourth type of interlocking tie—**the indirect directorship interlock (IDI)**. For example, assume that two of General Electric's BOD's were also directors for New York's electrical utility, Consolidated Edison. In addition, assume that two directors from Citicorp were also on Consolidated Edison's board. This is termed an IDI between General Electric and Citicorp. In this particular example, a total of *four* directorships are interlocked—two from Citicorp and two from General Electric. Consider the following illustration:

II

Citicorp—"A" and "B" are directors on Citicorp's board.
G.E.—"C" and "D" are directors on G.E.'s board.
Con-Ed—"A," "B," "C," and "D" are directors on Con-Ed's board.

Therefore, Citicorp and G.E. have *four* indirect directorship interlocks via Con-Ed.

In addition, these four IDI's occur through just *one* **indirect institutional interlock (III)**; that is, the four directorships are interlocked at one institution—Con-Ed. By knowing the absolute number of IDI's, coupled with the number of III's through which these IDI's take place, one can compute two important statistics. For instance, using General Electric as our example, and by knowing the number of III's, coupled with the knowledge that boards meet approximately 12 times yearly, one can compute from the data in Table 10 that directors from General Electric have approximately 96 meetings with CPC directors per year (8 III's times 12 BOD meetings per year), just through III's. In addition, by dividing the absolute number of IDI's by the number of III's, we can compute that there are approximately 4.25 directorships involved per meeting (34 IDI's divided by 8 III's). Thus, we also know that in each of these 96 meetings per year between General Electric and the CPC they have approximately 4.25 directorships interlocked. The number of IDI's per meeting is indicative of both the variety and intensity of the information exchanged at any particular meeting, while the number of meetings per year is more indicative of both the variety and intensity of information shared over time.

Upon examining each of the five basic types of administrative ties—(a) direct BOD *inter*locks, (b) indirect BOD *intra*locks, (c) indirect BOD *inter*locks, (d) indirect *directorship* interlocks, and (e) indirect *institutional* interlocks—between and among the corporations and industries in Table 10, we can see that all 12 institutions are, from an administrative viewpoint, *structurally interconnected*, quite solidly via the CPC. As one example, just through IDI's, on the average, directors from each of the 12 companies in Table 10 meet approximately 72 times a year with CPC directors. One final observation is in order concerning the specific data in Table 10. Whenever the symbol (*) appears, it signifies that the corporation's Chief Executive Officer (CEO) is also a

CPC director. Seven of the CEO's of the 12 corporations illustrated are also CPC directors.

In summary, from a purely structural point of view, we now have several industries, each dominated by a small number of corporations, that are:

- technologically and financially interdependent in terms of production, prices, and profits; and
- structurally interlocked via the CPC through (1) the CPC's control of large blocks of stock and (2) an intricate system of intra- and interlocking administrative ties.

Before examining the last of the formal and/or legally binding planning instruments (the corporate debt instrument), we direct a few comments at the use of administrative intra- and interlocking ties at the board of director level as a *functional* planning instrument.

Boards of Directors as a functional planning instrument. To organize and coordinate the production and distribution of various corporations and industries in a complex industrial society requires a well-developed, stable, and effective information processing system. In this regard, the board of director planning instrument performs two distinct, yet interdependent, functions. First, the veritable labyrinth of intra- and interlocking board of director ties allows—or, more precisely, dictates—that an intensive and constant flow of information between and among the various corporations and industries be maintained. The word *dictate* is certainly not too forceful a term in this context, unless one assumes that corporations do not hold board meetings on a regular basis and, further, that when such meetings are held board members refrain from talking to one another about business matters. The more plausible and obvious assumption, particularly in light of the various structural interdependencies that exist between these corporate institutions, is that attitudes and habits of cooperation and collective decision making would, quite naturally, evolve as the most efficient, practical, and *profitable* modes of operation.

Second, since each of the industries is represented in the CPC, the CPC becomes the focal point where information exists concerning *all* industries. Being a director for, say, Exxon, does not provide one with the variety and intensity and/or the kinds and types of information that one is the beneficiary of by virtue of being a CPC director. Being a CPC director gives one access to a broad range of data and information— information and data that are not available elsewhere. From a functional perspective, then, the intra- and interlocking administrative ties are structurally arranged so that the CPC becomes the focal point of the

CPSP process. Stated somewhat differently, a CPC director is uniquely situated so as to develop a holistic or macro perspective of the economy. In turn, the existence of a cohesive group with a macro economic perspective may function, for instance, so as—

• to facilitate the planning involved in mergers and acquisitions—mergers and acquisitions undertaken in order to create the most technically efficient industry, in terms of both optimum plant size and the optimum number of corporations (this would be an example of intraindustry planning); and,

• to facilitate and plan for the sharing of technical information between industries that are technologically and financially interdependent in terms of the quantity of products produced, prices, costs, and profits, that is, a sharing of technical information necessary to the production and integration of various component parts which, when joined together, constitute a final product, such as jet engines, jet aircraft, tires and tubes, jet fuel, etc. (this would be a typical example of interindustry planning).

Let us now turn our attention to the corporate debt instrument.

Corporate debt

The growing importance of debt financing. Under law, a corporation has at its disposal two legal mechanisms for obtaining funds from sources other than retained earnings or profits. First, the corporation may sell stock. Stock is usually referred to as *equity capital.* Individual equity stockholders (relative to their shareholdings as a percentage of the corporation's total equity stock issued) have a legal right to participate in the election of the corporation's management team and to share in any profits. Second, corporations may borrow money by issuing bonds.* Borrowed monies, or bonds, are generally referred to as *debt*

---

*On the one hand, the term "bond" is usually used to refer to a corporation's "long-term debt." Long-term debt, in turn, usually signifies a debt that matures or is due for repayment more than one year from the date the debt was incurred. On the other hand, "short-term debt" is usually referred to as a "note," and these normally have a relatively short maturity date—usually less than one year from the date the debt was incurred. In actual practice, the two terms (notes and bonds) are often used synonymously. In this study, the term "bonds" is used solely to refer to long-term debt. In addition, long-term debt is often used in referring to all of a corporation's current debt obligations not due for repayment within 12 months of a specified date.

capital. A corporation's principal creditors may, under certain circumstances, also have a legal right to participate in the election of a corporation's management team but are not legally entitled to share in the corporation's profits. Instead, creditors are paid an agreed-upon fixed interest rate for their investments in the corporation. When a corporation seeks monies by incurring a long-term debt, three separate legal contracts are generally involved—the *bond certificate* itself, the *bond indenture*, and the *trustee agreement*. The bond certificate is the initial or primary contract between the corporation and the investor, or bondholder. The typical certificate will state the amount of the bond, normally in $1000 denominations; the time, place, and percentage rate of periodic interest payments; and the bond's maturity date, i.e., the date when the loan must be repaid. Finally, the certificate contains a reference to the bond indenture.

The bond indenture is an additional, or supplementary, contract (quite often several hundred pages in length) stating in specific detail the rights and responsibilities of the corporation and the bondholders.* It is customary for a bond indenture to include the following:

• a restatement of the general information contained in the bond certificate;

• a detailed description of the corporation's property offered to guarantee or secure the loan;

• a statement specifying the responsibilities of the corporation in maintaining the property offered as security for the loan, such as—

    a. paying taxes,

    b. replacing obsolete equipment,

    c. making timely and necessary repairs, and

    d. maintaining adequate reserves necessary for depreciation requirements;

• a statement specifying restrictive covenants, such as—

    a. limiting the size of dividends to equity stockholders and/or requiring the maintenance of a specified amount of working capital,

    b. limiting the corporation's ability to make additional investments without prior creditor approval,

    c. limiting the corporation's ability to sell off assets without prior creditor approval, and

    d. limiting the corporation's ability to incur further debt without prior creditor approval;

*The bond indenture is also often referred to as a "mortgage indenture," "corporate indenture," a "trust agreement," and/or a "trust indenture."

• a statement specifying the rights of creditors representing a specific percentage (say, 60 percent) of the corporation's outstanding debt, in case the corporation defaults on its agreements to—

a. declare the corporation's entire debt to be due and payable within a specified time period (say, 30 days), and

b. elect a certain percentage (say, 25 percent) of the corporation's board of directors at the next scheduled meeting; and, finally,

• a statement setting forth the exact duties and responsibilities of the "trustee," if the bonds are being sold to the public at large.

As with stock, when bonds are sold to the public at large, the number of bondholders is quite numerous and they are geographically dispersed. In order to protect the legal rights of such bondholders, it is required by law that corporations offering public bond issues appoint a trustee to act on behalf of the bondholders. The trustee's role will be discussed more fully in the next section. It is mentioned here solely for the purpose of identifying the tripartite legal structure inherent to the issuance of long-term debt—the bond certificate, the bond indenture, and the trustee agreement.

The limitations and restrictions listed in points 4 and 5 above, while quite typical, nonetheless appear to infringe heavily on decisions that have been traditionally thought of as solely management prerogatives. As the late Senator Lee Metcalf appropriately pointed out:

> . . . the more discrete and lesser understood pressures that can be exerted by major creditors have generally gone unrecognized outside of corporate and financial circles . . . major corporate creditors are not only able to influence the policies and operations of a corporation through representation on the board of directors like equity holders; they are also able to limit normal corporate activities through contractual restrictions contained in loan indentures.[28]

A corporation's management would never be compelled to subject itself to such restrictions, however, unless it actually needed to use long-term debt as a mechanism for obtaining money. One criterion indicating the importance of long-term debt financing to today's corporations is the actual amount of such debt they have presently incurred. As of 1 January 1978, of the 138 corporations within the Central Planning Tableau, 25 percent had more than $800 million in long-term debt outstanding, while approximately 50 percent owed more than $500 million (see Table 11). The data in Table 11 seem to indicate that selling

Table 11

Approximate Amount and Cumulative Percentages of Long-Term Debt of Corporations within the Central Planning Tableau (1 January 1978)

Range (millions of dollars)	Number of corporations	Cumulative numerical total	Cumulative percentage
3,000 and over[a]	3	3	2.2
2,000 and 3,000	9	12	8.7
1,000 and 2,000	18	30	21.7
900 and 1,000	3	33	23.9
800 and 900	2	35	25.4
700 and 800	9	44	31.9
600 and 700	10	54	39.1
500 and 600	11	65	47.1
400 and 500	12	77	55.8
300 and 400	12	89	64.5
200 and 300	14	103	74.6
100 and 200	20	123	89.1
50 and 100	5	128	92.7

Source: See the Appendix.

Note: The phrase "long-term debt" may refer: (1) to debt that matures, or is due for repayment, more than one year from the date the debt was incurred; or (2) to all of a corporation's current debt that is not due for repayment within 12 months of a specified date. The figures on long-term debt in this table are in accord with the latter usage.

[a]As of 1 January 1978, American Telephone and Telegraph had approximately $32.5 billion of long-term debt obligations outstanding.

bonds is a major source of capital for many business enterprises. In addition to corporations using bonds as a major source for obtaining capital in the normal course of business, under adverse financial circumstances (which occasionally beset even the most Brobdingnagian enterprises), access to substantial sums of credit becomes even more crucial. Need one be reminded of Lockheed Corporation's problem in the early 1970s or of the more recent precarious circumstances confronting Chrysler Corporation. Anaconda Corporation, the world's largest copper mining company, likewise experienced severe financial strains in the early 1970s (although much less widely publicized in the popular press). Anaconda's predicament was reported in *Fortune* magazine as follows:

Anaconda picked a banker to become its new president and chief executive officer. John B. M. Place, 45, who has spent all his working years with Chase Manhattan Bank, most recently as board vice chairman, is replacing C. Jay Parkinson, 62, who will retain his title of chairman. The choice of a banker rather than a miner may have been dictated by Anaconda's financial condition. Now that its major mines in Chile, which had accounted for two-thirds of its production, are well on their way to nationalization by President Salvador Allende's government, Anaconda is under intense pressure to develop new income-producing properties, and that takes a lot of money. For example, it cost $200 million in a six-year period before Anaconda could realize a single pound of copper from its Twin Buttes mine in Arizona. Place's presumed ability to arrange financing undoubtedly led to his selection by the Board.[29]

It appears that Anaconda's board of directors viewed access to capital markets so important that they selected a CPC banker as their Chief Executive Officer—supreme testimony to the significance for modern corporations of having ready access to long-term credit.*

Before we analyze the role of corporate debt as a structural and functional planning instrument, a brief note regarding the debt statistics used in this study is warranted. Corporations, as a general rule, are not required to report the sources from which they obtain their loans in any systematic manner. Further, commercial loan creditors are likewise not required to systematically disclose information pertaining to their debtors—the major exception being that the Civil Aeronautics Board (CAB) does require air carriers to report annually the major holders of their indebtedness. Therefore, with the exception of the corporations in the commercial air transportation industry, the statistics on indebtedness are, for the most part, grossly underestimated and must be understood as such. Yet, without necessitating untoward extrapolations from the data obtained in CAB reports, as well as scattered data collected from various government studies, the statistics provided are nonetheless clearly noteworthy.

Corporate debt as a structural planning instrument. As indicated in Table 12, as of 1 January 1978, the CPC held 51.1 percent of the

---

*Previous to being made Anaconda's Chief Executive Officer, Place had served on Anaconda's board of directors for several years. On 12 January 1977, Anaconda became a wholly owned subsidiary of Atlantic Richfield, at which time Place also became a director and executive vice president for Atlantic Richfield. As indicated in Table 10, as of January 1978, Atlantic Richfield had 5 direct BOD interlocks, 44 indirect directorship interlocks, and 10 indirect institutional interlocks with the CPC.

Table 12

Common Stocks, Boards of Directors, and Corporate Debt As Important Interstitial Elements in Forming an Organizational Structure Conducive to CPSP, for Selected Industries and Corporations (1 January 1978)

Industries and corporations	Concentration ratios (percent)	Minimum[a] CPC stockholding (percent)	Number of direct BOD, indirect directorship (IDI), and indirect institutional (III) interlocks with CPC — Number		Minimum[b] of outstanding debt held by CPC (percent)
			Direct	IDI-III	
I. Commercial aircraft engines	90-95				
General Electric Company		9.3	7	34-8	11.6
United Technologies Corporation		9.2	2*	20-4	6.4
II. Commercial aircraft	90-95				
The Boeing Company		10.4	2	15-3	53.5
McDonnell Douglas Corporation		4.5	0	3-1	6.7

III. Commercial air transportation	30-40				
UAL, Inc.		13.3	3*	27-6	51.1
American Airlines		10.5	3	49-7	70.1
Eastern Airlines		4.7	2	30-7	42.4
IV. Jet aviation fuel	60-70				
Exxon Corporation		10.4	7*	24-5	5.0
Mobil Corporation		11.2	4*	54-11	14.2
Standard Oil (California)		8.3	3*	21-4	6.5
Standard Oil (Indiana)		16.6	4*	20-4	1.0
Atlantic Richfield Company		13.0	5*	44-10	24.9

Source: See the Appendix.

[a]See Chapter 5, the section on The Planning Instruments, Corporate Stock, for a more detailed analysis of the CPC's stockholdings.

[b]Corporations, as a general rule, are not required to report the sources of their loans. The major exception is that the Civil Aeronautics Board (CAB) does require air carriers to report annually the major holders of their indebtedness. Therefore, with the exception of the corporations in the commercial air transportation industry, the figures on indebtedness are, for the most part, grossly underestimated.

*Signifies that the corporation's Chief Executive Officer (CEO) is also a CPC director.

indebtedness of UAL, Inc., 70.1 percent of American Airlines' indebtedness, and 42.4 percent of Eastern Airlines'. Also, the CPC held, at a minimum, 53.5 percent of the Boeing Company's debt and 24.9 percent of Atlantic Richfield's indebtedness. The logical presumption is that the figures would be similar for the other corporations in the table were the data available. Concisely put, from the CPC's macro or holistic perspective, the debt instrument is also a very important interstitial element for structurally binding these corporations and industries together into a unified production and distribution system.

Corporate debt as a functional planning instrument. Of course, debt may also be used as a very important functional planning instrument. As illustration, a corporation's major creditor often has almost automatic access to the corporation's strategic planning documents. As already noted, such access to inside information is usually guaranteed to principal creditors by stipulations written into the bond indenture. In turn, having inside information concerning, for example, the discovery of new raw material (lead, zinc, petroleum, etc.) deposits, the creation of a new wonder drug, or a technological breakthrough in a manufacturing process can be quite useful for developing sound long-run planning strategies in terms of coordinating the allocation of debt and equity capital in the economy; positioning key personnel in important policy positions (as in the Anaconda example mentioned above); coordinating intra- and interindustry expansion or contraction plans; and, lastly, encouraging or discouraging acquisitions and/or mergers.

Throughout this chapter, considerable emphasis has been placed on the idea that habits of cooperation and coordination among the business elite in solving shared economic problems would be the most natural and evolutionary outcome to be derived from the economy's basic structural characteristic, i.e., economic interdependency. Nonetheless, in any form of centralized economic planning, a certain amount of coercion may occasionally be necessitated in order to create consensus or to create a unified approach to the solution of a particular problem. As the following quotation illustrates, corporate debt may, at times, be used quite well as a coercive tool:

> A Senate hearing earlier this year was told that Mohawk Airlines was forced to merge with Allegheny because it was unable to increase the size of its credit. It was Chase Manhattan which told Mohawk it would call its loans unless the airline found new capital to buy replacement aircraft. The only place Mohawk could find the money was with Allegheny.

While many marriages are made in Heaven, this one was made in the vaults of Chase Manhattan Bank, claimed Reuben B. Robertson III, a consumer advocate on aviation issues. While the stockholders' interests were substantially diluted, Chase and the other participants emerged unscathed.[30]

The merger between Mohawk Airlines, Inc., and Allegheny Airlines, Inc., took place 12 April 1972. Those in favor of the merger pointed to the increased efficiencies which often accompany larger scale operations and which, in turn, might lead to a more effectively "competitive enterprise." In terms of CPSP, though, the crucial point was not whether the merger was economically sound but, rather, that the merger came about because of the leverage a CPC institution was able to exert on its debtors. In short, the corporate debt instrument, within the context of CPSP, is a key functional component and is quite often so used.

In summary, when one simultaneously focuses on all of the *structural* and *functional* characteristics presented in Table 12 (i.e., the small number of firms in each industry; the financial interdependencies in terms of costs, prices, and profits; the physical interdependencies in terms of both technological interfusion and quantities produced; and the many intra- and interlocking interdependencies in terms of stock, debt, and board directors), Adam Smith's invisible hand and impersonal market forces may appear to some to have undergone a rather dramatic metamorphic transformation. In any event, this brings us to a consideration of the informal and/or influential planning instruments.

Informal and/or influential planning instruments

A collage of informational conduits

To detail and explain the number of financial services provided by CPC institutions for corporations would be a monumental study. A partial listing of these services, however, is in order so that one may more readily understand how these services, provided over a long period of time, further strengthen and add an additional dimension to the planning process. David Leinsdorf and Donald Etra supply the following list of services which most wholesale banks provide to corporations:

> . . . equity financing advice; arranges for the presentation and clearance of drafts by collecting checks, drafts with securities attached,

acceptances, coupons for bills, dividend warrants, documentary and clean drafts, etc.; purchases commercial paper and banker's acceptances for clients; acts as agent for the exchange of securities in reorganizations and mergers; collects bond coupons on called and due bonds; gives out credit information; transfers funds by mail, wire, and telephone; works with freight forwarders to assist clients in collecting from their customers; acts as escrow agent; does old-line factoring and accounts receivables financing; purchases conditional sales contracts, chattel mortgages, and leases; processes and collects freight bills; collects customers' interest and principal on bonds issued by corporations; maintains bondholders' ledgers; audits and countersigns stock certificates as registrar; provides vault space; documents, prepares, and delivers stock certificates; maintains shareholders' lists and ledgers; prepares and mails cash and stock dividends; prepares meetings and mails proxies; assists at shareholders meetings and mails reports to shareholders; prepares, issues, and forwards subscription warrants to shareholders; buys and lends against receivables; advises on the money markets and issues certificates of deposit; acts as trustee for corporate securities; transfers and delivers share certificates; acts as a depository of public money by receiving from corporations manufacturers' excise taxes and employees' withholding taxes; issues commercial and travelers' letters of credit; advises on foreign trade and banking; receives deposits and makes loans through overseas branches; quotes exchange rates on foreign currencies; provides complete payroll services; acts as a clearing house for capital investors and merger-minded companies; conducts cash flow studies; and finally, provides corporations with overall financial planning advice and introductions to additional sources of capital . . . [31]

By providing a corporation with all these services, one would undoubtedly develop an in-depth understanding of the corporation. It is also just as apparent that, over several decades, these additional working relationships would further strengthen the strong ties that already exist due to the presence of BOD, stock, and debt intra- and interlocking ties. Herein, only three of these services—that of the trustee, the transfer agent, and the stock registrar—will be examined. These three were chosen because the statistical data were readily available for comparison purposes and because of the stock exchange and/or legal requirements surrounding the performance of these particular functions. In terms of specific relevance to the actual planning process, the trustee's role is, by far, the most important of the three.

Trustee

Each time a corporation undertakes a bond issue, wherein the bonds are to be sold to the public at large, it must submit the bond indenture to the Securities and Exchange Commission (SEC) for review. The SEC will not approve a bond issue unless the bond indenture specifically provides for a trustee. The trustee may be an individual, another corporation, or a commercial bank's trust department. This procedure is mandated by law through the Trust Indenture Act of 1939. Each bond indenture must state specifically the duties and responsibilities of the trustee. Such duties normally include:

- furnishing individual bondholders with annual reports explaining the status of the loan agreement;
- notifying the bondholders in case of default and representing their interest in any foreclosure proceedings;
- arbitrating any disputes between individual bondholders;
- certifying that each bond certificate issued is covered by the bond indenture; and
- generally making sure that the corporation issuing the bonds abides by the provisions in the bond indenture by promptly taking steps to rectify any irregularities, including notifying bondholders of such irregularities.

In short, a trustee is charged with the overall responsibility of protecting and enforcing individual bondholders' rights (perhaps tens of thousands of individual bondholders) by acting as if the trustee were the sole owner of the entire bond issue. In order to fulfill these responsibilities, a trustee must have a sound working knowledge of the debtor corporation's economic conditions. This, in turn, requires that the bond indenture be written so as to provide the trustee wih adequate rights and powers vis-à-vis the debtor corporation. While the trustee is the bondholder's legal representative, the debtor corporation appoints and pays the trustee. A trustee must be assigned for each individual bond issue. As indicated in Table 13, General Electric had 8 bond issues outstanding as of 1 January 1978, and the CPC acted as trustee for 7 of the 8 issues. United Technologies, on the other hand, had 5 bond issues outstanding; the CPC acted as trustee for all five. As a group, the 12 corporations listed in Table 13 had 54 bond issues outstanding, and the CPC acted as trustee 37 times. Therefore, by acting as "the" major trustee for the corporate world's

Table 13

Trustee, Transfer Agent, and Registrar As Important Interstitial Elements in Forming an Organizational Structure Conducive to Economic Planning, for Selected Industries and Corporations (1 January 1978)

Industries and corporations	Trustees (TR)		Transfer agents (TA)		Registrars (R)	
	Total number of bond issues	CPC as (TR)	Total number	CPC as (TA)	Total number	CPC as (R)
I. Commercial aircraft engines						
General Electric Company	8	7	2	0	2	1
United Technologies Corporation	5	5	2	1	1	1
II. Commercial aircraft						
The Boeing Company	NA	NA	1	0	1	0
McDonnell Douglas Corporation	2	2	2	1	2	1
III. Commercial air transportation						
UAL, Inc.	4	3	3	2	3	0
American Airlines	5	2	2	0	2	0
Eastern Airlines	3	1	1	1	1	1
IV. Jet aviation fuel						
Exxon Corporation	2	2	4	2	4	2
Mobil Corporation	3	2	4	2	4	2
Standard Oil (California)	4	0	CO	CO	1	0
Standard Oil (Indiana)	8	7	3	2	3	2
Atlantic Richfield Company	10	6	3	1	3	1

Source: See the Appendix.

NA = Not available.

CO = Standard Oil (California) acts as its own trasfer agent.

debt obligations, the CPC gains yet—

• another valuable information processing system, a system that is intra- and interindustry in structure, thus further strengthening structural ties; and

• another valuable functional tool, a tool which adds still greater flexibility to the CPC's organizing and coordinating capabilities.

Transfer agents and registrars

The CPC, as also indicated in Table 13, is quite active as both a transfer agent and registrar. Literally tens of millions of shares of corporate stock are bought and sold each day on the New York Stock Exchange. Any corporation listing its stock with the Exchange is required (by the Exchange) to maintain both a transfer agent and a stock registrar. The transfer agent may be the corporation itself but is normally a large commercial bank's trust department. The Exchange also requires that both the transfer agent and the registrar reside in New York's financial district. The basic responsibilities of a transfer agent are to maintain an up-to-date record of a corporation's current stockholders and registered bond owners—names, addresses, Social Security numbers, and the number of stock or bond certificates held; to cancel a previous owner's stock or bond certificates and to issue new certificates to the new owner; to serve as a disbursing agent for dividends and interest payments; and to distribute annual reports, proxy solicitations, and notifications for shareholder meetings. The basic responsibilities of a stock registrar are—

• for new stock issues, to certify that the number of shares issued does not exceed the amount of shares authorized,

a. by comparing the number of shares authorized with the number of shares represented by new stock certificates, and

b. by registering, recording and signing each new stock certificate; and

• for corporate stock already outstanding, to check the work of the transfer agent when stock is bought and sold,

a. by certifying that each stock certificate issued by a transfer agent to a buyer is accompanied by a certificate representing a like number of cancelled stock certificates, and

b. by countersigning all stock certificates issued by the transfer agent.

The stock registrar, then, provides a check on the transfer agent's work.

On the one hand, the transfer agent's and registrar's work may be viewed solely as a routine processing procedure. On the other hand, one may take notice of the fact that the transfer agent knows, before any other person or corporate entity, who actually owns a corporation at any given moment. The transfer agent obtains this information even before the corporation whose stock is being bought and sold knows who its new stockholders are. In essence, the transfer agent occupies the most favorable position for obtaining information on possible corporate takeover attempts. When large blocks of stock begin to be bought and sold, the transfer agent is the first to know who the major participants are.

Nevertheless, the primary emphasis in terms of informal and/or influential planning instruments is not on the importance of any individual service that the CPC performs for corporations. Remember, the CPC performs literally scores of such services in addition to the three highlighted in our discussion. The important point to be emphasized is the impact of these services in their totality and in light of the formal and/or legally binding planning instruments which also exist.

When the information presented in Tables 12 and 13 becomes centrally focused, or begins to form a gestalt, in one's mind, the image created is similar to that envisioned by David T. Bazelon. Bazelon noted that:

> . . . the only existential meaning of *enterprise* is what businessmen generally happen to be doing at the moment, and *free* is merely the accompanying demand that they be left alone to do it.[32]

By way of summary, it was stated at the beginning of this chapter that the Central Planning Tableau consisted of (a) the Central Planning Core (CPC), and (b) those industries that actually engage in the production and distribution of goods and services. The various industries used as examples were each dominated by a relatively small number of corporations. In turn, these corporations were technologically and financially interdependent in terms of output, costs, prices, and profits. Abstractly, the interstitial elements introduced which bond these industries together consist of—

- direct interlocks,
- indirect intralocks,
- indirect interlocks,
- indirect directorship interlocks (IDI), and

• indirect institutional interlocks (III).

The first three types of intra- and interlocking ties may take the form of BOD, stock, debt, trustee, transfer agent, etc. The later two, as used in this study, refer specifically to the board of director type of interlock. The CPC was noted as being the vehicle through which the various intra- and interlocking ties were created and, thus, was designated as the focal point of the CPSP process. Specifically, the CPC was characterized as a cohesive group of banks and insurance companies that functions as a vehicle for organizing and coordinating the production and distribution activities between and among the various industries. Attention will now be directed to an examination of the CPC.

Notes

1. Joan Robinson, quoted in John Kenneth Galbraith's *Economics and the Public Purpose* (Boston: Houghton Mifflin Company, 1973), p. 12.

2. John Kenneth Galbraith, *Economics and the Public Purpose*, p. 7.

3. John Kenneth Galbraith, *The New Industrial State* (Boston: Houghton Mifflin Company, 1967), pp. 6–7.

4. Gunnar Myrdal, *Beyond the Welfare State*, 2nd ed. (New York: Bantam Books, Inc., 1967), pp. 28–29.

5. Ibid., p. 9.

6. David T. Bazelon, *The Paper Economy* (New York: Vintage Books, 1963), p. 203.

7. Ibid., p. 35.

8. Michael D. Reagan, *The Managed Economy* (London: Oxford University Press, 1963), p. 18.

9. Herman E. Kroose, ed., *Documentary History of Banking and Currency in the United States*, 4 vols., (New York: Chelsea House Publishers in association with McGraw-Hill Book Company, 1969), Vol. 1, pp. 249–250.

10. Ibid., p. 256.

11. William H. Husband and James C. Dockeray, *Modern Corporation Finance*, 7th ed. (Homewood: Richard D. Irwin, Inc., 1972), p. 204.

12. Harry G. Guthmann and Herbert E. Dougall, *Corporate Financial Policy*, 3rd ed. (Englewood Cliffs, N.J.: Prentice-Hall, Inc., 1955), p. 57.

13. Adolph A. Berle and Gardiner C. Means, *The Modern Corporation and Private Property*, revised ed. (New York: Harcourt, Brace and World, Inc., 1967), p. 66.

14. Ibid., pp. 208–209.

15. Robert J. Larner, "Ownership and Control in the 200 Largest Nonfinancial Corporations, 1929 and 1963," *American Economic Review*, Vol. 56, No. 4, Part I (September 1966), p. 779.

16. U.S. Congress, House, Staff Report for the Subcommittee on Domestic Finance, Committee on Banking and Currency, *Commercial Banks and Their Trust Activities: Emerging Influence on the American Economy*. H. Dept. 90th Congress, 2nd Sess., 8 July 1968, p. 2.

17. Ibid., p. 831.

18. U.S. Congress, Senate, prepared by the Subcommittees on Intergovernmental Relations, and Budgeting, Management, and Expenditures, of the Committee on

Government Operations, United States Senate, *Disclosure of Corporate Ownership*, 93rd Congress, 2nd Sess., (Washington: 1974), p. 9.

19. U.S. Congress, Senate, Hearings before the Subcommittee on Budgeting, Management, and Expenditures and the Subcommittee on Intergovernmental Relations of the Committee on Government Operations, *Corporate Disclosure*, S. Dept., 93rd Congress, 2nd Sess., 1974, Part 3, p. 427.

20. U.S. Congress, Senate, *Commercial Banks and Their Trust Activities*, pp. 831–832.

21. Ibid., p. 25.

22. Adam Smith, *An Inquiry Into the Nature and Causes of the Wealth of Nations* (New York: The Modern Library, 1937), p. 128.

23. Louis D. Brandeis, "Breaking the Money Trust," *Harpers Weekly*, 6 December 1913 (The Endless Chain), p. 13.

24. U.S. Congress, Senate, Staff Report to the Federal Trade Commission, released through Subcommittee on Monopoly of Select Committee on Small Business, *The International Petroleum Cartel*, 83rd Congress, 2nd Sess., 1952, p. 307.

25. The Conference Board, "Corporate Directorate Practices," *Studies in Business Policy No. 125* (New York: The Conference Board, 1969), pp. 93–94.

26. The Business Roundtable, *The Role and Composition of the Board of Directors of the Large Publicly Owned Corporations* (New York: Business Roundtable, January 1978), pp. 9–11.

27. Ibid., p. 6.

28. U.S. Congress, Senate, prepared by the Subcommittee on Reports, Accounting and Management of the Committee on Government Operations, *Corporate Ownership and Control*, S. Dept., 94th Congress, 1st Sess., November 1975, p. 153.

29. Businessmen in the News, "Banking on an Outsider," *Fortune*, June 1971, p. 33.

30. "Rockefeller Family Holdings Touch Every Economic Sphere," *Washington Post*, 13 September 1974, p. A5.

31. David Leinsdorf and Donald Etra, *Citibank* (New York: Grossman Publishers, 1973), pp. 77–78.

32. David T. Bazelon, *The Paper Economy*, p. 25.

Chapter Four

Centralized Private Sector Planning: The Central Planning Core

> *In a deterministic interpretation of history, the recurrent periods of intense merger activity would be attributed to broad, underlying economic forces, beyond the control or influence of any man or small group of men. But to ignore the pivotal role played by particular individuals who are in positions of power is to do violence to historical accuracy. A recognition that the course of economic events can be influenced by individuals who have the imagination and the power to take advantage of prevailing conditions does not constitute acceptance of a "conspiracy" theory of history.* [1]
>
> John M. Blair, 1972

> *In spite of all this Babel of discussion, accusation and crimination, it is believed that the Trust-doctors and Trust-busters are for the most part as far from the real cause and real remedy (if, indeed, a "remedy" is needed) as daylight is from darkness. Instead of the growth of the Trust movement being an achievement to be laid at the door of Mr. Morgan or Mr. Rockefeller, or any other leader of men, it should be laid at the door of nature. For if anything in this world is true, the following proposition is:*

> The modern Trust is the natural outcome or evolution of societary conditions and ethical standards which are recognized and established among men to-day as being necessary elements in the development of civilization. [2]
>
> John Moody, 1904

In conversations concerning the economy's structural characteristics, two distinct, yet interdependent, questions are always heatedly debated: (1) What are the economy's main structural characteristics—competitive market structures, oligopolistically competitive market structures, etc.? and (2) What *are* the causative forces that determine any particular industry's market structure? The conventional wisdom, of course, is that most markets in the American economy are typified by competitive market structures. In those few cases where it is admitted that monopoly markets exist (the telephone, electric, gas, etc., industries), it is usually argued that such monopolies have "naturally" arisen due to the economies of scale which automatically accompany bigness. In addition, those who argue that corporate leaders are quite capable of actively promoting monopoly situations and/or other varieties of cooperative arrangements and, in many instances, have done so, are routinely and automatically labeled "conspiracy theorists."

In this study, the idea that corporate leaders are simply pawns of the market place, totally entrapped by their cultural surroundings, has been labeled the "people neutrality concept." For many who believe that this concept is valid, it logically follows that corporate leaders should not be held accountable for any of society's economic ills, such as inflation, unemployment, or pollution. Blame for these types of unfortunate economic maladies is usually attributed to impersonal market forces, "unfair" foreign competition, and/or ill-conceived government policies. No attempt to set forth an elaborate illustration portraying the various arguments and counterarguments surrounding this controversy will be made. Let it suffice to state—without elaboration or equivocation—the positions subscribed to herein:

• People do count. The decisions made by corporate leaders are not always based on, or constrained by, impersonal market forces. Nor should a given market's structure automatically be viewed as the end result of the laws of nature.

• The assertion that people do count is certainly not tantamount to accepting a conspiracy theory of history. To assert that corporate leaders have created an institutional structure that promotes intra- and interindustry cooperation, as opposed to competition, *is not an endorsement* of the conspiracy theory of history.

• Those who have the power to make the economic decisions which ultimately determine how and what goods and services are to be produced and distributed should be held accountable for their decisions via some *formal and democratic* institutional process. Such is certainly not the case at the present time.

In any event, the task now before us is to describe and explain the structural and functional characteristics of the Central Planning Core (CPC).

The Central Planning Core—a structural reality

A descriptive sketch

As mentioned in Chapter 2, one of the first and most thoroughly documented works concerning monopoly enterprise in America was John Moody's *The Truth About the Trusts*, published in 1904. Mr. Moody was a great admirer of monopoly enterprise:

> For monopoly, as pointed out by all well-balanced, thoughtful men . . . is one of progress. . . . Business could not be carried on under present high social conditions and ethical standards without at least a tacit recognition of the legitimacy of the monopoly factor. The natural law which engenders monopoly is fundamental. [3]

Two of Moody's primary empirical findings were: (1) that the Rockefeller and Morgan families had each centralized the control of many different industrial trusts by interlocking these trusts with financial institutions, and (2) that the two groups were themselves closely allied. Moody noted:

> The great Rockefeller alliances in the railroad and industrial fields are supplemented and welded together, as it were, through the New York City financial interest of the group. [4]

He further stated:

> The Morgan domination, like the Standard Oil, makes itself felt through the means and influence of large metropolitan financial institutions and great banks . . . [5]

In summary, Moody said:

> It should not be supposed, however, that these two great groups of capitalists and financiers are in any real sense rivals or competitors for power, or that such a thing as "war" exists between them. For, as a matter of fact, they are not only friendly, but they are allied to each other by many close ties, and it would probably require only a little stretch of the imagination to describe them as a single great Rockefeller-Morgan Group. . . . *It will be only a matter of a brief period when one will be more or less completely*

*absorbed by the other, and a grand close alliance will be the natural
outcome of conditions which, so far as human foresight can see, can
logically have no other result.*[6]

The financial institutions which Moody cited as being under the influence or control of the Rockefeller-Morgan group are shown in Table 14. These 16 institutions were among the largest banks and insurance companies in the country and, almost without exception, were located in New York City. Indirectly linking industrial corporations via interlocking ties with financial institutions was merely a logical extension of the trust concept. The petroleum trust, for instance, essentially brought the production (oil fields), transportation (pipelines), manufacture (refineries), and distribution (filling stations) processes in the petroleum industry under a common management. The linking of several trusts or several industries together (especially industries that primarily bought and sold products from each other), by creating interlocking financial communities of interest, was merely the next logical step, offering—on a somewhat larger scale—the same types of technological and financial benefits that accompanied the establishment of trusts in individual industries.

Table 14

Financial Institutions Cited as Part of the Rockefeller–Morgan "Grand Alliance" (1904)

The Rockefeller group	The Morgan group
Hanover National Bank*	National Bank of Commerce
National City Bank*	First National Bank*
Second National Bank	Liberty National Bank
Equitable Life*	New York Life*
Mutual of New York	Mercantile Trust
United States Trust Company	Central Trust
Farmers Loan and Trust Co.	Guaranty Trust*
Central Realty Bond and Trust Co.	J. P. Morgan and Company*

Source: John Moody, *The Truth About the Trusts*, reprinted ed., (New York: Greenwood Press, 1968), pp. 491–492.

Note: By 1910, Chemical National Bank and Chase National Bank had become members of the Morgan—Rockefeller financial coterie. See Frederick Lewis Allen's *The Great Pierpont Morgan* (New York: Harper and Brothers Publishers, 1949), pp. 270-271.

*These institutions (having undergone numerous mergers, acquisitions, and name changes) are now members of the Central Planning Core.

Assuming that Moody was reasonably accurate in his prognosis concerning the economy's evolutionary trends, an examination of the intralocking ties between and among the country's largest banks and insurance companies seemed warranted. With this viewpoint in mind, the country's 10 largest banks and 5 largest insurance companies were selected for examination. The end result was the designation of 7 banks (Citicorp, the Chase Manhattan Corporation, Manufacturers Hanover Corporation, J. P. Morgan and Company, Incorporated, Chemical New York Corporation, Continental Illinois Corporation, and First Chicago Corporation), 4 insurance companies (the Prudential Insurance Company of America, Metropolitan Life Insurance Company, Equitable Life Assurance Society of the United States, and New York Life Insurance Company), and one diversified financial enterprise (Continental Corporation) as CPC institutions (see Table 15). On the one hand, Continental Corporation was not among the original 15 institutions studied, but it was eventually added to the core due to the magnitude of its interlocking ties with the other banks and insurance companies. On the other hand, 1 insurance company and 3 banks were dropped from the original group.

Among the 12 CPC institutions are 7 which Moody predicted would eventually form a "grand alliance." Through a long series of mergers, acquisitions, and name changes, National City Bank and First National Bank are now Citicorp; Guaranty Trust and J. P. Morgan and Company are now J. P. Morgan and Company, Inc.; and Hanover National Bank is now Manufacturers Hanover Corporation. New York Life and Equitable Life have both undergone minor name changes. In addition, by 1910, Chemical National Bank and Chase National Bank had also become members of the Morgan-Rockefeller financial coterie.* The Chase National Bank is now the Chase Manhattan Corporation while the Chemical National Bank has become the Chemical New York Corporation. In short, 9 of the 12 CPC institutions were closely "welded" together as early as 1910.

In terms of sheer size, as of January 1978, the CPC accounted for approximately $410 billion in assets and $230 billion in deposits-premiums; the trust departments of the 7 banks controlled approximately $100 billion in trust assets. Nine of the institutions are headquartered in New York City, one in Newark, and two in Chicago. In the banking industry—ranked according to assets—Citicorp ranked

*See Frederick Lewis Allen's *The Great Pierpont Morgan* (New York: Harper and Brothers Publishers, 1949), pp. 270-271.

Table 15

Rank, Assets (deposits or premiums), Trust Assets, Headquarters, and Number of Employees of the CPC Institutions (1 January 1978)

Industries and corporations	Rank[a]	Assets (thousands)	Deposits or premiums (thousands)	Trust assets (thousands)	Headquarters (city)	Employment
Banking						
1. Citicorp	2	77,112,434	55,651,250	24,542,985	New York	47,200
2. Chase Manhattan Corporation	3	53,180,295	43,508,258	14,473,907	New York	30,760
3. Manufacturers Hanover Corporation	4	35,787,568	29,782,691	10,892,233	New York	18,809
4. J. P. Morgan and Company	5	31,663,815	23,831,026	24,236,011	New York	9,932
5. Chemical New York Corporation	6	30,705,933	23,296,823	8,506,434	New York	16,285
6. Continental Illinois Corporation	7	25,800,280	18,753,785	7,312,683	Chicago	10,132
7. First Chicago Corporation	9	22,613,959	17,054,104	8,813,377	Chicago	8,586
Insurance						
8. Prudential Insurance Company	1	46,423,607	6,742,457		Newark	61,863
9. Metropolitan Life	2	39,575,922	5,521,311		New York	52,300
10. Equitable Life Assurance	3	24,798,678	3,850,290		New York	23,856
11. New York Life	4	15,848,213	2,194,734		New York	19,744
12. Continental Corporation	10[b]	6,410,950	2,772,928		New York	23,096
TOTALS		409,921,654	232,959,657	98,777,630		322,563

Source: See the Appendix.

[a]Ranked by assets and by industry. For example, Citicorp is the second largest bank in the country while Metropolitan Life is the second largest insurance company.

[b]Continental Corporation is usually classified as a diversified financial institution and not as an insurance company.

second, Chase was third, Manufacturers Hanover was fourth, J. P. Morgan was fifth, Chemical was sixth, Continental Illinois was seventh, and First Chicago was ninth. Among U.S. insurance companies, Prudential, Metropolitan, Equitable, and New York Life ranked first, second, third, and fourth in terms of assets. Last, Continental Corporation ranked tenth in terms of assets among U.S. diversified financial institutions. The interstitial elements which tightly bond these institutions into a cohesive and solid "grand alliance" will now be considered.

Direct board of director (BOD) intra-core interlocks

The *direct* BOD and non-BOD intra-core interlocks between and among the CPC institutions are depicted in Table 16. An example of a typical *non*-BOD institutional interlock would be where a member of one core institution's board has a relative who is a member of another core institution's senior operating management. This would certainly constitute an important intra-core institutional interlock between the two institutions even though it is not a BOD interlock. Another typical example would be where the *same individual* was a board member for one of the core institutions while simultaneously serving on another core institution's—say, for illustrational purposes—international advisory committee.

On the average, each core corporation has 5 direct intra-core interlocks (BOD and non-BOD combined) and 4 direct BOD intra-core interlocks with the other core institutions. As illustration, New York Life has 1 director who is also a director for Citicorp, 3 directors who are also directors for Manufacturers Hanover, 1 director who is a director for J. P. Morgan, and, finally, 2 directors who are also directors for Chemical Bank. In addition, 1 of the 3 BOD interlocks with Manufacturers Hanover is Manufacturers Hanover's Chief Executive Officer, while New York Life's Chief Executive Officer is a director for J. P. Morgan. In other words, whenever New York Life has a BOD meeting, directors from Chemical, J. P. Morgan, Manufacturers Hanover, and Citicorp are present. In all, 7 directors from 4 banks are on New York Life's BOD. Conversely, whenever J. P. Morgan has a BOD meeting, Prudential, Metropolitan Life, New York Life, and Continental Corporation each have one director present. In essence, then, the banks have *intra*locked the insurance companies, while the insurance companies have *intra*locked the banks. It is noteworthy that 7 of the 12

Table 16

Total and Individual Institutional Breakdown of the *Intra-core*, Direct BOD Interlocks and the Direct Non-BOD Institutional Interlocks (II) Between and Among the CPC (January, 1978)

Column → Row ↓ Industries and corporations	Total interlocks II and BOD	Direct (BOD and non-BOD) interlocks between each of the CPC institutions												Total interlocks BOD
		CIT	CMB	MH	JP	CB	CIC	FC	PL	ML	EL	NYL	CC	
Banking														
1. Citicorp	4									D,F	D			4
2. Chase Manhattan Corporation	8					2A				D	2D		2D	5
3. Manufacturers Hanover Corporation	7*						A					2D,*	3D,O	7*
4. J. P. Morgan and Company	4								D	D		D	D	4
5. Chemical New York Corporation	8		2A						A	2D	A	2D		4
6. Continental Illinois Corporation	3		A							A	D			1
7. First Chicago Corporation	0													0

Insurance

8. Prudential Insurance Company	2			D	A		1
9. Metropolitan Life	7*	O,F	*	D	2D	A	6*
10. Equitable Life Assurance	5*	D	D,*		A	D	4*
11. New York Life	7*	D		3D	*	2D	7*
12. Continental Corporation	7*		2D	3D,*	D		7*

Source: See the Appendix.

Note: The number of interlocks in the column "Total interlocks, II and BOD" may differ from the number in "Total interlocks, BOD" column since the former column includes both BOD and non-BOD interlocks. For example, an individual may be a BOD member for one core institution and also be on another core institution's international advisory committee. This would constitute an institutional interlock (II) but not an interlock between the two institutions' boards of directors. Another example would be where a member of one core institution's board had a relative who was a member of another core institution's senior operating management but who was not on its board of directors.

Legend: D = board of directors; O = officer and board member; * = Chief Executive Officer and board member; A = institutional interlock, but not a BOD interlock (see note above); F = family BOD interlock—for example, a father and son each sitting on the board of a different core institution. When a number appears before a symbol, such as "3D," "2A," etc., it signifies the actual number of whatever type of interlock is indicated.

Caution: To interpret symbols correctly, read from left to right. For example, Metropolitan Life's Chief Executive Officer (*) is a member of Chase's board.

companies have senior operating officers who are directors for other core institutions. For instance, both Metropolitan Life's and New York Life's chief executive officers are on Chase Manhattan's BOD.

A careful examination of Table 16 will reveal many different patterns of intralocking relationships between the core institutions. The symbols used to depict the various types of intralocks are as follows:

D—an interlock between and/or among the BOD's of various companies.

O—an interlock between and/or among the BOD's of various companies involving a senior officer(s) (but not Chief Executive Officers).

*—an interlock between and/or among the BOD's of various companies involving a Chief Executive Officer(s).

A—an interlock between and/or among various companies involving corporate officials who are not BOD members.

F—an interlock between and/or among various companies affected via relatives, e.g., a father sitting on the board of company A, while the son sits on the board of company B.

3F, 3D, or 2A—signifies the actual number of whatever type of interlock is indicated.

Finally, to interpret the symbols in Table 16 correctly, one must read from left to right and then up. For example, the letter "O" that appears at the intersection of the Metropolitan Life row and the Citicorp column indicates that one of Metropolitan's senior operating officers, but not its Chief Executive Officer, sits on Metropolitan's BOD as well as on Citicorp's BOD. Further, the asterisk (*) that appears at the intersection of the Metropolitan Life (row) and the Chase Manhattan (column) indicates that Metropolitan's Chief Executive Officer, who is also a member of Metropolitan's BOD, is also a member of Chase's BOD.

Indirect directorship interlocks (IDI)

While the above types of direct *intra-core* interlocks may be noteworthy (and are usually the types of interlocking ties that are discussed in the literature), it is the indirect directorship type of interlock that is crucial to the planning process. For purposes of clarity it is essential to maintain a clear distinction between the two concepts—direct BOD intralocks and indirect directorship interlocks. The former signifies a connection involving only CPC institutions, while the latter connotes an interlock that involves two or more CPC institutions, each of which has one or more of its directors sitting on the board of a third, non-core, corporation. As illustration of the indirect directorship interlock (IDI), consider the following:

I

Chase Manhattan Bank—"X" and "Y" are on Chase's BOD.
J. P. Morgan—"M," "N," and "O" are on Morgan's BOD.
General Motors—"X," "Y," "M," "N," and "O" are on G.M.'s BOD.

Since this example is factually accurate (see Central Planning Tableau), when General Motors has a board meeting, Chase and J. P. Morgan have 5 directorships indirectly interlocked. It is important to note that these 5 directorship interlocks occur in just *one* indirect institutional interlock (III). As is indicated in Table 17, Chase and J. P. Morgan have 9 additional III's. Also, since each of the 10 corporations in which these III's occur have around 12 BOD meetings annually, directors from Chase and J. P. Morgan are in meetings with each other approximately 120 times per year—just through III's. Clearly, then, the data presented in Table 17 are indicative of both the volume and the variety of information and responsibilities shared in common by J. P. Morgan's and Chase's directors. In addition, the specific corporations and industries wherein Chase and Morgan have IDI's and III's are illustrated in the Central Planning Tableau, as are the interlocking directorship data for each of the other 10 CPC institutions.*

The data in Table 17 also allow one to compute the average number of CPC directorships interlocked per each III. For example, Citicorp has a total of 134 IDI's with the other 11 CPC institutions. In turn, these 134 IDI's occur in 29 III's. Therefore, on the average (134 divided by 29), there are 4.6 CPC directorships interlocked in each III. In short, just through III's, Citicorp's directors are in around 348 meetings annually—with other CPC directors—where approximately 4.6 CPC directors are present. Clearly, the data in Tables 16 and 17

---

*The 12 CPC institutions, as a group, have 263 board members. On the average, each director holds four directorship positions within the 138 corporations included in the Planning Tableau. This would indicate that each individual was responsible for attending around 50 board meetings per year.

Table 17

Total and Individual Institutional Breakdowns of the Indirect Directorship Interlocks (IDI) and Indirect Institutional Interlocks (III) Between and Among the CPC—within the Boardrooms of 126 CPT Institutions (January 1978)

Industries and corporations	Total interlocks IDI–III	Indirect institutional interlocks between and among each of the 12 CPC institutions											
		CIT	CMB	MH	JP	CB	CIC	FC	PL	ML	EL	NYL	CC
Banking													
1. Citicorp	134–29		11	11	14	14	4	3	8	5	2	2	4
2. Chase Manhattan Corporation	129–30	11		13	10	10	6	6	4	6	1	7	4
3. Manufacturers Hanover Corporation	123–25	11	13		14	10	3	2	4	8	3	6	6
4. J. P. Morgan and Company	105–26	14	10	14		11	3	1	2	4	5	3	3
5. Chemical New York Corporation	121–26	14	10	10	11		4	3	4	3	7	2	5
6. Continental Illinois Corporation	74–16	4	6	3	3	4		10	1	3	1	0	2
7. First Chicago Corporation	84–19	3	6	2	1	3	10		2	4	0	1	2

Insurance

8. Prudential Insurance Company	57–12	8	4	4	2	4	1	2		3	2	0	3
9. Metropolitan Life	90–22	5	6	8	4	3	3	4	3		3	7	4
10. Equitable Life Assurance	51–12	2	1	3	5	7	1	0	2	3		3	3
11. New York Life	65–17	2	7	6	3	2	0	1	0	7	3		5
12. Continental Corporation	69–14	4	4	6	3	5	2	2	3	4	3	5	

Source: See the Appendix.

Notes: The numbers represent indirect directorship interlocks among the CPC institutions that are accounted for solely through interlocks with the other 126 institutions within the planning model. Many others obviously exist.

A word of caution is in order concerning the interpretation of the data in the table. Totalling the III's between, say, Citicorp and each of the other eleven institutions will *not* produce the same number that appears in the III total column. Summing these data would amount to double counting. Assume, for instance, that Citicorp, Chase, Manufacturers Hanover, and Prudential each have *one* direct BOD interlock with General Motors. On the one hand, Citicorp and Chase have an III at GM, Citicorp and Prudential have an III at GM. On the other hand, however, GM counts as only *one* III between Citicorp and the other CPC institutions, *not three*.

suggest that the 263 CPC directors are in almost constant—that is, daily—contact. In any event, let us now turn our attention to the stock, debt, trustee, and other *intra*-core interlocks that also exist in considerable abundance.

Stock, debt, trustee, and other intra-core interlocks

The data presented in Table 18 illustrate that CPC institutions control significant amounts of each other's stock, as well as performing the trustee, transfer agent, and registrar functions for each other. In large measure, for the reader who has mastered the ideas and concepts developed in this and in the preceding chapter, the meaning and significance of the data in Table 18 will be self-explanatory. A close examination of this information, however, will reveal several peculiarities and important comparative relationships which it may prove helpful to have explicitly pointed out.

First, the four insurance companies are "mutual" companies and, as such, have no capital stock outstanding. Having no stock to be issued or to be bought and sold on the exchange, these companies have no need for registrar or transfer agent services.

Second, the debt statistics would appear to indicate that the debt instrument is not used as a significant intra-core interlocking tie. This may be an erroneous conclusion, however, since the data presented do not include any debt held by the banks. The insurance companies annually publish a detailed investment portfolio, showing every government and private institution to which they have loaned monies, including the amount, rate of interest, and due date. The banks, on the other hand, do not provide a listing of their loans; thus, no information on bank loans was obtainable. The debt statistics, therefore, are incomplete, and must be viewed as such. The trustee data, though, may be viewed tentatively as criteria indicating the closeness between and among the banks in their debtor relationships. Chemical Bank, for example, has six debt instruments outstanding, and, in all six instances, other core banks act as the trustee for Chemical's bond indenture.

Third, one core institution, First Chicago, does not have any direct BOD intra-core interlocks. But, it is also the only bank in which the core institutions, as a group, control over 20 percent of the common stock. This points up the relevance of (1) viewing each of the interstitial elements individually, and (2) then doing a comparative analysis. In other words, while each of the interstitial elements—from a structural standpoint—is an important bonding agent, *each* specific corporation and industry must be analyzed to determine which particular interstitial element is the most significant for that particular corporation or industry.

Finally, the statistics on stock holdings must also be viewed tentatively.* As with bonds, the insurance companies publish an annual, detailed investment portfolio showing every institution in which they hold stock, including the number of shares and their market value. Likewise, banks that belong to the Federal Reserve System are required at the end of each year to submit to the Securities and Exchange Commission a list detailing every institution in which the bank's trust department has stock holdings, including the number of shares and their market value. The data on stock presented in Table 18 were computed primarily from these two sources and, as such, do not include, for the most part:

• stock held by the banks in custodial or corporate trust accounts over which the banks normally do not exercise any investment or voting authority; or

• stock that individual BOD members within the core may own personally or control through foundations.

Many members of the country's more wealthy families and/or financial elite are also CPC board members, and the combined total of their personal stock holdings is undoubtedly quite significant in and of itself.

Yet, from the perspective of stock being an important structural and functional planning instrument, it is most important to understand that vast personal wealth and/or stock *ownership* is not as significant a factor as is being a CPC member. Just within the trust departments of the seven core banks, CPC members control approximately $100 billion in stock holdings (see Table 15). As Louis D. Brandeis so correctly pointed out several decades ago:

> If the banker's power were commensurate only with their wealth, they would have relatively litle influence on American business. Vast fortunes like those of the Astors are no doubt regrettable. They are inconsistent with democracy. They are unsocial. And they seem peculiarly unjust when they represent largely unearned increment. But the wealth of the Astors does not endanger political or industrial liberty. It is insignificant in amount as compared with the aggregate wealth of America, or even of

*For a more thorough discussion of the magnitude of the CPC's stockholdings, see Chapter 5, the section on The Planning Instruments, Corporate Stock.

Table 18

Total Number of Indirect Directorship Interlocks (IDI), Indirect Institutional Interlocks (III), Direct BOD *Intra*-core Interlocks; BOD Intralocks, Stock and Debt Intralocks; and Trustee, Transfer Agent, and Registrar *Intra*-core Interlocks (1 January 1978)

Industries and corporations	IDI–III	Direct BOD	Number on board	BOD's intra-locked (percent)	Minimum CPC stock and debt holdings intralocked — Stock (per-cent)	Debt (per-cent)	Trustee (TR) — Number of bond issues	CPC as TR	Registrar (R) — Total	CPC as R	Transfer agent (TA) — Total	CPC as TA
Banking												
1. Citicorp	134–29	4	29	14	14.2	4.4	7	0	3	0	2	1
2. Chase Manhattan Corporation	129–30	5	27	19	6.1	<1.0	4	4	1	0	CO[a]	CO
3. Manufacturers Hanover Corporation	123–25	7	20	35*	16.9	1.0	6	2	2	1	2	2
4. J. P. Morgan and Company	105–26	4	22	18	14.7	6.2	4	2	1	1	CO[a]	CO
5. Chemical New York Corporation	121–26	4	23	17	8.4	14.4	6	6	1	0	CO[a]	CO
6. Continental Illinois Corporation	74–16	1	20	5	12.1	4.7	3	0	2	1	1	1
7. First Chicago Corporation	84–19	0	24	0	21.3	4.3	3	0	2	1	1	1

Insurance

8. Prudential Insurance Company	57–12	1	24	4	NA	NA	NA	NA	NA	NA		NA	
9. Metropolitan Life	90–22	6*	25	24*	NA	NA	NA	NA	NA	NA		NA	
10. Equitable Life Assurance	51–12	4*	32	12*	NA	NA	NA	NA	NA	NA		NA	
11. New York Life	65–17	7*	24	29*	NA	NA	NA	NA	NA	NA		NA	
12. Continental Corporation	69–14	7*	18	39*	11.3	1.5	0	0	3	3	2	3	1

Source: See the Appendix.

Notes: See Chapter 5, the section on The Planning Instruments, Corporate Stock, for a more detailed analysis of the CPC's stock and debt holdings.

NA = Not applicable.

[a]These companies act as their own transfer agents.

*Chief Executive Officer.

New York City. It lacks significance largely because its owners have only the income from their own wealth. The Astors' wealth is static. The wealth of the Morgan associates is dynamic. The power and the growth of power of our financial oligarchs comes from wielding the savings and quick capital of others.[7]

In other words, the CPC's capacity (1) to organize itself into a tightly bonded, cohesive group; and (2) to organize, coordinate, and plan the production and distribution activities of the economy's key core industries, comes, at least partially, from its ability to aggregate and use vast sums of, as Brandeis noted, other people's money.

In the American economy, the link between ownership and power has been nonexistent for many decades. Paradoxically, however, as the nexus between ownership and power widened, the actual concentration of power increased. In short, whenever necessary, the CPC can easily obtain control of 50 to 60 percent of any corporation's outstanding stock. Therefore, the statistics on CPC stock holdings must, as with the debt statistics, be viewed as a *minimum threshold*. And perhaps more importantly, the CPC's stock holdings must be viewed as a dynamic and fluid structural and functional planning instrument, as opposed to something static.

When one carefully examines the entire web of direct and indirect intralocks (administrative, financial, and technological) among the core institutions, a very clear structural reality emerges. Furthermore, a conscious recognition of these structural interdependencies and shared responsibilities would more or less automatically lead to extensive cooperation and coordination in the economic activities of the participants. Stated somewhat differently, from a purely logical perspective, for CPC members to act as if these interdependencies did not exist would be suggestive of irrational behavior, if not outright addleheadedness. To state the case in Nietzschean terms:

> Weakness of the Will: that is a metaphor that can prove misleading. For there is no will, and consequently neither a strong nor a weak will. The multitude and disaggregation of impulses and the lack of any systematic order among them result in a "weak will"; their coordination under a single predominant impulse results in a "strong will": in the first case it is the oscillation and the lack of gravity; in the later the precision and clarity of the direction.[8]

Clearly, the CPC is the hub, or nerve center, of the American economy, that "predominant impulse" which provides its members with both "precision and clarity" of purpose. The analysis will now shift to an examination of several specific examples wherein CPC institutions have cooperated in and coordinated their economic activities.

The Central Planning Core—a functional reality

The following examples were chosen in order to—
  • illustrate not only that the CPC is a cohesive group from a structural standpoint, but, also, that the CPC functions as such; and
  • further illustrate, from the CPC's macro perspective, the logic of both *intra-* and *inter-*industry CPSP.

Howard Hughes and TWA: ownership versus control

In December 1960, after a five-year battle, Howard Hughes lost control of Trans World Airways (TWA) to his creditors. A *Fortune* article, in 1959, characterized the conflict, in part, as follows:

> Hughes is struggling to preserve his power as the proprietor of the largest pool of industrial wealth still under the absolute control of a single individual.

> What he is struggling to do is keep a fortune intact, and hold a sanction: *the right to manage this concentration of industrial wealth without having to abdicate to bankers or stockholders a significant part of his present unique power.*

> . . . he cannot hope to enlist any outside help unless he is first ready to accept a monitoring of his affairs by the bankers, investment houses, insurance companies or the investing public to whom he must turn.[9] (emphasis added)

In the 1950s, Hughes's personal fortune was estimated to approach $750 million. The market value of Hughes Tool Company, TWA, and Hughes Aircraft Company, combined, was approximately $675 million. These three companies formed the core of Hughes's industrial empire. TWA was the country's largest domestic and international air transportation carrier. Hughes Tool Company was the oil industry's primary supplier for many types of drilling equipment. Hughes Aircraft Company was a major source of electronic equipment for the military.[10]

Hughes's financial problems began in the mid-1950s when Pan

American and American Airlines, his major air transportation competitors, began to modernize their fleets by switching to very expensive
jet aircraft. At that time, Hughes exercised undisputed control over
TWA, owning 78.2 percent of the company's common stock. In order
to remain competitive with Pan American and American Airlines,
Hughes needed to invest approximately $500 million in jet aircraft and
jet-related equipment. Hughes, unfortunately, contracted for hundreds
of millions of dollars worth of new jet planes before securing the loans
necessary to pay for them.

Eventually, in December 1960, to forestall the sale of one of his
companies in order to meet his contractual obligation, Hughes was
forced to borrow money from the CPC. As reported in an article in
Business Week, the restrictions written into the bond indenture which
Hughes was forced to agree to were quite severe:

> The final plan, which was signed late in December, 1960, was even harder
> on Hughes. It required him to give up voting rights on his stock for 10
> years to a trust composed of two men named by the lenders and one named
> by Toolco. Hughes tried mightily to avoid this stricture, but the two big
> institutions who were willing to lend the bulk of the required $165 mil-
> lion, Metropolitan Life Insurance Co., and Equitable Life Assurance
> Society, insisted on it. At the time, all TWA's competitors were ordering
> additional jets by the dozens, and if TWA didn't keep up it was doomed.[11]

Once in control of TWA's voting stock, the CPC's appointed trustees
for the bond indenture—

1. elected a board of directors to represent their interest;
2. had one of themselves appointed chairman; and
3. sued the Hughes Tool Company for mismanagement, obtaining:
   a. $137,600,000,

   b. a restraining order against Hughes specifically forbidding
him from having any contact with, or control over, TWA's management
for at least ten years, and

   c. a court order stating that, at the end of the ten-year period,
the Civil Aeronautics Board would hold hearings to determine if it
would be in the public interest for Hughes to regain control of TWA.[12]

Several colleagues, upon hearing this story, quickly pointed out that
Hughes was an eccentric, that he was indeed mismanaging TWA, and,
finally, that the courts had ruled in a responsible way. While these
contentions may be quite true, they simply miss the whole point of the
matter. The point is that the CPC used the debt, trustee, and board of
director planning instruments—as functional tools—to achieve its goals
and objectives.

From a structural and functional planning perspective, the sequence of the above events was as follows:

• CPC institutions structurally bonded themselves to TWA through both the debt and trustee planning instruments.

• Then, the CPC used the trustee instrument as a functional tool for creating several direct BOD interlocks with TWA.

• Finally, these direct BOD interlocks and/or administrative ties were, in turn, used as functional tools to completely oust Hughes from control of an airline in which he *owned* 78.2 percent of the common stock.

This example also illustrates how *withholding* credit can adversely impact on a corporation. If the CPC had determined that there were too many airlines in the air transportation industry, they could have undoubtedly destroyed TWA's ability to function effectively (that is, to compete with Pan American's and American Airlines' new jet fleets) simply by refusing to loan TWA money. Another such instance, as noted in the previous chapter, was the merger between Allegheny Airlines and Mohawk Airlines in 1972. This was brought about by a CPC bank threatening to bankrupt Mohawk by calling the airlines' loans due and payable. And, as also noted in Chapter 3, Anaconda's board of directors, in 1970, chose a CPC banker to be Anaconda's Chief Executive Officer so as to assure itself access to debt capital. Subsequently, Anaconda merged with Atlantic Richfield (see Chapter 3, Corporate Debt, The Growing Importance of Debt Financing). Here, then, are three instances where the CPC used the debt, the trustee, and the board of directors planning instruments to reorganize and/or restructure industries.

In conclusion, some are always quick to point out that, in 1966, Howard Hughes sold his 6,584,937 shares of TWA stock for a cash value of almost $500,000,000—as if to show that, in the end, Hughes's "will to power" prevailed against the CPC. Yet, the facts are just the reverse. In the exercise of raw economic power, a family's personal fortune, even if several billions of dollars in magnitude, is simply no match for the hundreds of billions of dollars controlled by the CPC. One can easily imagine that Howard Hughes would both understand and appreciate the following comment from John Kenneth Galbraith:

> . . . this reminds me of the most popular Polish story: Do you know the difference between Capitalism and Communism? Under Capitalism, man exploits man. Under Communism, it is just the reverse.[13]

Long Island Lighting Company: "the ties that bind" and the invisible hand

In 1967, the Long Island Lighting Company (LILCO) selected the engineering firm of Stone and Webster to do the architectural and engineering work for its Shoreham nuclear power plant. In all, five corporations submitted bids to LILCO. Stone and Webster submitted the second highest bid, which was approximately $2,000,000 higher than the lowest bid. The total contract amounted to $16,750,000.* LILCO's president, Edward C. Duffy, stated:

> We didn't award this on the basis of price. We examined the work they had done . . . the people they had and how long they had been with them, for stability of organization . . . [14]

Obviously, there are always other important criteria besides money that one must consider when awarding contracts. This particular example illustrates quite clearly, however, that, given the structural relationships and/or interdependencies that existed between and among the CPC, LILCO, and Stone and Webster, it would normally be in the best interest of all three institutions for LILCO to choose Stone and Webster over those contractors who submitted lower bids.

Stone and Webster is one of the leading engineering and construction companies engaged in designing and building fossil fuel, hydroelectric, and nuclear power plants for the electrical utility industry. For at least the last 12 years, two of Stone and Webster's ten-member board of directors have been interlocked with the CPC—one with Citicorp and one with the Chase Manhattan Bank. During this same time period, the CPC provided the corporation with trustee, transfer agent, and registrar services. And, at least since 1 January 1974, the CPC has controlled a minimum of 12 percent of the corporation's common stock.† Finally, in the early 1970s, Chase Manhattan provided Stone and Webster with a $5,000,000 open credit line.

---

*This particular example was taken from an article written by Kenneth Crowe entitled "Corporate Closeness: LILCO's Ties That Bind," which first appeared in *Newsday*, 22 March 1973. It was subsequently reprinted in U.S. Congress, Senate, *Disclosure of Corporate Ownership*, prepared by the Subcommittee on Intergovernmental Relations and Budgeting, Management and Expenditures of the Committee on Government Operations, 93rd Congress, 2nd Session, 4 March 1974, pp. 387–391.
†Stock ownership data prior to January 1974 were not obtainable.

Similarly, at least since 1 January 1971, the CPC has controlled approximately 15 percent of LILCO's common stock and has likewise provided LILCO with trustee, transfer agent, and registrar services. In the late 1960s and early 1970s, First National City Bank (now Citicorp) provided LILCO with a $12 million open credit line. In addition, as of January 1978, LILCO had 28 long-term bond instruments outstanding, and the CPC was the trustee on all 28.

Finally, Eben W. Pyne, a senior vice-president at Citicorp, has also been a director for LILCO for at least the last 12 years. Pyne's wife (Hilda Holloway Pyne) is William R. Grace's great granddaughter, and J. Peter Grace sits on Citicorp's board with Pyne and is also a director on Stone and Webster's board. Likewise, both Pyne and Grace are directors for W. R. Grace and Company. Whitney Stone, of Stone and Webster, was also a director for W. R. Grace and Company from May 1959 to March 1964. Stone and Webster also owned approximately 8 percent of Transcontinental Gas Line Corporation's common stock, and Transcontinental was LILCO's major supplier of natural gas.

In summary, at least since the late 1960s, the CPC has been closely interlocked with both LILCO and Stone and Webster through stock, debt, board of director, trustee, and other interlocks. An important question that arises is, How could a director conscientiously fulfill his responsibilities to the stockholders of, say, Citicorp, Stone and Webster, and LILCO—simultaneously? On the one hand, Stone and Webster's prosperity would be enhanced if it received the contract from LILCO as opposed to one of its competitors. How, then, could a CPC director encourage LILCO to accept a bid from someone besides Stone and Webster when the CPC is, in part, legally responsible for tending to Stone and Webster's economic prosperity? On the other hand, if one of Stone and Webster's competitors were equally capable from a design and engineering standpoint and had submitted a lower bid, encouraging LILCO to accept Stone and Webster's bid might initially appear not to be in LILCO's economic self-interest. All of this, of course, is reconcilable, if one does not view each of these economic enterprises as separate entities, but, instead, looks at the matter from the standpoint of each institution's being a separate, yet interdependent, link in a unified production process. Directors who were simultaneously responsible for the economic prosperity of the CPC, LILCO, and Stone and Webster would, given even a modicum of common sense, realize the economic gains to be reaped from carefully planning and coordinating the economic decisions between and among the three institutions. Note:

1. If LILCO chose a high bidder,

    a. the banks would make more money because the amount of their loans to LILCO would be greater, and

    b. the deposits placed in the banks by Stone and Webster would also be greater in amount since they would be making larger profits than would be the case given competitive conditions; and

2. LILCO would,

    a. given an expanded rate base, be allowed to collect a greater amount of money from its electric customers by the regulatory commission,* and

    b. be assured of obtaining ample credit, even as others—perhaps its competitors—were being frozen out of the credit market.

In short, from a purely monetary viewpoint, it would be in the economic self-interest of all three institutions for LILCO to chose Stone and Webster—as opposed to choosing a company with a lower bid—to do the architectural work for its nuclear plant. On the other hand, though, it would most certainly not be in the best interest of LILCO's customers, who would ultimately be forced to pay higher utility bills, nor would it be in the best interest of those companies who had submitted lower bids. When asked about these types of business arrangements, Charles Ross, a former Federal Power Commissioner said:

> Unfortunately, this is the way the world of big business operates. It's not illegal as far as I know. From my standpoint, this is one of the most discouraging situations from a regulatory standpoint. You're trying to regulate from the point of view of cost of services. You're trying to make sure the consumer is getting the least costly product. . . . It's the function of the regulator to act as if we had a free competitive society whereby everybody is out cutting each other's throats. When you have interlocks, human nature dictates you're going to try to minimize the risk involved.[15]

The whole process works quite well because customers either pay whatever price the utility charges or do without electricity. Yet, similar

---

*A utility's rate base may be defined as the dollar value, established by a regulatory commission, of the utility's physical plant, equipment, and intangible capital used and useful in serving the public (minus depreciation), on which the utility is entitled to earn a reasonable rate of return or profit. Thus, as the dollar value of a utility's rate base increases, the utility will be allowed to collect more money from its customers.

types of profit pyramiding procedures are just as applicable to those enterprises where the end product is not produced by a "regulated" monopoly.

As a case in point, the following scenario appeared in a Ralph Nader study group report:

> Examples of the profit pyramiding game are not hard to find. For instance, Western Electric was able to play the game to the tune of a 6,684 percent profit without doing any work. In the early 1950's, the Army needed launcher-loaders for its Nike missiles. Western Electric already had the contract for the launcher-loader too. Western Electric then subcontracted the job to Douglas Aircraft. Douglas proved to be even more adept at the game than Western Electric. It gave a sub-contract to Consolidated Western Steel Company, a division of United States Steel, which actually manufactured and delivered 1,032 launcher-loaders directly to the Army.
>
> Assuming that Consolidated correctly reported its costs (although this is not clear from congressional hearings), we start at the bottom of the pyramid with a figure of $13.5 million, including its profit. Then Douglas, which invested a grand total of $3,361 making plastic rain covers for the launcher, took its profit, $1,211,771—a 36,531 percent return on investment. It then became Western Elecric's turn. Western Electric's total effort was $14,293 "for checking over the equipment at Army bases," but it based its profit on Douglas's "costs" of $14.7 million. Even so, it managed to take $955,396 profit on the $14,293 effort—a pyramided profit of 6,684 percent. The government, therefore, paid $16.4 million for $13.5 million worth of equipment and services, Douglas nosed out Western Electric in the game of pyramiding costs, and only the taxpayer lost.[16]

Western Electric is a wholly owned subsidiary of American Telephone and Telegraph (AT&T), and both U.S. Steel and AT&T have historically been closely tied to the CPC. As of January 1978, 7—or 37 percent— of AT&T's board of directors were also CPC directors; 6—or 40 percent—of U.S. Steel's board were CPC directors. In addition, directors from AT&T and U.S. Steel were indirectly intralocked at Citicorp, Manufacturers Hanover, and Chemical Bank; McDonnell Douglas Corporation had IDI's with both Metropolitan Life and J. P. Morgan and Company.

The above examples (both LILCO, Stone and Webster, and the CPC as well as Western Electric, Douglas Aircraft, U.S. Steel, and the CPC), have important characteristics in common. In addition, these examples also share important similarities with the aircraft engine–aircraft–air transportation–jet fuel–CPC example introduced in Chapter 3. By way of illustration, from the CPC's macro perspective, it would not have been economically rational for either LILCO, Western Electric, or Boeing (in Galbraithian terms) to exert a countervailing force toward reducing cost. More specifically, from a CPSP viewpoint, it was not economically rational for either LILCO, Western Electric, or Boeing to attempt to minimize the prices they paid for the goods and/or services that they received from Stone and Webster, Douglas Aircraft, or General Electric, respectively. As LILCO's president, Edward C. Duffy, stated, "We didn't award this on the basis of price." Stated somewhat differently and in a more positive manner, these various types of profit pyramiding schemes may appropriately be viewed as *one* of the CPC's most important mechanisms for—

• transferring capital from the rest of the economy to the CPSP group; and

• allocating capital between and among the various industries within the economy's CPSP sphere.

In brief, by each corporation or industry in the production chain reaping higher-than-competitive profits, the revenues flowing into the economy's CPSP sphere from the economy's less organized sectors are enhanced—that is, *CPSP profits are enhanced.*

In summary, then, when firms are *structurally* bonded tightly together, they usually tend to *function* in a highly organized, coordinated, and cooperative manner in their pricing and production decisions; i.e., corporations and industries that are structurally interdependent seldom tend to function as if such were not the case. Finally, one would normally assume that, in an economy characterized by CPSP—especially where the planners are motivated by self-interest and profit maximization—the overall economic results would be quite different than would be the case under competitive market structure conditions. For instance, those individuals (white-collar, blue-collar, executive-collar, etc.) who are part of the CPSP sphere will, for the most part, fare much better than their counterparts in the less well-organized sectors of the economy, from both an economic and cultural standpoint. Furthermore, given the existence of CPSP, coupled with the country's attitude toward the values of self-interest and profit maximization, it would be quite ridiculous to expect otherwise. Why, indeed, should the CPC be expected to act in the general public's self-interest at the expense of their own self-interest? One should hasten to add, however, that, from a psychological perspective, CPC members no doubt firmly believe that by profit maximizing and acting in their own self-interest they are also acting in the general public's self-interest.

Steinberg and Chemical Bank: the mythical Jewish connection

The following appeared in an article in *Business Week*, 25 July 1970:

> As institutions buy and sell ever larger blocks of stock, they develop greater power in corporate affairs—power they occasionally exercise with the impact of a sledgehammer. Probably the best known case of such influence was when Leasco Data Processing Equipment Corp. tried to take over Chemical Bank New York Trust Co. in 1969. Leasco's stock plunged from 140 to 106 in two weeks. Though even Leasco's Saul P. Steinberg would never admit it publicly, it appeared that bank trust departments and perhaps other institutions dumped their shares to protect Chemical. "I always knew there was an Establishment," said Steinberg at the time, "I just used to think I was part of it."[17]

This example highlights several important points. First, the CPC is quite capable of protecting its own structural integrity. Second, when CPC institutions function as a cohesive group—as they did in this instance to protect Chemical Bank—they can have a devastating impact on even the largest corporations. Third, as was discussed in Chapter 3, from a purely functional perspective, the CPC's ability to sell large quantities of a corporation's stock can be just as effective a tactic as their ability to quickly acquire significant amounts of a corporation's stock. Fourth, young Jewish entrepreneurs should not be brash. Regardless of the nonsense prattled about by ultraconservatives, Jewish entrepreneurs in America do not, almost without exception, occupy positions that possess real economic power, i.e., power at the level of national and international affairs. The CPC contains less than one-half of one percent Jewish membership. One might say that the Jewish connection myth ranks alongside the myth that the American economy is basically a market system composed of competitive economic institutions. Finally, it is undoubtedly true that many others—Jewish and non-Jewish—who, by most standards, have been quite successful in their business activities, nonetheless, do not really understand the economics of the game in which they are playing, regardless of their real achievements and triumphs.

As illustration, in 1978, Hanes Corporation (headquartered in Winston-Salem, North Carolina) ranked (per sales) as the country's 437th largest manufacturing enterprise with $471,600,000 in sales, a 15,000 plus work force, and a quite respectable 14.6 percent rate of return on equity. The Hanes family owned 17 percent of the corporation's common stock, and Gordon Hanes was chairman of the corporation's board of directors. The company was a major producer of men's and boy's undergarments and had been remarkably successful in hosiery. Its "L'eggs" line of women's hosiery was stocked in supermarkets and drugstores throughout the country. Enter Consolidated Foods. As reported in *Fortune*, the scenario, in part, went as follows:

> Last June Con Foods accumulated 4.9 percent of Hanes' shares—just under the amount that would have required it to report the purchases to the Securities and Exchange Commission. Then, after a pause of several weeks, the company began buying again, rapidly and secretly. Within ten days Con Foods had accumulated 21 percent of Hanes' stock, notified the SEC, and proposed merger.

> Told by his financial advisors that a takeover by someone seemed inevitable, Gordon Hanes gave in—though with some lingering bitterness. Says Hanes: *"It was hard for me to believe that there were people who didn't give a damn about anything except money—the lawyers, the bankers. The Hanes family spent three generations building this business, and it was taken away from us in ten days."*[18] (emphasis added)

Assuredly, both Steinberg and Hanes considered themselves part of "the Establishment." Likewise, both men probably found it hard to believe that, in fact, they were not. One cannot help but wonder how many of the country's less influential and powerful business leaders do not fully understand how the system actually works. No doubt, it must be frustrating to suddenly *be forced to become consciously aware* that the world one has promoted, defended, and believed in does not really exist.

In any event, in 1978 Consolidated Foods ranked (per sales) as the country's 78th largest manufacturing corporation. In 1979, after the Hanes Corporation takeover, Consolidated Foods ranked as the country's 64th largest manufacturing corporation, with $4.7 billion in sales.* In conclusion then, the Steinberg and Hanes examples illustrate

---

*As of January 1978 the CPC had two board of director interlocks with Consolidated Foods (one at First Chicago and one at Equitable Life); controlled approximately 5 percent of its common stock; and provided Consolidated with trustee, transfer agent, and registrar services.

how CPC institutions can, and in fact do, coordinate their activities in order to (1) forestall the takeover of CPC institutions by an outsider (Chemical) and (2) bring other corporations (Hanes) into the economy's CPSP sphere.

Dick Goodwin and Johns-Manville Corporation: "the man who never came to dinner"

Johns-Manville Corporation is the largest producer of asbestos fiber in the world (excluding the USSR) and the second largest producer of fiberglass insulation in the United States. In terms of sales, in 1979 the corporation ranked 156th among all U.S. manufacturing companies. In the early 1970s Johns-Manville was literally transformed from a rather stodgy, slow-growth enterprise into a very dynamic and much talked about corporation, primarily due to the leadership of Dick Goodwin. As reported in *Fortune*:

> He had reorganized and rejuvenated the once torpid building-materials company. Sales had risen 91 percent, from $578 million in 1970 to $1.1 billion in 1975. Net profits had gone up 115 percent between 1970 and 1974, and although last year's recession wiped out almost all of that gain, earnings had rebounded sharply during the first half of 1976 to set a company record. As Goodwin was planning to tell his fellow directors, 1976 was shaping up as a great year for Johns-Manville. Perhaps the best year ever.[19]

Goodwin was appointed Johns-Manville's Chief Executive Officer in December 1970. Between 1970 and 1976, he had—
- completed 11 major acquisitions and 12 divestitures;
- moved the company's headquarters from New York to a magnificently scenic cattle ranch just outside of Denver;
- attempted to remove J. P. Morgan and Co., Inc., as the corporation's major banker; and
- attempted to increase the corporation's 12-member board of directors to 20 members.

Evidently, the last three points mentioned proved too much for Johns-Manville's existing directors. After a meeting in Sun Valley, Idaho, where Goodwin informed the board of his desire to seek out a different investment banker and to increase the size of the board, John P. Schroeder (also a vice-chairman and board director for J. P. Morgan and Co., Inc.) said:

"We had here a fellow who had no experience working with a group of people who held ultimate responsibility for the company." . . . "He was used to working as an individual before he joined Johns-Manville [J-M]. We gave him a lot of room, and we tried to teach him, but he had trouble working with a board. We came away from that meeting in Sun Valley a disturbed bunch."[20]

Goodwin's dismissal was reported in the October 1976 issue of *Fortune*.* The rather lengthy quotation to follow is indeed a conclusive statement, well deserving of attention:

Aboard the flight to New York with Goodwin on September 1 were several aides, including Francis H. May, Jr., J-M's executive vice president and a director. Another director, John A. McKinney, a senior vice president and the company's top legal officer, met them there. On Thursday, the group conducted routine business in Manhattan. As the busy day ended, Godwin asked his colleagues to gather in his suite at the Tuscany Hotel for a pre-dinner drink. He would meet them there and take them all to dinner at Joe's Pier 52.

Goodwin arrived at the suite at seven o'clock to find May, McKinney, and the others sipping drinks and munching cheese and crackers. He also found a message that William F. May, chairman of American Can Co. and for nine years a director of Johns-Manville, had phoned and would call back in a few minutes. When he did, May said that he and two other directors would like to meet with Goodwin before the next morning's board meeting.

"Fine," said the cheerful and unsuspecting Goodwin, for whom such last-minute meetings were not unusual. "Now, after dinner, or over breakfast?"

"We'll be there in ten minutes," replied May.

Goodwin sent the others, including Francis May and McKinney, ahead to Pier 52. He said he would probably join them after the meeting broke up. William May arrived a few minutes after the group departed. With him were J-M directors John P. Schroeder, vice chairman of Morgan Guaranty Trust Co., and Charles J. Zwick, president of Southeast Banking Corp., in Miami.

---

*Herbert E. Meyer's article, "Shootout at the Johns-Manville Corral," is a classic and is certainly well worth examining in its entirety. Reprinted from *Fortune*, October 1976, pp. 146–154. Copyright © 1976 Time Inc. All rights reserved.

Schroeder came directly to the point. He told Goodwin that the trio represented the nine outside directors on J-M's twelve man board, and that they wanted him to resign.

"Why?" stammered Goodwin who was caught totally by surprise.

"Under the bylaws of this corporation," replied Schroeder evenly, "we don't have to give you a reason."

Off balance and outgunned, Goodwin agreed to resign. . . . Goodwin, whose appetite disappeared along with his job, decided not to join his ex-colleagues at the restaurant.[21]

At the time of Goodwin's dismissal, Johns-Manville had board of director interlocks with three CPC institutions—New York Life, Manufacturers Hanover, and J. P. Morgan and Co., Inc. In addition, the CPC provided Johns-Manville with trustee, transfer agent, and registrar services and controlled, at a minimum, 10 percent of its common stock. The Dick Goodwin case clearly emphasizes several important points:

• A corporation's board of directors not only has the legal responsibility for firing and hiring management; they freely exercise this authority.*

• CPC directors expect corporations that are structurally tied to the CPC to adopt a cooperative attitude.

• The interlocking director ties between the CPC and non-core corporations are quite effective as functional tools in eliminating individuals who exhibit a noncooperative attitude.

In conclusion, for those interested in the subtle nuances which surround and permeate the exercise of power, note that—while

---

*Other recent examples where boards have fired or removed Chief Executive Officers include Bob R. Dorsey at Gulf Oil Corporation (see "Morality Play," *Wall Street Journal*, 15 January 1976, p. 1) and A. Robert Abboud at First Chicago Corporation (see "After the Carnage at First Chicago," *Fortune*, 2 June 1980, p. 15). In commenting on the attitude taken by First Chicago's board of directors, Ben Heineman, board spokesman and chairman of the bank's executive committee, was reported in the *Fortune* article as having stated, "Sometimes it's necessary for the coaches to select a new quarterback." The sentiments expressed by Heineman appear to aptly sum up the attitude taken by boards of directors toward their company's Chief Executive officers. In short, boards of directors are self-perpetuating, but Chief Executive officers are not. First Chicago hired an executive vice-president from Chase Manhattan Bank—Barry Sullivan—as its new Chief Executive Officer.

Johns-Manville's headquarters is located in Colorado—the board of directors meeting at which Mr. Goodwin was forced to resign was held in New York. Throughout history, trips to the Meccas of the world have always evoked both jubilation and trepidation on the part of travelers.

J. P. Morgan and United States Steel: the arrogance of power

Above all else, J. P. Morgan and John D. Rockefeller abhorred competitive market structures. Each continually exhorted his colleagues, the public, and the politicians about the economic inefficiencies inherent to competitive enterprise and, conversely, about the economic efficiencies to be gained from cooperation. In turn, they allowed only those with similar sentiments to sit as directors on the boards of the trusts they created. For instance, Judge Elbert H. Gary, U.S. Steel's first board chairman, initiated the much-celebrated "Gary Dinners" as a means of achieving and maintaining intraindustry cooperation and coordination among steel producers. As F. M. Scherer noted in his book *Industrial Market Structure and Economic Performance*:

> Judge Gary once explained that the "close communication and contact" developed at these dinners generated such mutual "respect and affectionate regard" among steel industry leaders that all considered the obligation to cooperate and avoid destructive competition "more binding . . . than any written verbal contract."[22]

When U.S. Steel was formed in April 1901, the corporation's board of directors included, in addition to Judge Gary, J. Pierpont Morgan, John D. Rockefeller, and John D. Rockefeller, Jr. In 1913, in testimony before the Subcommittee of the House Committee on Banking and Currency, Morgan—in a very arrogant and begrudging fashion—offered the following comments pertaining to how board members were chosen:

> UNTERMEYER: At the time of the organization of the United States Steel Corporation did you name the entire board of directors?
> MORGAN: No. I think I passed on it.
> UNTERMEYER: Did you not, as a matter of fact, name the board and pass out a slip of paper containing the names of the board?
> MORGAN: I cannot say that no one else helped me in it.
> * * *
> UNTERMEYER: Did you not only pass on it and approve it, but did you

not further select the board and determine who should go on and who should stay off?

MORGAN: No, I probably did the latter.

UNTERMEYER: Yes; and having determined who should stay off, you necessarily determined who should go on?

MORGAN: I am quite willing to assume the whole responsibility.

UNTERMEYER: I only want the fact.

MORGAN: Whoever went on that board went with my approval.

UNTERMEYER: And from time to time . . . whoever has gone on the board has gone on with your approval, has he not?

MORGAN: Not always.

UNTERMEYER: Has he gone against your protest?

MORGAN: No, sir.[23]

In 1978, 65 years after Morgan's congressional testimony, 40 percent of U.S. Steel's board of directors were also CPC directors. Twenty-seven percent of Inland Steel's directors were CPC directors, as were 23 percent of Bethlehem Steel's directors. In addition, the Chief Executive Officers for each of the nation's six largest steel producers—with the exception of National Steel and U.S. Steel—were CPC directors. Finally, (a) U.S. Steel and Bethlehem Steel were indirectly intralocked at Citicorp, (b) U.S. Steel and Armco, Inc., were indirectly intralocked at Chase, (c) U.S. Steel, National Steel, and Republic Steel were indirectly intralocked at Chemical, and (d) U.S. Steel, Bethlehem Steel, and Republic Steel were indirectly intralocked at Metropolitan Life (see the Central Planning Tableau). In addition, as is also illustrated in the Central Planning Tableau, directors from U.S. Steel, Bethlehem Steel, Armco, Inc., National Steel, Republic Steel, and Inland Steel, on the average, have 38 IDI's and 7.5 III's with the CPC.

On the one hand, from a purely structural perspective, corporations in the steel industry are solidly bonded together through a veritable maze of indirect intraindustry administrative ties. On the other hand, from a purely functional perspective, these administrative ties have proven every bit as effective as Judge Gary's dinners in creating a spirit of cooperation within the steel industry so as to "avoid destructive competition." Price competition within the CPC's domestic steel industry has been nonexistent for decades. In short—

- competitive market structure prices have been replaced by administered prices; and, in turn,
- the steel industry's pricing policies are affected through the

existence of indirect intraindustry administrative ties within the CPC.

Alas, if only our steel executives could convince the Japanese of the futility of competition in the world's international steel markets.

Lao-Tsu—"The more ingenious and clever men are, the more strange things happen": and, of course, there are joint ventures

A very common method of harmonizing and coordinating the intraindustry activities of corporations is the joint venture. From a legal standpoint, joint ventures between corporations may take numerous forms. The purest form of joint venture is the *joint ownership of the means of production*. This type of joint venture may be effected through a simple contractual relationship between two or more corporations, or, more typically, through the creation of a jointly owned subsidiary. As illustration, the Arabian American Oil Company (ARAMCO) is a very typical "subsidiary type" of joint venture. Since December 1948, ARAMCO has been jointly owned by Standard Oil Company of New Jersey (now Exxon), Standard Oil Company of California, Texaco, and Mobil Oil Corporation (see Table 19). Also, since 1948, ARAMCO has been the sole petroleum producer in Saudi Arabia. At present, the oil shipped from Saudi Arabia—primarily to Japan and Western Europe—accounts for 35 percent of the Middle East's total petroleum production. Throughout most of the period since World War II, Saudi Arabia has ranked fourth in worldwide petroleum production—behind the United States, Russia, and Iran. Today, ARAMCO produces approximately 9.2 million barrels of oil per day (slightly more than half of the daily petroleum consumption in the U.S.) and has estimated reserves in excess of 145 billion barrels. In short, one corporation—ARAMCO—accounts for approximately 25 percent of the entire world's (excluding the Communist bloc countries) petroleum production.

Concerning the relationship between ARAMCO's four owners and the CPC, Exxon, Mobil, and Standard of California have indirect BOD *intra*locks at Citicorp, including Exxon's and Standard of California's Chief Executive Officers. Exxon and Mobil also have indirect BOD *intra*locks at both Chemical Bank and Equitable Life, including Mobil's Chief Executive Officer and one of Exxon's senior executive officers. Exxon and Standard of California have indirect BOD *intra*locks at Prudential Life. Finally, Texaco is intralocked with Exxon and Mobil at Chemical Bank through an "A" type of interlock

---

Table 19

Ownership of the Major Petroleum Producing Operation in Saudi Arabia (January 1980)

Company ownership and fields	Percentage of ownership	Production (barrels per day)
Arabian American Oil Company (ARAMCO)		9,200,000
Standard Oil Company, California	28.3	
Standard Oil Company, New Jersey (Exxon)	28.3	
Texaco, Inc.	28.3	
Mobil Oil Corporation	15.0	

Fields: Khurais, Manifa, Ghawar, Abqaiq, Berri, Abu Sa'Fah, Abu Hadriya, Safaniya, Qatif, Khursaniyah, Fadhili, Dammam, Shaybah

Source: James C. Tanner, "Mobil to Expand Stake in ARAMCO to 15% by 1979," *Wall Street Journal*, 10 April 1975, p. 3, and John R. Munkirs, "Joint Ventures in the International Petroleum Industry: Production and Pipelines," Ph.D. dissertation, University of Oklahoma, 1973, p. 125.

(institutional interlock, but not a BOD interlock—see note to Table 16). In total, the four corporations have 14 direct BOD interlocks with the CPC. In addition, Exxon has 24 IDI's with the CPC; Mobil, 54; Texaco, 14; and Standard of California, 21. A quick perusal of the Central Planning Tableau reveals additional III's, as well as numerous stock, debt, trustee, and other intra- and interlocking ties. When the multifarious intra- and interlocking ties that these corporations have with the CPC are considered—in addition to the fact that they "jointly own" ARAMCO—one cannot help but conclude that these corporations are technologically, legally, and financially bound to a common course of action. One is reminded of J. P. Morgan's statement, "I like a little competition, but I like combination better."[24] It would, indeed, be hard to imagine how the CPC could have created a more tightly bonded or highly coordinated enterprise.

When one sees a traffic intersection with Mobil, Exxon, Texaco, and Chevron (Standard of California) filling stations, one on each corner, an image of competition is evoked. On the other hand, though, when one is confronted with the structural realities that are behind these outward images, one can more fully understand from whom the Organization of Petroleum Exporting Countries (OPEC) learned about the benefits of combining and coordinating one's economic activities with others.

Just as ARAMCO dominated the petroleum industry in Saudi Arabia, the same kind of joint venture monopoly enterprise dominated the petroleum industry in every other Middle Eastern country. In turn, each joint venture was itself dominated by some combination of the same seven corporations—Standard Oil Company of New Jersey (Exxon), Texaco, Standard Oil of California, Mobil Oil Corporation, Gulf Oil Corporation, British Petroleum, and Royal Dutch Shell. These seven corporations are usually referred to as "the International Majors." As of June 1972, the International Majors had 68 interlocking ownership ties in 16 separate joint ventures which accounted for 58 percent of the petroleum production in the OPEC countries (see Table 20). In addition, the International Majors owned another 20 percent of OPEC's total production—16 percent in one-owner operations and 4 percent in joint ventures with government-owned companies. Simply stated, OPEC is merely a combination of government institutions, much like the International Majors is a combination of private institutions.

It should not be assumed, however, that OPEC has reduced the economic effectiveness of joint ventures, such as ARAMCO. The following was noted in a 1975 *Wall Street Journal* article:

> None of the stock of ARAMCO, a Delaware corporation, has ever left the U.S. despite widely publicized reports of the Saudi government having taken over 60% ownership of the company. The Saudi government isn't a shareholder in ARAMCO, it was learned. The government's 60% participation is in the "producing assets" of ARAMCO, not in the company itself. The huge Ras Tanura, Saudi Arabia, petroleum refinery and certain other facilities, as well as all the stock of ARAMCO, continue to be owned 100% by the company's four U.S. shareholders: Exxon Corporation, Standard Oil Company of California, Texaco, Inc., and Mobil. Mobil currently holds 10% of the stock of ARAMCO. The remaining 90% of the stock is divided equally among the three other companies. Under the new arrangement, Mobil's interest will rise to 15% over a five-year period, while the proportionate interests of the others will decline to 28 1/3% each in 1979.[25]

Also, in 1975, it was revealed during the Senate hearings on "Multinational Oil Corporations . . . and U.S. Foreign Policy" that:

> [t]he multinational oil corporations are currently engaged in a series of

Table 20. Interlocking Ownership Ties in Petroleum Producing Operations among the International Majors—OPEC Countries (June 1972)

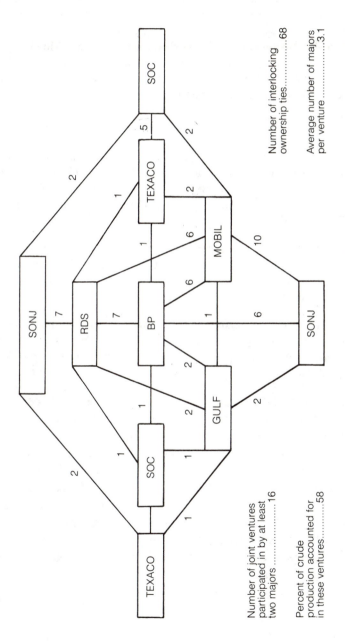

Number of joint ventures participated in by at least two majors 16

Percent of crude production accounted for in these ventures 58

Number of interlocking ownership ties 68

Average number of majors per venture 3.1

Source: John R. Munkirs, "Joint Ventures in the International Petroleum Industry: Production and Pipelines," Ph.D. dissertation, University of Oklahoma, 1973, p. 125.

Legend: SONJ = Standard Oil of New Jersey (Exxon); SOC = Standard Oil of California; RDS = Royal Dutch Shell; BP = British Petroleum.

negotiations designed to ensure their exclusive right to "buyback" oil—oil which has become the property of the producer countries by virtue of the various participation "arrangements," and which those countries now wish to sell back to the previous company concession holders. The four ARAMCO shareholders—Exxon, Texaco, SOCAL, and Mobil—by joint negotiations seek to establish a special relationship with Saudi Arabia which would give them preferential access to the Saudi crude oil supply at a discount off the going market price.[26]

Finally, in an article in the 26 May 1980 issue of *Forbes*:

Another reason for the huge jump in Exxon's refining and marketing earnings has been its "Saudi advantage." That refers to the oil Exxon has access to through its partnership in the Arabian American Oil Co. Three other companies, Mobil, Texaco, and Standard Oil of California, are ARAMCO partners.

The ARAMCO companies have exclusive access to 7.2 million barrels of oil a day, now at $26 a barrel, about $8.50 less than the average spot market price. Exxon's share of ARAMCO oil is 2.2 million barrels a day, 50% of its total supply.

Garvin estimates that in the first quarter the amount of earnings due to the Saudi advantage might have been $100 million. Some Exxon critics say the Saudi advantage is worth as much as $175 million a month to each of the ARAMCO partners.[27]

One might contend, then, that joint ventures in the petroleum industry, particularly ARAMCO, have withstood thus far the test of time and, further, that with the creation of OPEC—

• consumers now pay an additional tribute to the International Majors over and above the normal CPSP profits, additional monies which the majors usually attribute to OPEC or to changes in their accounting procedures (surely no one believes that even Americans would allow the petroleum companies to make such exorbitant profits, if OPEC were not handy as a psychological scapegoat); and,

• consumers also pay an additional public sector tribute (tax) to the OPEC countries themselves.

It is certainly no exaggeration to say that, from a purely profit perspective, OPEC has been a tremendous asset to the CPC.* It should

---

*Also, in Chapter 6, The Anational Corporation, there is a discussion illustrating how, from a global political-economic perspective, the CPC is *using or taking advantage* of the so-called "petroleum shortages" to make fundamental structural changes in the world's economy. For example, it is very probable that the not be assumed, however, that joint ventures in the petroleum industry are limited to the Middle East.* As is indicated in Table 21, the International Majors, in nine geographic areas (Africa, Alaska, Asia-Pacific, Australia, Central America, the Middle East, the North Sea, South America, and Western Europe), had 916 joint interlocking ownership arrangements. As noted by James I. Sturgeon in his Ph.D. dissertation:

> . . . three-fourths of the crude production, 60 percent of the pipeline mileage, and 50 percent of the refining capacity in the nine areas is jointly owned. Given the magnitude of joint ownership of these productive means, it may be concluded that the means of production in the international petroleum industry are substantially jointly owned.
>
> Joint ownership of the means of production, eventuated through joint ventures, serves as one mechanism to bring order and organization into the international petroleum industry. The nature of joint ventures demands cooperation among the participants. Cooperation, in turn, demands planning and a sophisticated communication network. Joint ventures provide both of these prerequisites to order and organization.
>
> Cooperation, planning, order, and organization may work to the benefit of the consumer; however, they may also work to the vested interest in the pecuniary gain of the participants in the oil industry.[28]

In addition, it must not be assumed that joint ventures are peculiar to the petroleum industry.† For, as Michigan State University's

---

American-based automobile companies, within the next several decades, will produce the majority of their cars outside the continental United States. Such fundamental changes which dramatically impact on the lives of American workers—workers who are also voters—can be negotiated much more smoothly and successfully, from a political perspective, during times of economic crisis. For instance, as the auto industry is closing plants in this country, it is simultaneously opening new ones in other countries. In short, what may appear to be a crisis in the auto industry, from a narrow and provincial domestic perspective, may, in fact, given the CPC's global political-economic perspective, be an opportunity for the CPC to make fundamental and, from their viewpoint, much-needed changes.

*For a detailed and exhaustive analysis of joint ventures in the petroleum industry, see James I. Sturgeon, "Joint Ventures in the International Petroleum Industry: Exploration and Drilling," Ph.D. dissertation, University of Oklahoma, 1974; also, John R. Munkirs, "Joint Ventures in the International Petroleum Industry: Production and Pipelines," Ph.D dissertation, University of Oklahoma, 1973.

†For a very concise and thorough analysis of joint ventures in the iron and steel industry, see Gordon Bova, "The Concentrated Control of Iron Ore by Major Steel Companies as an Unfair Method of Competition," *Southern California Law Review*, Vol. 46, No. 4, September 1973, pp. 1116–1167.

Table 21

Joint Interlocking Ownership Arrangements in Exploration and Drilling, Producing Operations, Pipeline Systems, and Refining Operations (International Majors, 9 geographic areas, 1957-1972)

Company \ Company	Jersey	Shell	Texaco	Mobil	Gulf	SOCAL	BP	TOTAL
Standard Oil, New Jersey/Exxon								
Royal Dutch Shell Group	186							186
Texaco	32	45						77
Mobil Oil	59	46	31					136
Gulf Oil	21	22	23	14				80
Standard Oil of California	19	98	100	31	15			263
British Petroleum	33	44	22	37	25	13		174
TOTAL	350	255	176	82	40	13		916

Source: James I. Sturgeon, "Joint Ventures in the International Petroleum Industry: Exploration and Drilling," Ph.D. dissertation, University of Oklahoma, 1974, p. 166.

Note: The data in this table cover nine geographic areas: Africa, Alaska, Asia-Pacific, Australia, Central America, the Middle East, the North Sea, South America, and Western Europe.

economics professor Daniel R. Fusfeld concluded from his research on jointly owned subsidiaries in the iron and steel industry:

> More significant, perhaps, is the new light thrown on the structure of the industry. The more than seventy joint subsidiaries is a substantially larger number than heretofore was thought to exist—and there are probably others that this study was not able to discover. The interest groupings into which they fall indicate that we can no longer think of the steel industry as comprising some dozen large and ten smaller integrated producers. . . . *The joint subsidiaries are quasi-mergers . . .*

> It is evident that further study of joint subsidiaries is needed, both in the iron and steel industry and in the economy as a whole.[29] (emphasis added)

For the most part, the "jointly owned subsidiary" variety of joint venture is most common in the extractive industries, such as petroleum, iron ore, copper, and aluminum. *Intra*-industry consultation, coordination, and planning does not occur in these industries through cartel agreements, trade associations, oligopolistic market structures, or "Judge Gary"-type dinners. Rather, consultation, coordination, and planning is called for because the means of production, in large measure, are jointly owned by the participants.

Finally, in terms of the structural-functional bifurcation of the CPSP planning instruments, the argument goes as follows:

• The various corporations in each of the major extractive industries were initially tightly bonded together, from a structural standpoint, through various types of BOD, stock, and other indirect intralocking ties.

• Because of the way in which nature stores its petroleum and mineral deposits in highly centralized locations—for example, Saudi Arabia contains almost one-fourth of the world's petroleum reserves—several different companies, in order to survive, had to have access to the same petroleum fields and/or mineral deposits.

• The CPC used its BOD, stock, debt, and other planning instruments as functional tools in facilitating the organization and coordination of the joint venture type of operation.

The data in the Central Planning Tableau reveal that 28, or approximately 10 percent, of the CPC's 263 members are petroleum company directors. In addition, in III's, petroleum company and CPC directors are in almost constant contact. For example, just through III's, directors from Exxon and Mobil, respectively, have approximately 60 and 132 meetings annually with CPC directors. In brief, then, these two facts are quite clear: (a) joint ventures are a way of life in many of the country's extractive industries, and (b) the CPC, in terms of both its means and self-interest, would appear to be the most likely vehicle for facilitating the organizing, coordinating, and planning of such ventures.

In any event, intraindustry contractual relationships between corporations within the Central Planning Tableau are not limited to the jointly owned subsidiary variety. "Parts-swapping" in the automobile industry, for example, is very typical of the more loose-knit types of intraindustry cooperative relationships that are also commonplace. A partial listing of the parts that General Motors (GM), Ford, Chrysler, American Motors (AMC), and Volkswagen (VW) manufacture and sell to each other is shown in Table 22. As a case in point, GM sells ball bearings to Ford, Chrysler, and AMC; air conditioning compressors, power brake boosters, and electric solenoids to Ford; automatic transmissions to Fiat for the Fiat 131; catalytic converters to AMC; and,

Table 22

A Partial Listing of "Parts-Swapping" in the Automobile Industry, for Selected Corporations (1978)

Producing corporations	Buyer corporations				
	General Motors	Ford	Chrysler	American Motors	Fiat 131
General Motors		Ball bearings Air conditioning compressors Power brake boosters Electric solenoids	Ball bearings Steering columns Bumper components Power steering pumps Emissions-controlling air pumps Engine castings Wire harnesses	Ball bearings Steering columns Bumper components Automatic transmissions (for Jeep)	Automatic transmissions
Ford	Diesel engine parts Transmission transfer cases Instrument clusters		Raw glass	Two-barrel carburetors	
Chrysler		Diesel engine parts Transmission transfer cases Instrument clusters		Automatic transmissions	
American Motors			Plastic parts (various)		
Volkswagen			Engine and manual transmissions for Dodge Omni and Plymouth Horizon	Four-cylinder engines for Gremlin and Concord	

Source: "The Great Engine Switch and Other Magic Tricks Performed by the One-and-Only Auto Industry," *Consumer Reports*, April 1978, pp. 190-191.

finally, bumper components and steering columns to both Chrysler and AMC. On the other hand, Chrysler sells truck parts—including diesel engine parts—transmission transfer cases, and instrument clusters to both GM and Ford; it also sells automatic transmissions to AMC. Ford sells raw glass to Chrysler and two-barrel carburetors to AMC. Not to be outdone, VW sells Chrysler the engines and manual transmissions for the Dodge Omni and the Plymouth Horizon. AMC buys the four-cylinder engines that it uses in its Gremlin and Concord automobiles from VW. The article in *Consumer Reports* from which the data on "parts-swapping" were taken concluded with the following observations:

> There's considerable incest among foreign automakers, as well. *A single supplier makes automatic transmissions for both Datsun and Mazda—* under license *from Ford. The Porsche 924 uses an Audi engine. The discontinued Porsche 914 had a VW engine. The Fiat 131 uses an automatic transmission built by GM in Europe.* . . . And if anyone out there is about to invest $55,900 in a Rolls Royce to gain its legendary engineering, be aware that you'll be using a legendary automatic transmission made by General Motors.[30]

Parts-swapping in the industry arises, in part, because of joint ventures among the corporations in their research activities. The controversial "smog conspiracy" case is quite illustrative of this point.* In 1966, a federal grand jury was convened to investigate GM's, Ford's, Chrysler's, and AMC's joint research activities in pollution control devices. The Anti-Trust Division of the Justice Department summarized the grand jury's findings, in part, concerning a cross-licensing agreement between the four automakers as follows:

> . . . The evidence adduced before the Grand Jury clearly developed that the signatories to the cross-licensing agreement had the following understandings and agreements: (A) not to publicize competitively any solution to the motor vehicle air pollution problem; (B) to adopt a uniform date for announcement of the discovery of any air pollution control device; and (C) to install devices only on an agreed date.[31]

---

*For an excellent and detailed discussion of the "smog conspiracy" case, see Mark J. Green, Beverly C. Moore, Jr., and Bruce Wasserstein, *The Closed Enterprise System* (New York: Grossman Publishers, 1972), pp. 254–265.

The covenants in this agreement would prohibit a company that developed a new technology from introducing such (a) until the other companies had also developed a similar technology, or (b) until an agreement was reached wherein the patent owner would produce and sell the part or parts to its "competitors." In this particular instance, the Justice Department attorneys became convinced that the licensing scheme, developed primarily by the Automobile Manufacturer Association (AMA), was used primarily to slow down the introducion of new pollution control devices. For instance, as early as 1961, Chrysler's engineers had developed a more pollution-free exhaust system, and Du Pont (E. I.) de Nemours and Company's D. C. Diggs summarized a conversation between himself and a Chrysler engineer, as follows:

> While admitting that favorable publicity would result, he was very forceful in telling me that if this was done Chrysler would be severely chastised by the rest of the industry. He reminded me that the AMA agreement says that no one company will gain any competitive advantage because of smog, and that Chrysler was a relatively small cog in the industry. He indicated that Ford and GM were calling the shots. . . .[32]

Upon completion of the grand jury's investigation in 1967, the Anti-Trust Division's attorneys left little doubt as to their own conclusions:

> We are convinced that we have shown the grand jury and are in possession of evidence to prove beyond a reasonable doubt the existence of an industry-wide agreement and conspiracy among the auto manufacturers, through AMA, not to compete in the research, development, manufacture and installation of motor vehicle air pollution control devices for the purpose of achieving interminable delays, or at least delays as long as possible. The cross-licensing agreement was used as a cover and focal point of the conspiracy.[33]

Three of the four attorneys assigned to the case and the grand jury itself wanted to indict the four automobile companies, as well as several of their employees, on both *criminal* and *civil* charges. Criminal suits, upon conviction, may be accompanied by fines and/or imprisonment. Civil suits do not involve inflicting punishment; rather, upon conviction, civil suits usually (a) enjoin the defendant from proceeding with a certain action, for example, a proposed merger, or (b) forbid repetition of past acts determined to be illegal. In 1969, a *civil* suit was filed against the Automobile Manufacturers Association and the four automobile companies. (The Assistant Attorney General and the Attorney General make the final decision concerning both whether the Justice Department will prosecute a particular case and what type of suit—civil or criminal—will be filed.) Assistant Attorney General Donald Turner, in correspondence with Ralph Nader, demurred:

> . . . the joint research venture among the auto companies, though in my view unlawful (as the later civil suit charged), was not in the category of "per se" offenses and . . . most of the alleged restricted agreements were arguably ancillary to the joint undertaking. . . .[34]

In 1969, the Justice Department issued a *consent decree* which enjoined the defendants from continuing their cross-licensing agreement. Civil suits may be terminated before a court decision is reached, if the government and the defendant reach a compromise or an agreement. The compromise reached is always published in what is officially called a consent decree. Under law, the signing of a consent decree by the defendant(s) is not an admission of guilt. Ninety percent of all civil suits are ended by the consent decree method. In any event, this particular cross-licensing joint venture among the auto companies has ostensibly been terminated. Nonetheless, joint ventures are still both numerous and useful in assuring intraindustry cooperation and consultation and in developing technological, pricing, and production strategies.

One last comment is in order concerning joint ventures. Traditionally, an industry's market structure classification has been decided by determining the amount of total sales or assets accounted for by the 4, 8, or 12 largest firms in the industry. For instance, in an industry where the 4 largest firms account for more than 50 percent of the industry's total sales, the industry is classified as having an oligopolistically competitive market structure. But, if each of these 4 firms produced the majority of their output in joint ventures with each other, would not the industry's actual market structure be much more concentrated than the oligopoly classification implies? In other words, are not joint ventures "quasi-mergers," as suggested above by Daniel R. Fusfeld? In short, joint ventures have become so numerous in many industries as to render the traditional industrial organization taxonomy obsolete. And, in market structure studies where joint ventures are not thoroughly analyzed, the analysis must be considered both incomplete and inadequate.

In conclusion, the above examples could be supplemented with literally hundreds of similar scenarios. Scores of government reports, business-oriented periodicals, and books are filled with such references. Further, the words of Adam Smith come echoing through the centuries—those who imagine " . . . that masters rarely combine . . . " are " . . . as ignorant of the world as of the subject." However, these few examples may be sufficient to provide an initial indication as to the existence of a collective consciousness among CPC members:

• a collective consciousness which stems directly from the manner in which the CPC institutions are tightly bonded together as a structurally integrated and cohesive group;

• a collective consciousness which views intra- and interindustry cooperation as both (a) rational and (b) essential; and

• a collective consciousness regarding the methods available for effecting intra- and interindustry cooperation.

The central point in all this is that when intra- and interindustry cooperation and coordination reach a certain degree of regularity and intensity, the words ''cooperation'' and ''coordination'' should be superceded by the more appropriate label—intra- and interindustry economic planning, i.e., CPSP. Nonetheless, it must be recognized that most of the corporate leaders engaged in these activities would themselves eschew the concept of CPSP as being descriptive of their actions. This is partly so because of the deeply rooted psychological antipathy against the very concept of economic planning that is itself undoubtedly rooted in our country's association of planning with communism and/or government institutions. In any event, equipped with the ideas and conceptual tools developed in this chapter and in Chapter 3, we find the task now at hand is to begin an examination of the Central Planning Tableau.

Notes

1. John M. Blair, *Economic Concentration, Structure, Behavior and Public Policy* (New York: Harcourt, Brace, Jovanovich, Inc., 1972), p. 262–263.

2. John Moody, *The Truth About the Trusts*, reprinted ed. (New York: Greenwood Press, 1968), p. 494.

3. Ibid., pp. 494–495.

4. Ibid., p. 491.

5. Ibid., p. 492.

6. Ibid., pp. 492–493.

7. Louis D. Brandeis, quoted in Blair, *Economic Concentration, Structure, Behavior and Public Policy*, pp. 262–263.

8. Friedrich Nietzsche, *The Will to Power*, Walter Kaufmann and R. J. Hollingdale, trans.; Walter Kaufmann ed. (New York: Vintage Books, 1968), pp. 28–29.

9. Charles J. V. Murphy and T. A. Wise, "The Problem of Howard Hughes," *Fortune*, January 1959, pp. 79, 171.

10. Ibid., p. 79.

11. "What's Behind the Big TWA Sale," *Business Week*, 16 April 1966, p. 146.

12. Ibid., pp. 145, 146, 148, 150.

13. John Kenneth Galbraith, *Journey to Poland and Yugoslavia* (Boston: Harvard University Press, 1958), p. 57.

14. U.S. Congress, Senate, prepared by the Subcommittees on Intergovernmental Relations and Budgeting, Management, and Expenditures of the Committee on Government Operations, *Disclosure of Corporate Ownership*, 93rd Congress, 2nd Sess., 4 March 1974, p. 390.

15. Ibid., p. 391.

16. Mark J. Green, ed., *The Monopoly Makers* (New York: Grossman Publishers, 1973), pp. 231–232.

17. "Why the Big Traders Worry Industry," *Business Week*, 25 July 1970, pp. 53–55.

18. "John Bryan Rewrites the Gospel According to Nate Cummings," *Fortune*, 4 June 1979, p. 104.

19. Herbert E. Meyer, "Shootout at the Johns-Manville Corral," *Fortune*, October 1976, p. 146.

20. Ibid., p. 154.

21. Ibid., pp. 147–148.

22. F. M. Scherer, *Industrial Market Structure and Economic Performance* (Chicago: Rand McNally College Publishing Company, 1970), p. 158.

23. Blair, *Economic Concentration, Structure, Behavior and Public Policy*, p. 77–78.

24. J. P. Morgan, quoted in Robert L. Heilbroner's *The Economic Transformation of America* (New York: Harcourt, Brace, Jovanovich, Inc., 1977), p. 110.

25. James C. Tanner, "Mobil to Expand Stake in ARAMCO to 15% by 1979," *Wall Street Journal*, 10 April 1975, p. 3.

26. U.S. Congress, Senate, Hearings before the Subcommittee on Multinational Corporations of the Committee on Foreign Relations, *Multinational Oil Corporations and U.S. Foreign Policy: Report Together with Individual Views of the Committee on Foreign Relations of the United States Senate*, 93rd Congress, 2nd Sess., 2 January 1975, p. 10.

27. Carol E. Curtis, "Exxon's Nuclear Frustration," *Forbes*, 26 May 1980, pp. 34–35.

28. James I. Sturgeon, "Joint Ventures in the International Petroleum Industry: Exploration and Drilling," Ph.D. dissertation, University of Oklahoma, 1974, pp. 194–195.

29. Daniel R. Fusfeld, "Joint Subsidiaries in the Iron and Steel Industry," American Economic Association *Papers and Proceedings of the Seventieth Annual Meeting* (Philadelphia, 1958), pp. 586–587.

30. "The Great Engine Switch and Other Magic Tricks Performed by the One-and-Only Auto Industry," *Consumer Reports*, April 1978, pp. 190–191.

31. Mark J. Green, Beverly C. Moore, Jr., and Bruce Wasserstein, *The Closed Enterprise System* (New York: Grossman Publishers, 1972), p. 255.

32. Ibid., p. 256.

33. Ibid., p. 257.

34. Ibid., p. 258.

Chapter Five

Centralized Private Sector Planning: The Central Planning Tableau (CPT)

> . . . . . *we have suggested that our evolution and genetic heritage, our subsequent physical and mental development, the learning process, the culture in which we have developed, and especially the process of perception are all involved in how the organism "organizes" itself and the environment. I suggest that all of these forces are manifestations of what I regard as the key concept for the development of meaning— namely the concept of structure. I am suggesting that the manner in which structure is provided, outside and inside the organism, determines the meaning there is for the organism. . . . My thesis is that the concept of structure pervades everything, and that it is the clue to the problem of meaning.* [1]
>
> Joseph R. Royce, 1964

Familiarization with both the structural and the functional characteristics of the various planning instruments and the concepts of intra- and interindustry cooperation and coordination will allow one, for the most part, to read and understand much of the data presented in the Central Planning Tableau (CPT). Nonetheless, there are several aspects of the tableau that require additional elaboration. First, a general description of the corporations and industries contained in the CPT is in order. Second, it is extremely important to make explicit note of some of the corporations and industries that are *not* shown in the tableau but that are, nonetheless, controlled and/or heavily influenced by corporations which are depicted in the tableau. Third, further elaboration is also necessary so that the symbols and data in the tableau can be read and interpreted accurately from a purely mechanical perspective. Fourth, several additional characteristics of the various planning instruments need to be explicitly set forth. Finally, a few additional observations are in order regarding the CPSP theory itself. In essence, then, this chapter is a potpourri of observations and elaborations that do not, in themselves, represent a logically integrated argument but rather are intended to provide a fuller and more complete understanding of the ideas and concepts developed in Chapters 3 and 4.

The Central Planning Tableau

The exterior: a brief description

The CPT consists of 138 corporations with 11,043,818 employees; $992,596,298,000 in revenue; and assets totalling $1,071,792,046,000—as of 1 January 1978.* In turn, the tableau contains two basic divisions—the CPC and the non-core corporations. At this point, a description of the CPC would be redundant. The 126 non-core corporations are subdivided into three categories: (a) manufacturing, transportation, and public utilities; (b) retailing; and (c) miscellaneous. Industries in the manufacturing, transportation, and public utilities subdivision are quite diverse, including, but not limited to, electrical utilities, soaps and detergents, chemicals, soft drinks, and television broadcasting. Also, the 94 corporations within the 28 industries in this subdivision are arranged as much as possible in a "buy from" and "sell to" sequence—i.e., aircraft engines, aircraft, air transportation, jet fuel; steel, aluminum, metal containers, soft drinks, and so on.

The retailing subdivision is restricted solely to general merchandising, and only seven corporations are included—Sears, K-Mart, R. H. Macy, J. C. Penney, Montgomery Ward, Federated Department Stores, and Associated Dry Goods.

Finally, the miscellaneous subdivision contains 25 corporations including such companies as W. R. Grace and Company (chemicals), Avon (cosmetic products), and Ralston Purina Company (commercial livestock and poultry feeds and pet foods). For the most part, these are corporations that were found to be closely tied to the CPC but did not,

---

*The $992 billion revenue figure was computed by adding together the demand deposits of the banks; the premiums and annuity income of the insurance companies; the operating revenues of the electric utilities, transportation companies and diversified financial institutions; and the total sales of the retailing and manufacturing corporations. Of course, some of these figures are stock variables while others are flow variables; therefore, they are not precisely comparable. Nonetheless, by adding them together one can obtain an existential understanding of the magnitude of dollars involved without treating reality with undue harshness.

as individual institutions, constitute the greater part of any specific market. This observation, though, is tempered by the fact that several of the corporations in this category do account for a substantial percentage of the total sales in their respective markets. As illustration, Owens-Illinois (glass containers), Owens-Corning Fiberglas (home insulation), and Cummins Engine Company (truck engines) each account for more than 50 percent of the total sales in their respective markets. In addition, many of these corporations are major suppliers for other industries within the tableau. For example, (1) Borg-Warner and Bendix Corporation are major suppliers of original equipment automobile parts to the auto industry; (2) Cummins Engine Company is the primary supplier of truck engines to the "big four" automobile companies; (3) Owens-Illinois supplies glass containers for the pharmaceutical and soft drink industries; (4) Whirlpool Corporation supplies Sears with household appliances; and (5) Norton Simon is a major cosmetic supplier for many of the retailing corporations (Sears, Penney's, etc.). In short, these corporations are, from a structural and functional perspective, closely linked—technologically, financially, and administratively—to the other industries in the tableau.

The interior: a brief description

While the CPT may appear to be rather comprehensive, the data do not reveal the true magnitude of the concentration of economic power that actually exists within the economy's CPSP sphere for two basic reasons. First, some industries were simply omitted. The initial tableau very quickly became too large and cumbersome to be readily understandable. In addition, a comprehensive study would have required more resources than were available. Thus, from a practical viewpoint, it became necessary to institute limitations. For example, the CPC is closely tied to the electrical utility industry. Yet, there are only three of the country's major utilities depicted in the tableau—New York's Consolidated Edison, Chicago's Commonwealth Edison, and New Jersey's Public Service Electric and Gas. Likewise, many of the railroads are closely tied to the CPC, but this industry is left out of the tableau.

Second, many CPT corporations own other *corporations* that do not explicitly appear in the tableau.* As is shown in Table 23, United

---

*Actually, from an organizational standpoint, these companies are wholly owned subsidiaries or consolidated companies.

Table 23

Partial Listing of CPT Corporations That Own Other Corporations (January, 1978)

Central Planning Tableau corporations and parent companies	Wholly owned subsidiary(ies) or consolidated company(ies)*
Northwest Industries	Acme Boot Company, Inc. Union Underwear Company, Inc. Lone Star Steel Company
TWA	Canteen Corporation
Atlantic Richfield	Anaconda Copper
Pepsico	Wilson Sporting Goods
Beatrice Foods	Peter Eckrich & Sons
United Technologies	Otis Elevator
Phillip Morris	Seven-up
Mobil Corporation	Container Corporation of America
R. J. Reynolds Industries	Del Monte Corporation†
Black and Decker	McCulloch Corporation

Source: Moody's Industrial and Transportation Manuals, 1978, 1979, and 1980.

*Corporations that are often thought of by the general public as being independent economic enterprises.

†As of April 1979.

Technologies owns Otis Elevator, TWA owns Canteen Corporation, Pepsico owns Wilson Sporting Goods, Phillip Morris owns Seven-Up, and Black and Decker owns McCulloch Corporation, to mention only a few.

Also, many *industries* that do not explicitly appear in the CPT are nonetheless heavily influenced—if not actually controlled—through this same mechanism of CPT corporations owning other corporations. As depicted in Table 24, industries as varied as car rentals, coffee roasting, uranium milling, cosmetics, coal mining, and fast food chains fall within the economic domain of the CPSP sphere. Therefore, one must consider the CPT merely as a transitory view or a snapshot, not a comprehensive description that embodies the entirety of the economy's CPSP sphere.

Table 24

Partial Listing of Industries Controlled and/or Heavily Influenced by CPT Corporations But Not Included in the CPT (January, 1978)

Industry and Central Planning Tableau parent corporation(s) (rank in parenthesis)[1]	Wholly owned subsidiary(ies), consolidated company(ies), and/or brand name(s) (rank in parenthesis)[2]
I. Car rentals	
1. RCA (30)	Hertz (1)
2. Norton-Simon (145)	Avis(2)
II. Coffee roasting	
3. General Foods (40)	Maxwell House (1)—brand names include: Yuban, Mellow Roast, Sanka, Brim, and Maxim
4. Proctor and Gamble (20)	Folgers (2)
5. Coca-Cola (61)[3]	Brand names include (3): Admiration, Butter-nut, and Huggins Gourmet Mocha Java
III. Credit cards	
6. American Express (3)[4]	American Express
7. Continental Corporation (10)	Diners Club
8. Citicorp (2)[5]	Carte Blanche
IV. Coal mining	
9. Boeing (49)	Peabody Coal (1)[6]
10. Equitable Life (3)[7]	Consolidated Coal (2)
11. Continental Oil (17)	Consolidated Coal
12. Standard Oil of California (6)	Amax Coal Company (3)[6]
13. Occidental Petroleum (27)[8]	Island Creek Coal (4)
14. Standard Oil of Ohio (66)[8]	Old Ben Coal (13)
15. Gulf Oil Corporation (8)	Pittsburg and Midway Coal (15)
16. Exxon (2)	Monterey Coal Company (NA)
17. Ashland Oil Company (42)[8]	Arch Mineral Corporation (7)
18. U.S. Steel Corporation (15)	U.S. Steel Corporation (6)
19. Bethlehem Steel (35)	Bethlehem Mines Corporation (9)
20. Inland Steel (94)	Bishop Coal Company (NA)[9]
V. Uranium milling	
21. Kerr McGee (116)[8]	Kerr McGee (1)
22. Atlantic Richfield (13)	Anaconda (3)
23. General Electric (8)	Pathfinder Mines (4)
24. Exxon (2)	Exxon Nuclear (5)
25. Continental Oil (17)	Continental Oil (6)
26. Union Carbide (21)	Union Carbide (7)

Industry and Central Planning Tableau parent corporation(s) (rank in parenthesis)[1]	Wholly owned subsidiary(ies), consolidated company(ies), and/or brand name(s) (rank in parenthesis)[2]
27. Phelps Dodge (250)	Phelps Dodge (8)
28. Standard Oil of Ohio (66)[8]	Standard of Ohio (9)
29. Commonwealth Edison (6)	Cotter (14)

VI. Cosmetics

30. Colgate Palmolive (54)	Helena Rubinstein
31. Pfizer (126)	Coty Cosmetics
32. Norton-Simon (145)	Max Factor and Elizabeth Arden
33. Avon (149)	Avon

VII. Publishing

34. RCA (30)	Random House, Inc., Publishing—labels include: Knopf, Ballantine, Pantheon, Vintage, and Modern Library
35. CBS (91)	*Education Division*: Holt, Rinehart and Winston *Consumer Division*: Road & Track, Cycle World, PV4, World Tennis, Sea, Woman's Day, Field & Stream, Mechanix Illustrated, Fawcett Gold Medal and Popular Library *Professional Division*: W. B. Saunders Company
36. ABC (152)	World Inc., Prairie Farm, Wallaces Farmer, Wisconsin Agriculturist, Modern Photography, High Fidelity

VIII. Restaurants and fast food chains

37. Mobil Corporation (4)	Golden Bear (Illinois) Putsch's (Kansas City, Missouri) Sign of the Beefeater (Michigan)
38. Ralston Purina (55)	Boar's Head Hungry Hunter Stag & Hound Jack-in-the-Box
39. CPC International (88)	Dutch Pantry
40. Squibb (187)	Steak and Eggs
41. General Mills (83)	Red Lobster Inn York Steak House
42. Pillsbury (176)[8]	Burger King
43. General Foods (40)	Burger Chef
44. Great Western Sugar (NA)[8]	Shakey's Pizza
45. Pepsico (63)	Pizza Hut Taco Bell
46. Quaker Oats (162)	Magic Pan
47. W. R. Grace (51)	El Torito-La Fiesta
48. Royal Crown Cola (503)[8]	Arby's

158

Table 24 (continued)

Industry and Central Planning Tableau parent corporation(s) (rank in parenthesis)[1]	Wholly owned subsidiary(ies), consolidated company(ies), and/or brand name(s) (rank in parenthesis)[2]
IX. Pet foods	
49. Ralston Purina (55)	Brand names include: Chuck Wagon, Purina Dog Chow, Purina Puppy Chow, Purina Variety, Tender Vittles, Whisker Lickers, Purina Cat Chow, Purina Meow Mix, Purina Special Dinners
50. Quaker Oats (162)	Brand names include: Ken-L-Ration, Ken-L-Ration Burgers, Special Cuts, Ken-L-Ration Tender Chunks, Puss 'N Boots
51. Carnation (105)	Brand names include: Mighty Dog, Friskies, Friskies Buffet, Friskies (regular), Chef's Blend
52. General Foods (40)	Brand names include: Cycle, Top Choice, Gaines Burger, Gravy Train

Source: Moody's Industrial and Financial Manuals, 1978.

Note: NA = not available.

[1]Unless otherwise noted, rank for the parent company category refers to Fortune's 500 Largest Industrial Corporations.

[2]Unless otherwise noted, rank for the subsidiary category refers to the subsidiary's rank within a given market. For example, Hertz is the largest car rental agency; Avis ranks second.

[3]Coca Cola does not manufacture its coffee in a separate subsidiary company, but simply has a coffee "division" within the corporation.

[4]Classified and ranked as a diversified financial institution.

[5]Classified and ranked as a bank.

[6]Standard of California (6) owns only 21.8 percent of Amax (169), the third largest coal producer in the country; Boeing (49) owns only 15 percent of Peabody Coal Company, the largest coal producer. Equitable Life owns another 5 percent of Peabody Coal.

[7]Classified and ranked as a life insurance company.

[8]Not a Central Planning Tableau corporation.

[9]Inland Steel (94) owns 67 percent of the Bishop Coal Company.

A casual perusal of the CPT and Tables 23 and 24 lends very real credence to a comment made by Art Buchwald. Buchwald imagined a scenario[2] where two corporations—Samson Securities and Delilah Company—asked the head of the Justice Department's Anti-Trust Division if the two companies could merge. To make matters more intriguing, Samson Securities owned everything east of the Mississippi River, while Delilah Company owned everything west of the river. At first, the head of the Anti-Trust Division indicated that he might have reservations about the merger of the only two companies left in the United States:

"Our department," he said, "will take a close look at this proposed merger. It is our job to further competition in private business and industry, and if we allow Samson and Delilah to merge we may be doing the consumer a disservice."

The chairman of Samson protested vigorously that merging with Delilah would not stifle competition, but would help it. "The public will be the true beneficiary of this merger," he said. "The larger we are, the more services we can perform, and the lower prices we can charge."

The president of Delilah backed him up. "In the Communist system the people don't have a choice. They must buy from the state. In our capitalistic society the people can buy from either the Samson Company or the Delilah Company."

"But if you merge," someone pointed out, "there will be only *one* company left in the United States."

"Exactly," said the president of Delilah. "Thank God for the free enterprise system."

The Anti-Trust Division of the Justice Department studied the merger for months. Finally the Attorney General made this ruling. "While we find drawbacks to only one company being left in the United States, we feel the advantages to the public far outweigh the disadvantages."

"Therefore, we're making an exception in this case and allowing Samson and Delilah to merge."

"I would like to announce that the Samson and Delilah Company is now negotiating at the White House with the President to buy the United States. The Justice Department will naturally study this merger to see if it violates any of our strong antitrust laws.''*

The mechanics of reading the CPT

Table 25 contains illustrations of the types of mechanical considerations it is imperative to understand in order to be able to read the data in the tableau correctly. Of course, by now, much of the data in Table 25 will be readily understandable. Yet, there are still two mechanical

*Reprinted by permission of G. P. Putnam's Sons from *Down the Seine and Up the Potomac with Art Buchwald* by Art Buchwald. Copyright © 1977 by Art Buchwald.

peculiarities that have not been introduced. First, note the use of lowercase letters, that is, the "d" at the intersection of the Equitable Life (EL) column and the Sampson Securities row. This new form of notation is used to depict a situation where one individual is (a) on the board of a non-core corporation and (b) also on the board of *two* CPC corporations, so that the same *individual* will not be counted twice. In this particular illustration, an individual on Sampson Securities' board also sits on both CIT's and EL's boards. The number of CPC institutions interlocked with Sampson Securities is three—one, noted by the symbol "D," with CIT; one, noted by the symbol "d," with EL; and one family director interlock, noted by the symbol "F," with JP. Yet, in counting the actual number of Sampson Securities directors that are interlocked with the CPC, there are only two—one, noted by the "D," with CIT, and one, noted by the "F," with JP. The lowercase letter, then, is used to prevent double counting by differentiating between the actual number of "directors" interlocked and the actual number of "institutions" interlocked whenever one individual is a director for two of the CPC institutions.

Second, the data on stock and debt *cannot* be read, from a mechanical perspective, in the same manner as the data on administrative interlocks. On the one hand, as stated in Chapter 4, the CPT data on administrative interlocks should also be read from left to right. In other words, the symbol "*" at the intersection of Delilah Company's row and CIT's column indicates that Delilah's Chief Executive Officer is also a member of CIT's board of directors. On the other hand, if one reads the data on stock from left to right, one would conclude that Delilah Company controlled 1,300,000 shares of CIT's voting stock. The opposite is true, however; CIT controls 1,300,000 shares of Delilah's voting stock. In short, while the data on administrative interlocks must be read from *left to right and then up*, the data on both stock and debt must be read in just the opposite manner—*down and then from right to left*.

As illustration, let us now examine each of the interlocking ties between Delilah Company and the CPC, as depicted in Table 25:

1. There are five *direct* BOD interlocks and II's combined.
2. There are sixty IDI's and twelve III's.
3. Delilah's Chief Executive Officer (*) sits on CIT's board, while the two institutions have four III's.
4. There are two direct BOD interlocks between Delilah and EL and eight III's.

Table 25

The Basic Mechanics of the Central Planning Tableau

Structural and Functional Interconnecting Ties between the CPC Institutions and the Corporations in the "All Things" Industry, Individually and in the Aggregate (1984)

Industry/ corporation	Total interlocks		II's, BOD interlocks III's per individual CPC institution			Total family and BOD interlocks, total number on board and percentage of board interlocked with the CPC					Bond issues and trustee (TR) interlocks		Minimum CPC institutions and core family's (CF) stock control, aggregated (AGG), with total stock outstanding (TSO) and percentage controlled by the CPC (thousands)					
	II and BOD	IDI-III	CIT	EL	JP	BOD	F	Total	Total board	Per-cent-age	Number of bond issues	CPC as TR	CIT	EL	CF	AGG	TSO	Per-cent-age
All things																		
1. Sampson Securities	3	40-10	D-4	d-6	F-3	1	1	2	10	20	8	6	1,200	900	60	2,160	28,000	7.7c
2. Delilah Company	5	60-12	*-4	2D-8	2A-5	3	0	3	15	20	2	2	1,300	500	90	1,890	18,000	10.5

Note: The symbol "c" indicates that the corporation in question is subject to cumulative voting.

Legend: D = BOD member.

* = Chief Executive Officer and BOD member.

O = Senior officer and BOD member.

A = Institutional interlock (II), but not a BOD interlock.

F = Family BOD interlock (e.g., a father sitting on Sampson Securities' board and his son sitting on Citicorp's board).

3D or 2A = The actual number of whatever type of interlock is indicated.

d, a, f, o = Lower case letters are used to differentiate between the actual number of "directors" interlocked versus the number of "institutions" interlocked, to prevent double counting of the same "director."

5. There are two direct II's between Delilah and JP and five III's.

6. There are three direct BOD interlocks between Delilah and the CPC, accounting for 20 percent of Delilah's board, with no "F" BOD interlocks.

7. Delilah has two debt instruments outstanding, and the CPC acted as their trustee in both cases.

8. CIT controls 1,300,000; EL, 500,000; and CF, 90,000 shares of Delilah's voting stock.

9. Finally, the CPC controls 10.5 percent of Delilah's voting stock, and cumulative voting is not allowed.

Understanding the mechanics of reading the CPT is tedious. However, when one couples (a) the theoretical concepts of intra- and interindustry cooperation and coordination with (b) the concrete and structural realities of the economy's CPSP sphere presented in the CPT, one is on the threshold of understanding how the economy of the greatest empire in the world's history is structured and how it functions. For the reader who has mastered the material presented thus far, a visual exploration of the CPT is the next logical step.

The next section of this chapter will be devoted to a potpourri of observations that may be helpful in gaining a fuller and more complete understanding—especially from a macro perspective—of the CPC's key planning instruments.

The planning instruments—some sundry observations

Boards of directors

To begin, a few general statistical characteristics of the boards of the CPT corporations will be presented:

1. Size and composition
   a. The average size of a CPC institution's BOD is 24.
   b. The average size of a non-core corporation's BOD is 15.
   c. The majority of a board's membership consists of outsiders 95 percent of the time.

2. Location
   a. 49 of the corporations are headquartered in New York; 9 in New Jersey; 8 in Connecticut; 18 in Illinois; 11 in Ohio; 8 in Michigan; 7 in Pennsylvania; 4 in Minnesota; and 6 in California.
   b. 66, or nearly half, are headquartered in the Greater New York area.

c. 119 are headquartered in just 8 states.

3. Types and magnitude of interlocking BOD ties

a. Each CPC board member averages 3 direct BOD interlocks with non-core corporations.

b. Therefore, each CPC director is responsible for, on the average, around 48 formal "strategic planning" sessions per year—36 in non-core institutions and 12 within the CPC itself.

c. Each non-core corporation, on the average, has 3 direct BOD interlocks, 26 IDI's, and 6 III's with the CPC.

d. In most instances, the CPC is more heavily intra- and interlocked with the dominant corporations within each industry.

e. Finally, 59 of the 126 non-core corporations have their Chief Executive officers interlocked with the CPC institutions, while the Chief Executive officers of 5 CPC institutions are on the boards of other CPC institutions.

4. Election procedures

a. 95 percent of both the CPC and non-core corporations hold annual elections for the entire board (i.e., directors are elected for *one*-year terms, and the terms are usually not staggered).

b. A minimum of 26 of the corporations either require or allow cumulative voting.

Speaking specifically in terms of location, two geographical areas account for 84 of the 138 CPT corporations—66 are located in the Greater New York area, while 18 are in Illinois. Of these, 9 of the CPC institutions are headquartered in New York City; 1 in Newark, New Jersey; and 2 in Chicago.*

Perhaps it is also important to note—though, in a sense, redundant—that many corporations within a given industry will be headquartered in the same geographic area. For instance, Goodyear Tire and Rubber, Firestone Tire and Rubber, B. F. Goodrich and Company, and General Tire and Rubber are all headquartered in Akron, Ohio. International

---

*Some of the corporations categorized as being in the Greater New York area are actually headquartered in both New Jersey and Connecticut. It is often said that there has been a steady exodus of corporations from New York City over the last decade. While this is true, though often exaggerated, it is also true that 90 percent of those corporations moved to nearby counties, such as Fairfield County, Connecticut. Fairfield County is across Long Island Sound, just north of Long Island, which is occupied at its western end by two boroughs of New York City, Brooklyn and Queens. As reported in a 1976 *Newsweek* article, "By remaining close to New York City, Fairfield corporations draw on its resources without sharing its tax burden."[3] Further, as one young executive explained to a business client, " . . . on a clear day you can see Manhattan."[4]

Harvester (headquartered in Chicago), Caterpillar Tractor (headquartered in Peoria, Illinois), Deere and Company (in Moline, Illinois), and Allis-Chalmers (in West-Allis, Wisconsin) share a reasonably close geographic proximity. Also, International Harvester, Caterpillar, and Deere each have two BOD interlocks with First Chicago. Both International Harvester's and Caterpillar's Chief Executive Officers are on First Chicago's board. In addition, Deere and Company's Chief Executive Officer and two of International Harvester's directors are on Continental Illinois' board. Corporations in other industries whose headquarters also show a close geographic proximity include computers, metal containers, iron and steel, copper, pharmaceuticals, television broadcasting, telecommunications equipment, automobiles, and commercial aircraft engines.

Regarding the location of corporation headquarters, then, it should be clear from the above types of geographical patterns that spatial location is not an impediment to centralized planning. Clearly, the oft-heard comment that interlocking directorships of any magnitude would necessitate directors spending all of their time in airports and planes is simply not borne out by the facts. Rather, it would appear that the locality of many corporate headquarters could not have been better placed had such decisions been made originally from a CPSP perspective. Furthermore, given the extraordinary prescient business and industrial acumen of the early "captains of industry" (the Rockefellers, the Morgans, the Stillmans, the Bakers, etc.), perhaps they were.

In terms of size, the boards of the CPC institutions have many more directors than do the non-core corporations. As a case in point, Citicorp and the Chase Manhattan Corporation have 29 and 27 directors, respectively, while Exxon has only 17 and Mobil Oil Corporation only 19. On the average, CPC boards are 60 percent larger than the boards of non-core corporations. The greater size of the CPC institutions' boards is necessary so that the CPC can serve as the focal point of the planning process. Quite simply, being a director for Exxon or Mobil does *not* give one access to the same quantity, variety, or quality of information that is available to a CPC director.

In terms of access to information, of course, the composition of the boards of directors is just as important as size. Ninety-five percent of the boards of the CPT corporations (core and non-core) are composed primarily of outside directors; in particular, 80 percent of the directors of the CPC banks are outside directors. Therefore, when Citicorp has a BOD meeting, not only are two directors each from Exxon, Mobil, and

Standard Oil of California present (intraindustry coordination and planning), but information from every other industry in the CPT is also directly available (interindustry coordination and planning). Concisely stated, then:

- the BOD's of the CPT corporations—in terms of relative size, composition, and location—are admirably suited to creating the types and magnitude of intra- and interindustry administrative ties that, from a structural and a functional point of view, are essential to the CPSP process; and,
- they have done so.

In conclusion, no systematic attempt was made to find either the family type of BOD interlock (F) or the non-BOD institutional type of interlock (A). Several did emerge, by chance, while research was being done for the study and were included. Nonetheless, the data must be viewed as incomplete, since many such types of additional interlocking ties must undoubtedly exist.

Corporate stock

Commercial banks that belong to the Federal Reserve System and/or to the Federal Deposit Insurance Corporation and which also operate trust departments must prepare and submit a "Trust Department Annual Report" to various regulatory agencies. For reporting purposes, the only information that a bank's trust department is required to submit is that concerning its *trust assets*. Traditionally, the term "trust assets" has *included* primarily employee benefit trusts, employee agency trusts, personal trusts, and estates; it has specifically *excluded* custodial accounts, corporate trusts, and/or corporate agency accounts.

On the one hand, the terms *employee benefit trust* and *employee agency trust* are customarily used to refer to pension funds, retirement plans, and profit sharing plans (created by corporations, unions, and other types of institutional groups) that have been entrusted to the bank and over which the trust department almost *always* has sole investment and voting authority. In other words, the trust department determines where to invest these monies and how to handle whatever voting privileges accompany these investments.

On the other hand, the terms *personal trust* and *estates* are primarily used to refer to the assets of individuals who either own or are the beneficiaries of money or stock that has been entrusted to the bank and over which the trust department *usually* has sole or shared investment and voting responsibilities. A ''shared investment and voting'' arrangement is often referred to as a co-trusteeship. In essence, the asset owner and the trust department, through consultation, codetermine where to invest and how to handle voting privileges when such exist.

Finally, the terms *custodial account, corporate trust account*, and/or *corporate agency account* are customarily used to refer to assets over which the bank's trust department normally does *not* have any investment or voting responsibilities, but for which the bank may (a) act as the registrar and/or transfer agent; (b) provide secure storage; (c) collect and account for any earned income; (d) disburse dividends; or (e) in the case of bonds, give notification as to maturity dates. The federal regulations, then, are specifically designed to enable banks to omit from their reports those types of accounts over which their trust departments do not have any investment or voting authority.

Hereafter, in this study, those types of accounts over which trust departments *normally* have sole or shared investment and voting authority will be called *trust assets*, or *trust accounts*. Those accounts over which trust departments normally have no investment or voting responsibilities will be called *custodial accounts*.

As *trust assets* (especially employee benefit trusts) grew enormously after World War II, bank trust departments began investing more and more money in corporate stock. As reported in *U.S. News and World Report*, in 1974:

> U.S. banks, their size and sharply expanding role in the economy, suddenly are coming under fire from many sides.
>
> *Fear of lawmakers.* Congressional concern today centers on these trust departments, which hold 404 billion dollars in assets on behalf of individual investors, more than mutual funds and all other investment institutions combined . . .
>
> Stock Exchange Chairman James Needham asked a House committee last autumn:
>
> ''Must all of America's finance activities be concentrated in the banks of this country? This is a fearsome thought.''[5]

Bankers responded to their critics by pointing out—
   • that bankers, qua bankers, had no desire to control other corporations; and

Table 26

Bank Trust Department Voting Rights as a Percentage of Total "Trust Assets," for Selected Banks, and the Average Voting Rights for "Trust Assets" (December 1974)

Institution	Voting rights as a percentage of total trust assets		
	Sole voting (percent)	Shared voting (percent)	Total (percent)
J. P. Morgan and Company	69.2	7.4	76.6
Manufacturers Hanover[a]	63.4	18.4	81.8
Chemical Bank[a]	NA	NA	66.0
Mellon Bank	70.9	12.4	83.3
Average for 24-bank survey[b]	54.9	14.2	69.1

Source: Subcommittee on Reports, Accounting, and Management of the Committee on Government Operations of the U.S. Senate, *Institutional Investor's Common Stock: Holdings and Voting Rights*, 94th Congress, 2nd Sess., Senate, May, 1976, pp. 476-483.

Note: Traditionally, the term "trust assets" has not included stock held in custodial or corporate trust accounts. Bank trust departments, normally having no investment or voting authority over such accounts, were not required by law to report their holdings in these types of accounts to any of the federal financial regulatory agencies. The regulatory definition of "trust assets," then, includes only "employee benefit trust, personal trust, estates, employee benefit agencies, and certain other agency accounts." As of 1978, however, bank trust departments were also instructed to omit from their reports all assets held in these latter types of accounts over which they have no discretionary investment authority.

NA = Not available.

[a]These data were calculated from the 1977 trust department reports of each bank. The data are current as of 31 December 1977.

[b]This survey, carried out by the Congressional Research Service for the Subcommittee on Reports, Accounting, and Management, included the country's 66 largest banks, ranked by trust department assets. Only 24 banks responded with "quantified responses that could be aggregated."

• that, besides, trust departments did not actually have voting authority over *many* of the stocks which they held in personal trust and estate accounts.

The second point obviously created a problem for those contending that the banks were gaining undue influence over corporations by controlling vast amounts of stock through their trust departments' assets. Specifically, what did the term "many" actually mean.

As noted in Table 26, J. P. Morgan and Company in 1974 reported that it had *sole* and *shared* voting authority over 69.2 percent and 7.4 percent of its trust assets, respectively. Table 26 also contains data obtained from a survey of 66 banks, conducted by the Library of Congress' Congressional Research Services. Of the banks surveyed, 24 provided data that was comparable and quantifiable.* In terms of sole and shared voting authority, the data indicated that the respondents averaged 54.9 percent and 14.2 percent, respectively, in 1974.

Finally, as of 31 December 1977, Manufacturers Hanover reported its sole voting authority as 63.4 percent and its shared authority as 18.4 percent. Chemical Bank, lumping its sole and shared voting responsibilities together, reported having voting authority over 66 percent of its trust assets.

From a practical point of view, "sole and shared" voting authority should always be combined, or, more to the point, be viewed as synonymous. Why would anyone go against the advice of the trust department of a bank, when the bank probably has one or two direct BOD interlocks, as well as numerous IDI's and III's (i.e., inside information) with the corporations in question? Quite obviously, many personal trusts and estates are entrusted to large banks quite simply because people know that the banks actually do have inside information.

In any event, the data in Table 26 indicate that these bank trust departments reported having sole voting authority over 55 to 66 percent of their trust assets and sole and shared voting authority, combined, over approximately 66 to 80 percent of their trust assets.

The CPC banking institutions, as a group, appear to have investment and voting responsibilities for approximately 75 to 80 percent of their trust assets, as indicated by examples A and B in Table 27. By way of illustration, in 1977, the seven CPC banking institutions reported holding $98,777,397,000 in *trust assets*. Their reported holdings had fallen, in 1978, however, to $83,481,794,000. The 1978 decrease was because the federal banking regulatory agencies instructed the banks to omit reporting *all* assets over which the trust departments had no investment and/or voting authority. Assuming that the trust assets actually held by the banks in 1978 increased by around 10 percent over their 1977 holdings would indicate that the CPC banks had investment and/or voting authority over approximately 76.8 percent of their trust assets. Assuming a more modest growth rate of around 5 percent would

---

*The terminology used to classify and categorize the assets held by trust departments is not very uniform. This, of course, presents a real problem for researchers—a problem that the banks appear unwilling to help solve and that the regulatory agencies are either unwilling or unable to solve.

Table 27

Trust Assets Reported by CPC Institutions (1977 and 1978)

Corporations	1977 (thousands)	1978 (thousands)
Citicorp	$24,542,985	$19,693,883
Chase Manhattan	14,473,907	7,994,417
Manufacturers Hanover	10,892,000	9,747,683
J. P. Morgan and Company	24,236,011	25,517,207
Chemical New York	8,506,434	6,923,169
Continental Illinois	7,312,683	6,907,717
First Chicago	8,813,377	6,697,718
TOTAL	$98,777,397	$83,481,794

Source: Federal Deposit Insurance Corporation, *Trust Assets of Insured Commercial Banks—1977,* and Federal Deposit Insurance Corporation, *Trust Assets of Banks and Trust Companies—1978.*

Notes: The data in this particular report do not indicate the amount of stock held by trust departments in individual corporations; rather, the data are presented in aggregate form. Beginning with the 1978 report the data exclude all trust assets over which the trust departments have *no* investment and/or voting responsibilities.

Example A: Assuming a 10 percent rate of growth between 1977 and 1978, we have $98,777, 397 × 110 percent = $108,655,136; and $83,481,794 ÷ $108,655,136 = 76.8 percent.

Example B: Assuming a 5 percent rate of growth between 1977 and 1978, we have $98,777,397 × 105 percent = $103,716,266; and $83,481,794 ÷ $103,716,266 = 80.4 percent.

indicate that the banks had investment and/or voting responsibilities over approximately 80.4 percent of their trust assets.

On the one hand, since the data in the CPT exclude the trust departments' custodial accounts, the statistics must be viewed as indicating the *minimum* amount of stock *actually held* by the CPC. On the other hand, since the data include *all* stock held in trust asset accounts and since the CPC banks report having investment and/or voting responsibility over only 75 to 80 percent of their trust assets, the data may appear initially to invite an overestimation of the CPC's stock investment and/or voting powers. On closer examination, however, the data undoubtedly invite an underestimation of the CPC's actual investment and voting powers for four basic reasons.

First, beginning in 1974, the Office of the Comptroller of the

Currency required that the trust departments of banks belonging to the Federal Reserve System submit an "Annual Report of Equity Securities," containing a detailed listing of the shares of stock in the trust assets category, on a corporation-by-corporation basis, held by the banks' trust departments. Two CPC banks, Manufacturers Hanover Corporation and Chemical Bank, however, are not members of the Federal Reserve System.* The data in the CPT for Chemical Bank came from Chemical's *1977 Report of the Trust and Investment Bank* and for Manufacturers Hanover Corporation from its *Report of the Trust Division—1977*. In Manufacturers Hanover's report, only common stock holdings over $25 million are listed, while in Chemical's report the cutoff point was $5 million. In short, the data in the CPT do not include all of the stock held by both these banks' trust departments.

Second, for the most part, stock actually owned by individuals who are CPC members is omitted. No systematic procedure for finding this information exists. The limited data that are presented on core family stock holdings were obtained largely from newspaper articles and business-type publications that occasionally mention such facts. As a case in point, in Table 28, there is a partial listing of CPT corporations' stock owned by the Rockefeller family that was published in a 1974 *New York Times* article. For instance, the Rockefeller family owns more than 2 percent of the common stock of Eastern Airlines, Standard Oil Company (California), and Allis-Chalmers; and between one and two percent of the common stock of Exxon, Aluminum Company of America, Mobil Corporation, and the Chase Manhattan Corporation. The CPC consists of 263 individuals, many of whose names (Rockefeller, Goelet, Grace, Du Pont, Hewlett, Ingersoll, Milliken, Hillman, Prince, Hatfield, Houghton, McCormick, etc.) are synonyms for American industry. The stock owned by these individuals and their families (often held by bank trust departments in custodial accounts) must be taken into consideration when trying to determine the percentage of stock actually controlled by the CPC. As noted above, the trust departments of banks are not required to report stock held in custodial accounts. First National City Bank (now, Citibank), though, in submitting its first such report to the Comptroller in 1974, evidently did include information pertaining to these types of accounts. The transmittal letter accompanying its report contained the following paragraph:

*J. P. Morgan and Company is also not a Federal Reserve System member, but chose to voluntarily prepare and submit this report.

Table 28

Amount and Percentage of Shares Outstanding of Stock Held by the Rockefeller Family in Selected Corporations within the CPT (1974)

Company	Amount of stock held	Percentage of shares outstanding
Chase Manhattan Corporation	429,959	1.3
Eastern Airlines	925,000	4.7
Mobil Corporation	1,762,206	1.74
Standard Oil of California	3,410,148	2.0
Allis-Chalmers	430,000	3.45
Aluminum Company of America	405,783	1.2
Exxon	2,288,171	1.02
Merck & Company, Inc.	455,100	0.61
Monsanto Company	213,273	0.64
Texas Instruments	203,900	0.90
Eastman Kodak	535,973	0.49
International Business Machines (IBM)	384,042	0.26
General Electric	509,952	0.29
Minnesota Mining and Manufacturing	221,700	0.20
Kresge	336,800	0.28

Source: New York Times, 4 December 1974, p. 29.

Regarding category (C–2) Closely Held Companies, we are requesting that this section be considered confidential since it pertains to family owned accounts where the Bank acts as Custodial for over 10% of the outstanding shares.[6]

Several attempts have been made to obtain this information from the Comptroller's office, with the usual response being, "No, we do not consider it appropriate to reveal the business affairs of private citizens." If just twenty people owned one-fourth of one percent of the common stock of a corporation, however, as a group, they would control 5 percent of the corporation's stock. Here, then, is another compelling reason for viewing the stock statistics listed in the CPT as representing only a minimum threshold.

Third, one must also take into account the common stock that corporations *own* of other corporations. As illustration, the data in the CPT indicate that the CPC holds only 4.4 percent of Amax's common stock.

Table 29

Percentage of Stock Owned by Corporations of Other Corporations, for Selected Companies (January 1978)

Name and rank of company(ies) owning stock	Name and rank of company(ies) whose stock is owned	Percentage of shares owned
Manufacturing and transportation		
Standard of California (6)	Amax (169)	21.8
Amax (169)	Alumax (327)	50.0
Mobil Corporation (4)	Marcor (7)[1]	100.0
Sears (1)[1]	Whirlpool (130)	3.4
	Kellwood (421)	22.4
	Roper Corporation (471)	41.0
	DeSoto (518)	31.0
Kennecott (258)	Carborundum (300)	100.0
Bendix (73)	Asarco (235)	18.4
Reynolds Metal (104)	Robertshaw Control (585)	27.4
General Tire & Rubber (22)	Frontier Airlines (40)[2]	59.0
Northwest Industries (133)	B. F. Goodrich (111)	4.9
General Electric (9)	Honeywell (82)	9.2
Phelps Dodge (250)	Consolidated Aluminum (339)	40.0
E. I. Du Pont (16)	Remington Arms (631)	69.5
Gulf & Western Industries (59)	Simmons (412)	27.0
AT&T (1)[3]	Western Electric (18)	100.0
Dow Chemical (25) Corning Glass Works (221)	Dow Corning Corporation (450)	50.0 50.0
Owens Illinois (92) Corning Glass Works (221)	Owens Corning Fiberglass (172)	3.0 26.0
Life insurance companies		
Aetna Life and Casualty (1)[4]	Aetna Life Insurance Company (6)[5]	100.0
American Brands (86)	Franklin Life (26)[5]	27.5
Continental Group (58)	Life Insurance of Virginia (39)[5]	99.7
Property-casualty insurance companies		
Sears (1)[1]	Allstate Insurance Company (2)[6]	100.0
Aetna Life and Casualty (1)[4]	Aetna Casualty and Surety (4)[7]	100.0
Continental Corporation (10)[4]	Continental Insurance (5)[6]	100.0
ITT (11)	Hartford (6)[6]	100.0
American Express (3)[4]	Fireman's Fund (9)[6]	100.0

Source: Standard and Poor's Stock Reports; *Moody's Industrial Manual, Bank and Finance Manual, Transportation Manual*, and *Industrial Manual*; and the Securities and Exchange Commission's *Official Summary of Security and Exchange Transactions*.

On the other hand, though, the CPC has 3 direct BOD interlocks with Standard Oil of California (including Standard's Chief Executive Officer), 21 IDI's, and 4 III's, and it controls, at a minimum, 8.3 percent of Standard's common stock. In turn, Standard Oil of California *owns* 21.8 percent of Amax, while Amax itself owns 50 percent of Alumax.* As of January 1978, Standard, Amax, and Alumax ranked as the 6th, 169th, and 327th largest American manufacturing companies, respectively. In essence, by being tightly bonded to Standard Oil of California *directly*, the CPC is also *indirectly* tightly bonded to both Amax and Alumax. In short, in order to accurately determine the magnitude of the CPC's stock holdings, one must also consider the common stock that non-core corporations own of other non-core corporations.

A careful examination of the data in Table 29 will reveal that large blocks of stock of several of the companies on *Fortune*'s "largest industrial corporations" list are owned by other corporations. Just as with stock owned by individuals, the CPC banks' trust departments hold vast amounts of stock owned by corporations, in other corporations, in a specific type of custodial account called corporate trust and/or corporate agency account. Also, as with stock owned by individuals, there is no systematic way to determine the magnitude of such stock ownership arrangements. Such data emerge periodically in various private and governmental publications, but no one, except the trust departments of banks, has the necessary information to construct a reasonably thorough or complete list. This, then, is another compelling reason to view the statistics on stock holdings in the CPT as the tip of the iceberg.

*The CPT is replete with analogous types of examples that are not highlighted in the text.

Table 29 (continued)

Notes: Unless otherwise noted, rankings refer to *Fortune*'s 500 and second 500 largest "industrial" corporations.

[1]Classified as a "retailing" company; i.e., Marcor owns Montgomery Ward, which *Fortune* ranks as the 7th largest retailing company. Sears is ranked as the largest retailing company.

[2]Classified as a transportation company.

[3]Classified as a public utility.

[4]Classified as a diversified financial institution.

[5]Classified as a life insurance company.

[6]Classified as a property and casualty insurance company. Rankings for property and casualty insurance companies were taken from A. M. Best and Company and Standard and Poor's "Industry Surveys."

[7]Aetna Life and Casualty is ranked by *Fortune* as the largest "diversified financial institution." But, in addition, Aetna Life Insurance Company, a wholly owned subsidiary, ranks as the 6th largest life insurance company, and Aetna Casualty and Surety ranks as the 4th largest property and casualty insurance company.

Finally, and most importantly—
1. through its ability to control hundreds of billions of dollars; and
2. through having inside information from—
    a. its direct BOD interlocks, IDI's, and III's;
    b. its position as debt trustee, transfer agent, and registrar; and
    c. its position as manager of trust assets and custodial accounts,
the CPC knows precisely when, where, and how to go about using corporate stock as an effective organizing and coordinating planning instrument. In other words, consideration of the variety and quantity of inside information CPC members possess, coupled with their controlling hundreds of billions of dollars, tends to lead to the conclusion that their ability to easily acquire and sell large blocks of stock is much more significant—especially when corporate stock is viewed as an important structural and functional planning instrument—than is the actual amount of stock they might control in a corporation at any given moment.

In conclusion, then, the actual magnitude of the concentration of stock represented as being controlled by the CPC in the CPT must be interpreted carefully. First, many of the CPC's stock holdings are not shown, since the data were not available. Second, the CPC often uses indirect stock ownership arrangements. Finally, the CPC can increase its stockholdings in even the largest corporations from 1 or 2 percent to 20 or 30 percent in a very short period of time. Therefore, as stated above, the data in the CPT on the quantity of the CPC's stock holdings must be interpreted prudently.

Corporate debt

As stressed in Chapters 3 and 4, having access to debt capital is often crucial for survival in the corporate world. In turn, the CPC's ability to control the allocation of vast sums of debt capital is one of its most powerful planning instruments. It may be, however, that the terms "debt" and/or "loan," as commonly understood, do not actually connote what is occurring when the CPC transfers money from corporation to corporation. As illustration, assume that General Electric is reported as having negotiated a large loan, say, $500 million, from a group of banks and an insurance company (Citicorp, Chase Manhattan Corporation, Manufacturers Hanover, J. P. Morgan and Company,

Chemical Bank, and Prudential Life). A quick look at the CPT will indicate that General Electric (GE) has direct BOD interlocks with each of these institutions, as well as 34 IDI's and 8 III's with the entire CPC. Just through III's, then, directors from GE and the CPC are in approximately 96 BOD meetings annually. In addition, the CPC controls at least 9.3 percent of GE's common stock and has acted as trustee for seven of GE's last eight bond indentures. Is this "new" loan, then, to be viewed as one group loaning another group money? Or, would it be more appropriate to say that a group, in this case, the CPC, is transferring money from some of its institutions to another one of its institutions?

Stated somewhat differently, from a CPSP perspective, it may be more appropriate to view this transfer of money, not as a loan, but as a direct indication of the CPC's strategic planning. In other words, the allocation of money by the CPC may quite appropriately be viewed as a form of indicative planning, revealing fairly clearly the macro economic plans that the CPC is attempting to implement. Further, since the final decisions concerning debt allocation are made within the CPC itself, the CPC becomes the focal point (as was the case with the BOD and stock planning instruments) of the CPSP process.

Unfortunately (even more so than with the BOD and stock planning instruments), the information on the CPC's allocation of capital to individual non-core corporations was largely unobtainable.* Nonetheless, one can assume that the amount would be quite significant in size, since, as of January 1978, the seven CPC banks had capital allocations outstanding totaling approximately $160 billion.

On the other hand, the banks, in their "Annual Report of Equity Securities" to the Comptroller of the Currency, do report a form of bond holdings known as convertible subordinated debentures (CSD). As the term "convertible" suggests, these types of bonds may be converted into or exchanged for common stock by the bondholder. In terms of the CPC's aggregate bond holdings, CSD's are miniscule. In

---

*The investment departments of each of the CPC insurance companies publish a "Schedule of Investments" or a "Schedule of Securities" report on a yearly basis. In these reports, there is a detailed listing of all the stock and bonds in which the companies have invested money. No such reports were available from the banks, and, with the exception of the Civil Aeronautics Board, regulatory agencies do not require reports pertaining to debt statistics. Thus, the data on debt are grossly underestimated.

Table 30

Potential Number of Shares of Common Stock Represented by
Convertible Subordinated Debentures Held by the CPC, for
Selected Corporations (January 1975)

Corporations	Potential shares of common stock
American Airlines	362,300
Pan American World Airways	792,734
Trans World Airways	240,401
Pfizer Inc.	220,371
Xerox	304,981
R. H. Macy	294,713
Marcor	508,860
J. P. Morgan and Company	342,986

Source: Bank trust department reports to the Comptroller of the Currency entitled, "Annual Report of Equity Securities," Form CC7510-05.

some instances, however, they may be important in determining the CPC's potential for increasing its stock holdings. As is depicted in Table 30, as of January 1975, the CPC held CSD's representing 362,300 shares of common stock in American Airlines; 792,734 shares in Pan American World Airways; and 240,401 shares in Trans World Airways. Here again, then, is another important factor to be considered when attempting to determine the potential magnitude or size of the CPC's stock holdings.

In summary, the CPC's capital allocation strategies (or, in more conventional terms, corporate debt held by the CPC) are not readily obtainable. An accurate corporation-by-corporation breakdown of the CPC's money allocation strategies, however, is quite crucial to fully understanding how the CPC is actually using capital allocations (corporate debt) as a structural and functional planning instrument in terms of both intra- and interindustry economic planning.

Informal and/or influential planning instruments

Without undue harm to reality, CPC banks may be thought of as having three distinct, yet interdependent, types of *traditional banking relationships* with non-core corporations:

• They are a major depository for the trust assets and demand deposits of corporations.

• They are a major source of debt and equity capital for corporations.

• They perform the various types of bookkeeping chores that accompany the borrowing and investing of vast sums of money, as well as providing other depository types of services (e.g., transfer agent, trustee, registrar, collection of bond coupons, check processing, fund transfers, tax collection, etc.).* Many of the numerous services now provided by wholesale banks for corporations are, from a traditional banking perspective, said to be the end result of banks attempting to make money. In other words, banks get paid a fee for providing a corporation with, for example, transfer agent and trustee services.

From a macro point of view, however, the summation of these types of services may now more appropriately be viewed as a "demand deposit" centralizing tool. Corporations, quite naturally, are more apt to place their demand deposit and trust asset accounts with a bank that can provide the corporation with the most varied and sophisticated types of services. Viewing each of these services as an *individual* money-making device precludes understanding that the interdependencies that *now exist* provide a favorable framework for centralizing and coordinating the allocation of capital within the economy's CPSP sphere. More importantly, the CPC planners have now become acutely conscious of this fact. It is not exaggerated to say that *demand deposits* and *trust assets* are the lifeblood of CPSP.

First, non-core corporations transfer to the CPC hundreds of billions of dollars in the form of demand deposits and trust assets. As of 31 December 1977, the seven CPC banks accounted for approximately $210 billion in demand deposits and around $100 billion in "reported" trust assets.

Second, the CPC then allocates these monies (in the legal form of stock and bonds investments) to non-core corporations in such a manner as to coordinate the production and expansion plans adopted within the CPC. It is *not* accurate to assume that, when the CPC contemplates transferring the monies of this or that pension fund, their "investment" decision will be made specifically to maximize money returns in the micro sense. On the one hand, money may be transferred to one

*For a more complete listing of the types of services wholesale banks provide for corporations, see Chapter 3, Informal and/or Influential Planning Instruments, A Collage of Informational Conduits.

corporation to underwrite a merger; or, conversely, a "loan" may be called or additional money denied to another corporation in order to force that corporation to accept a merger proposal. In addition, money transfers may be given or denied so as to secure funds for, or to allocate manufacturing contracts between and among, the corporations and industries within the economy's CPSP sphere. On the other hand, as long as, say, domestic steel production is viewed as being necessary, the CPC will always transfer sufficient funds to *some* steel companies— regardless of the rate of return—in order to sustain the desired production levels. In essence, a circular flow of monies managed and controlled, but not owned, by the CPC provides the molecular force, or glue, that binds the system structurally and functionally into an integrated production process.

In short, then, the CPC—

• receives and transfers hundreds of billions of dollars from and to non-core corporations in the legal form of demand deposits, fees, loans, and equity investments; and

• provides many of the legal services that such money transfers require.

Finally, even a casual acquaintance with the data in the CPT will reveal that the technological, pricing, cost, profit, BOD, stock, debt, trustee, transfer agent, registrar, and other intra- and interindustry interdependencies have become so great in number and, thus, so visible to the participants that there is not only a very real but a very conscious understanding of these interdependencies. In turn, a conscious awareness of these interdependencies would almost automatically contribute to a great deal of intra- and interindustry coordination and cooperation, i.e., to CPSP.

Centralized Private Sector Planning—some sundry observations

In this concluding section, the topics to be considered are causation, coercion, efficiency, democracy, and macro economics.

Causation: technological determinism, conspiracy, or what?

Centralized Private Sector Planning (CPSP) in the United States may appropriately be viewed as the end result of a nonconspiratorial evolutionary process. As advances in the industrial system's technologically based production processes made it possible to concentrate administrative control over the country's key industries in fewer and fewer hands, corporate leaders simply adapted traditional market system economic ideas and concepts to create a centralized management process. In a very real sense, the CPC's planning instruments are simply modifications of traditional business devices (boards of directors, stock, bonds, etc.), modifications made in such a way as to *simulate*, from an administrative perspective, the concentration, or consolidation, that technological advances made possible in the country's production processes. After all, in a society that has enshrined the values of laissez-faire, self-interest, and profit seeking, one should expect corporate leaders to take full advantage of the entire spectrum of administrative and technological possibilities available for maximizing their personal power and prerogatives. As anyone who has had a basic college course in economics can attest, from an economic standpoint, self-interest, profit seeking, and laissez-faire are what America is all about.

Quite clearly the CPC may be viewed as the evolutionary end result of entrepreneurs creating, *albeit unconsciously*, the most centralized administrative and production system possible, given existing technology, because of their entirely *conscious, logical, and rational* pursuit of monetary gain, or profit. Obviously, this type of evolutionary process should *not* be categorized as the conscious work of some conspiratorial group. Most emphatically, however, this is not to say that the CPC's existence was *caused* by, or is a function of, modern technology.

To say that the use of *some* modern technologies in an efficient manner necessitates, is conducive to, or merely permits a form of centralized economic planning does *not* prejudge what specific form or type of planning process per se a society will, or should, adopt. Nor must a society always use a particular technology just because it exists. Neither should one assume that all modern technologies necessarily require some form of centralized planning. Unfortunately, in America, the real choices that our technological knowledge make possible (choices between different production and distribution systems, for example, centralized versus decentralized) have been circumscribed by, or encapsulated within, our capitalistic ideology and, in particular, by the values of self-interest, profit seeking, and laissez-faire. In brief, the particular type of centralized planning that exists in America today is due neither to technological determinism nor to conspiratorial machinations. Rather, CPSP is a direct result of combining the values of self-interest, profit seeking, and laissez-faire with certain technological possibilities.

Coercion—or just sound business?

If one takes the system's structural nature as given, some form of intra/interindustry economic planning is both rational and, indeed, absolutely essential, if the system is to function with even minimum efficiency.* Moreover, CPC members lack neither logical skills and reason nor a sense of self-preservation. Therefore, the extent to which the use of coercive tactics may at times become necessary *within* the CPSP sphere, does *not* stem from the fact that the underlying belief in the need for intra- and interindustry coordination and cooperation needs reinforcement. Rather, coercion may become necessary, at times, to ensure adherence to a specific decision—a specific decision that arouses genuine and deeply felt policy differences in a minority group within the CPC or within an individual corporate entity. In short, as long as the economy's existing *structural* characteristics remain unchanged, logic and reason dictate some form of centralized planning—a fact with which CPC members are familiar and which they readily accept. In his book *Nineteen Eighty-Four*, George Orwell commented on the power of the party and Big Brother:

> It has long been realized that the only secure basis for oligarchy is collectivism. Wealth and privilege are most easily defended when they are possessed jointly. The so-called "abolition of private property" which took place in the middle years of the century meant, in effect, the concentration of property in far fewer hands than before . . . collectively, the Party . . . controls everything. . . .[7]

Coercive tactics practiced by the CPC against those outside the planning umbrella, however, must be viewed somewhat differently. How the "maverick," Howard Hughes, was removed from the air transportation industry is one such example. The CPC had loaned Hughes's competitors hundreds of millions of dollars to modernize their air transportation fleets. In order to remain competitive, Hughes needed to borrow approximately $350 million to modernize TWA's fleet. Hughes decided to borrow the money from a coalition of several CPC institutions. Was Hughes coerced into borrowing money? In reality, no arms were twisted, no orders issued; Hughes made his choice. Although Hughes eventually lost control of TWA to his creditors, would this

---

*Always keep in mind, though, that there is nothing, from a technological point of view, that necessitates the economy having the specific types of structural arrangements that now exist.

normally be considered an aggressive or coercive act on the part of the CPC? Creditors are legally entitled to exercise, or act upon, whatever agreements are contained in the bond indenture. In turn, both parties must *freely* agree to the bond indenture covenants. For the most part, then, the CPC can attain its objectives without appearing explicitly or overtly coercive.

Soviet planners implement their decisions by issuing direct orders. A direct order, backed by the force of law, appears coercive to the Western mind, especially when an individual is not free to choose whether or not to be part of the system. CPC planners, on the other hand, implement their decisions by buying or selling stock and/or bonds. The CPC's more subtle tactics appear not be coercive and, therefore, are more effective. There is a saying that captures the spirit of this argument quite well. When Soviet leaders want to influence economic activities in another country, they garrison troops; when Americans want to influence economic activities in another country, they establish a bank.

In summary, the CPC is usually capable of achieving its goals without being perceived as using coercion. Indeed, it may be that the magnitude of the CPC's actual power is directly related to the degree of imperceptibility of its planning instruments as actually being planning instruments, as opposed to just sound business.

CPSP and economic efficiency

The inefficiency inherent in centralized economic planning is the topic of a folktale about a 600-pound nail. The story, usually related by an economics professor to his students after class, goes somewhat as follows. Whenever a factory manager in the Soviet Union failed to meet the quota established for his factory by the Gosplan, he was immediately shipped to some far corner of Siberia. Once upon a time, Ivan, the manager of Nail Factory No. 22, was 18,000 pounds short of his established nail quota, with only several days remaining before the production cutoff date. Fearing the long, cold Siberian nights and being very quick-witted, Ivan decided that the factory's quota of nails, in terms of weight, could not be met under current production procedures. Given the size and weight of the nails being produced, an additional 720,000 nails were needed. In order to meet the quota, Ivan devised a plan to produce thirty-two 600-pound nails. The plan worked, and Ivan received a bonus for exceeding the quota by 1,200 pounds, while four factory workers were awarded worker hero medals. Alas, the nails are to this day rusting in the factory yard—there appears to be no immediate need for thirty-two 600-pound nails. At this point, the economic professor relating the story smiles, the students giggle, and everyone orders another drink, satisfied that, in a market system oriented economy, the invisible hand would never send such signals that would result in the production of 600-pound nails.

Quite by accident one evening, several hours and a few drinks after having heard this story, a student asked the professor about the CPSP thesis. The professor immediately said, " . . . how could anyone see the mess that our automobile and steel industries are in and still contend that there was any rational planning being done by these corporations. Any sophomore could have told Chrysler to stop producing those 6,000-pound behemoth, gas-guzzling monsters several years ago." No attempt was made by the student to point out the rather glaring contradiction between the central thesis of the professor's earlier story and his latter statement about Chrysler Corporation. Specifically, the students were told, on the one hand, that the Soviet economy was inherently inefficient because economic planning does not work well; on the other hand, they were told that, if anyone had been doing any conscious, long-range planning in the U.S. economy, Chrysler Corporation would have shifted to smaller cars before it was confronted with bankruptcy. In short, when problems occur in the Soviet economy (such as the 600-pound nail), they are often seen as indicative of the failure of economic planning. But, when problems occur in the American economy (such as Chrysler's 6,000-pound cars), they are often viewed as evidence of no planning.

These types of double-edged arguments exist in abundance; only the subject matter of the tales changes:

• There is such poor communication and cooperation between the various planning agencies in the Soviet Union that it is no wonder their economy is in such a mess; how could anyone remotely aware of the lack of communication and cohesion between America's corporate leaders believe that any type of rational planning was going on.

• It is naive to believe that the Soviet's planning structure encompasses *all* economic activity; central planning could not work in the United States because no planning structure could be built that could possibly encompass all the many different varieties and types of economic activity.

The crucial point in all this has nothing to do with whether centralized planning is inherently inefficient. The point is simply that one cannot have it both ways. Or, more specifically, one cannot adhere to the formal rules of logic and use the inefficiency argument as evidence to prove both—

a. that centralized planning does not work well in the Soviet Union, and

b. that centralized planning does not exist in the United States.

CPSP and democracy

In Chapter 3, a brief review of the various approaches to economic planning was presented. It was suggested that economic planning could be done in either the public or private sector and that within these sectors the planning process could either be centralized or decentralized. Obviously, these pedagogical categorizations do not suffice to actually indicate the relative power position between the public and private sector institutions that prevail in various countries. For instance, in the Soviet Union (an example of Centralized Public Sector Planning), for all practical purposes, there really are not any well-developed private sector institutions that are involved with the planning process. In the United States (an example of Centralized Private Sector Planning), while public sector institutions certainly exist, they not only do not take part in the planning process, but most of our public servants are not even aware that the corporate world engages in centralized planning.

On the other hand, In Germany, Sweden, and France (all examples of Decentralized Public Sector Planning), both public and private sector institutions play an active role in the planning process. As Joan Robinson noted in her book *Freedom and Necessity*:

> It is possible to argue that in Sweden democratic public opinion has mastered the industrialists and made them its servants, while in the U.S.A. the state has become the servant of the industrialists. Other Western countries lie somewhere in between.[8]

While all the industrialized countries that engage in some form of Decentralized Public Sector Planning seem to agree that public and private sector institutions need to cooperate, there remain factual differences over which sector holds the real levers of power—or, who is the senior partner—in the planning process.

Only in the Soviet Union and the United States is one sector competely excluded from the planning process. Nonetheless, to suggest that the Soviet system of Centralized Public Sector Planning and the American system of Centralized Private Sector Planning are in any other way similar is to display an unforgivable ignorance of how the two systems work from an *operational* standpoint. This point cannot be overstressed.

The Soviet system is basically a totalitarian system. By comparison, the United States is quite democratic. The crucial problem now facing Americans, given the tremendous advances in central planning in the private sector since World War II, is to create the types of laws and institutional structures conducive to a fuller and more complete democratization of both our political and our economic institutions. Unfortunately, up to this point, our attempts to counter the growing powers of the CPC have been primarily devoted to creating a bloated federal bureaucracy. Both trends represent a dangerous threat to our traditional democratic liberties. We are rapidly approaching a critical crossroads. The issue is *not* whether centralized planning is to occur in the public or private sector—the critical issue is the centralization of power itself.

The answer is to begin creating institutional structures that allow all citizens (consumers, artisans, laborers, etc.) to take part in molding their own destinies, that is, to become part of the economic *goal-setting* process itself. In a modern industrial society worthy of the name democracy, economic planners would be technicians whose function would be to carry out or to implement the economic goals and policies established in institutional settings that maximized, rather than limited, citizen participation.

Finally, all attempts by grass-roots movements (a) to halt the ever increasing concentration of power and decision making within the CPC and (b) to further the democratization of the system's decision-making processes will ultimately fail—unless the participants in these movements are guided by a clear picture of the economy's structural and functional realities. Even then, success is not guaranteed. A movement solidly anchored in and/or informed by the economy's concrete realities, however, would at least have a chance. On the other hand, movements guided by the ideological prattlings of either the Left or the Right, even if its leaders succeeded in gaining power, would no doubt (if history be our guide) create an environment with even fewer of our democratic freedoms than now exist. Stated somewhat differently, conversations predicated on the idea that America is actually a *capitalist society* are very simply conversations where economic reality is not being discussed.* And, reforms that are not solidly rooted in economic reality not only usually fail to achieve their stated objectives, but, instead, usually bring about a great deal of chaos. In turn, chaos is *not* a breeding grounds for democracy; chaos is *the* breeding grounds for totalitarianism—be it totalitarianism of the Left or of the Right.

The term is also still very meaningful from a political perspective. How could a politician make a successful speech on the economy without (1) praising and glorifying competitive capitalism, or (2) condemning government's interference with the market system?

CPSP and macro economics

When oligopolistically competitive market structures became the dominant form of market structure in the economy, John Maynard Keynes constructed a macro economic analysis which provided government policymakers with both a theoretical justification, as well as a set of practical monetary and fiscal policy tools which could be used to prevent major depressions, while simultaneously assuring stable and steady economic growth within an environment of full employment and stable prices. Government policies based on macro economics, however, no longer work. Just as Adam Smith's competitive market structures gave way to oligopolistically competitive market structures, oligopoly markets have given way to CPSP. Stated quite simply, theories predicated on a structural economic reality that, in fact, does not exist, will *not* work. For example, in order to eliminate inflation by attempting to slow economic growth within the economy's CPSP sphere, the Federal Reserve Board would need to drive interest rates so tremendously high, or so severely constrict the money supply, that many of the country's middle-sized businesses would literally be destroyed. How

---

*One must not conclude from these remarks that the term "competitive capitalism" is meaningless. From a psychological point of view, it is not an overstatement to point out that the psychological well-being of many individuals in this country is dependent on their maintaining a belief in the existence of capitalism. Thus, in a psychological sense, the term has legitimate and profound meaning. Nonetheless, in terms of providing an accurate description of the economic realities of extant market structures, the term, for the most part, is (1) totally misleading, or (2) totally devoid of any meaning at all. Unless, of course, our economic savants can breathe meaning into the concept "competitive cooperation."

high, for instance, would the cost of capital (the interest rate) need to go to stop the CPC from *allocating* funds to, say AT&T? Consider the following:

• Thirty-seven percent of AT&T's BOD are CPC members; in addition, there are 102 IDI's and 20 III's—i.e., CPC directors are in approximately 240 meetings annually with AT&T's directors.

• The CPC has acted as the trustee for 21 of AT&T's 23 outstanding bond indentures, etc., etc.

In other words, while the cost of capital may be quite meaningful when a typical middle-sized business borrows money, it may not be so important from the point of view of the CPC allocating capital among non-core corporations.

In short, the CPC's ability to amass, control, and allocate vast sums of money, *for all practical purposes*, simply places the economy's CPSP sphere outside the purview of the traditional Keynesian analysis. This is *not* to say, however, that monetary and fiscal policies have no effect on the economy, but, rather, *as presently conceived and practiced*, that such policies are insufficient as tools for bringing about full employment and a stable price level.*

By way of summary, the description and analysis of the key sectors of our economy that have been set forth in this and the two preceding chapters are an attempt to demonstrate to the community—

• how the firms within many industries—from both a structural and a functional perspective—have become technologically, financially, and administratively intradependent;

• how many of these industries—from both a structural and a functional perspective—have also become technologically, financially, and administratively interdependent; and, finally,

• how, over the years, intra- and interindustry coordination and cooperation have *evolved* to the point where the term CPSP more accurately *describes and explains* the economy's structural and functional realities than do the terms market system, capitalism, or free private enterprise.

*For a provocative and thoughtful analysis concerning alternative types of public policy approaches, see Alfred S. Eichner's *The Megacorp and Oligopoly* (Cambridge: Cambridge University Press, 1976). See in particular the Preface and Chapter 8.

Notes

1. Joseph R. Royce, *The Encapsulated Man* (Princeton: D. Van Nostrand Company, Inc., 1964), pp. 91–92.

2. Art Buchwald, *Down the Seine and Up the Potomac with Art Buchwald* (5th impression) (New York: G. P. Putnam's Sons, 1977) p. 295.

3. "Runaways of Fairfield County," *Newsweek*, 16 August 1976, p. 64.

4. Ibid.

5. "Are the Nation's Banks Getting Too Powerful?" *U.S. News and World Report*, 25 March 1974, pp. 70–72.

6. First National City Bank, "Annual Report of Equity Securities," 21 March 1975, sent to the Office of the Comptroller of the Currency, Washington, D.C.

7. George Orwell, *Nineteen Eighty-Four* (New York: Harcourt, Brace and Company, Inc., 1949; reprint ed., New York: The New American Library, Inc., 1961), p. 170.

8. Joan Robinson, *Freedom and Necessity* (New York: Vintage Books, 1970), p. 90.

Chapter Six

The Anational Corporation: A Peek at the Future?

> *And since new ideas will not come if their entry into the mind is subject to conformity with old ones and with what we call commonsense, this book demands of the reader—as it demanded of the author—a willing suspension of commonsense. The aim is to open up a new point of view.*[1]
>
> Norman O. Brown

> *I have long dreamed of buying an island owned by no nation, and of establishing the World Headquarters of the Dow Co. on the truly neutral ground of such an island, beholden to no nation or society. . . . We appear to be moving strongly in the direction of what might be called "anational" companies, nationless companies.*[2]
>
> Carl A. Gerstacker, present board member and past Board Chairman, Dow Chemical Company

A thorough and comprehensive treatment of the anational corporation concept would demand a study several hundreds of pages in length. The task at present is much simpler. Specifically, the ideas and arguments set forth in this chapter are intended only:

- to further illustrate how truly immense the dichotomy between orthodox economic theories (whether Marxian or market system) and economic reality has actually become; and

- to illustrate how one *cannot* possibly understand or accurately surmise either the logic or the motives that lie behind many of the actions and policies of our corporate and political leaders unless one views these actions and policies within the context of an anational corporation perspective.*

*The technical aspects usually considered when discussing the economic impact of anational corporations include: inflation, employment levels, the balance of payments, capital formation, productivity, economic growth, and, finally, the distribution of income between various economic groups. None of these topics is examined

A descriptive and statistical topography

Trade and commerce between peoples have a long history. In 7000 B.C., Sumerian boats laden with goods plied the waters of the Tigris and Euphrates rivers, as well as the Persian Gulf. By 2000 B.C., sturdy Phoenician vessels were transporting goods throughout the Mediterranean littoral; the Armenians had created the great caravan routes of the Arabian and Persian deserts. During the latter Middle Ages, trade and commerce throughout Christendom were greatly facilitated by the Italian banking houses. By the middle of the 1800s, the East India Trading Company, for all practical purposes, ruled the Indian continent.

Moreover, by the close of the eighteenth century, English economists had rationalized trade among nations by formulating the Law of Comparative Advantage. The primary logical conclusion to be drawn from this abstract "law," first popularized by Adam Smith and later refined by David Ricardo, was that individual countries should not attempt to provide for all their needs through indigenous production. Rather, each country should specialize in the production of those goods that could be produced *relatively* more efficiently. With this procedure, the total world production of goods would be greater, and, after division of the bigger economic pie through trade, each country would be better off than it would have been without specialization and trade.

In short, trade and commerce between and among countries, from both a theoretical and a practical point of view, are most certainly *not* recent phenomena. But, the idea that the vehicle or institution responsible for carrying out the transfer of goods between nations would itself be "nationless," " . . . beholden to no nation or society . . . ," is somewhat peculiar to the modern mind, to say the least. Nonetheless, since many of our prominent intellectuals and business leaders are quite seriously suggesting that the anational corporation is, in fact, becoming—and, indeed, ought to become—an institutional reality, the idea certainly merits serious consideration.

As early as the middle decades of the twentieth century, fundamental changes were beginning to be perceived in the traditional relationship

explicitly in this chapter. For an excellent discussion of these considerations, see *Direct Investment Abroad and the Multinationals: Effects on the United States Economy*, prepared by Peggy B. Musgrave for the use of the Subcommittee on Multinational Corporations of the Committee on Foreign Relations, U.S. Senate, 94th Congress, 1st Session, 1975. In the present chapter, the discussion will center primarily on more broadly gauged philosophical and political concerns, from both a domestic and an international perspective.

between the corporation and the world's political institutions. Adolf A. Berle and Gardiner C. Means were among the first orthodox, or non-Marxian, American scholars to begin seriously questioning and examining these changing institutional relationships. In their book *The Modern Corporation and Private Property*, they stated:

> The rise of the modern corporations has brought a concentration of economic power which can compete on equal terms with the modern state—economic power versus political power, each strong in its own field. The state seeks in some aspects to regulate the corporation, while the corporation, steadily becoming more powerful, makes every effort to avoid such regulation. Where its own interests are concerned it even attempts to dominate the state. The future may see the economic organism, now typified by the corporation, not only on an equal plane with the state, but possibly even superseding it as the dominant form of social organization. *The law of corporations, accordingly, might well be considered as a potential constitutional law for the new economic state*, while business practice is increasingly assuming the aspect of economic statesmanship.[3] (emphasis added)

The ideas of "economic statesmanship" and "the new economic state" were also discussed by Adolf A. Berle in his 1954 book, *The 20th Century Capitalist Revolution*:

> Large corporations, like nations, have encountered the danger of world anarchy, have sought safety in balance of power, and from time to time have attempted their field experiments in world government. To this last point, attention may be directed. In point of surprising fact, the *large American corporations in certain fields have more nearly achieved a stable and working world government than has yet been achieved by any other institution.*[4] (emphasis added)

The two main points set forth by Berle and Means were—
• that modern corporations might well replace the nation-state as the dominant form of social organization in human affairs; and
• that, since the activities of the modern corporation are worldwide in scope, " . . . the new economic state" might evolve into an *economic world order*.

Before examining these hypotheses, some empirical data will be presented concerning the size and scope of the modern corporation's global activities.

Table 31

Number of Foreign-Based *Manufacturing* Subsidiaries Controlled by the Largest American-Based Manufacturing Corporations, by Area, for Selected Years (1901-1975)

Area	Year and number								
	1901	1913	1919	1929	1939	1950	1959	1967	1975
Canada	6	30	61	137	169	225	330	443	594
Europe	37	72	84	226	335	363	677	1,438	2,427
France	8	12	12	36	52	54	98	223	354
Germany	10	15	18	43	50	47	97	211	398
United Kingdom	13	23	28	78	128	146	221	356	565
Other Europe	6	22	26	69	105	116	261	648	1,110
Southern Dominions*	1	3	8	25	69	99	184	361	559
Latin America	3	10	20	56	114	259	572	950	1,325
Other	0	1	7	23	28	42	128	454	870
TOTAL	47	116	180	467	715	988	1,891	3,646	5,775

Source: Clair Wilcox and William G. Shepherd, *Public Policies Toward Business* (Homewood, Ill.: Richard D. Irwin, Inc., 1975), p. 37, and John P. Curan, William H. Davidson, and Rajan Suri, *Tracing the Multinationals* (Cambridge, Mass.. Ballinger Publishing Company, 1977), pp. 150-151.

Note: The data base for the years 1901 through 1967 includes foreign-based manufacturing concerns controlled by the 187 largest U.S.-based manufacturing companies, while the data base for the year 1975 includes foreign subsidiaries controlled by the 180 largest U.S. manufacturing corporations.

*The Southern Dominions include the countries of Australia, New Zealand, Rhodesia, and South Africa.

As of 1 January 1976, 180 of America's largest corporations held ownership interest in 11,198 foreign-based subsidiaries. In approximately 70 percent of these subsidiaries, the U.S. parent company owned between 95 and 100 percent of the common stock.* In only 14 percent of these companies did the U.S. corporation control less than 50 percent of the common stock. In Table 31, there is an illustration of the proliferation of foreign-based *manufacturing* subsidiaries controlled by American-base *manufacturing* corporations. For example, in

*See John P. Curan, William H. Davidson, and Rajan Suri, *Tracing the Multinationals*, (Cambridge, Mass.: Ballinger Publishing Company, 1977), p. 312. In this book, one will find a superb data base on the activities of foreign-based companies controlled by U.S. corporations. Topics include ownership patterns, employment statistics, financial statistics, and intrasystem sales flows.

Table 32

Percentage of Profits, Sales, and Assets Accounted for by Foreign Activities, for Selected Corporations (1977)

Corporation	Profits	Sales	Assets
Citicorp	NA	65.6*	NA
Chase Manhattan Corporation	NA	52.0*	NA
J. P. Morgan and Company	NA	51.1*	NA
Exxon Corporation	51.7	7.35	68.3
Mobil Corporation	43.9	71.3	59.9
Texaco Inc.	49.0	66.0	53.0
Ford Motor Company	42.1	29.4	40.4
Caterpillar Tractor Company	NA	50.7	NA
Pfizer Inc.	65.3	53.5	38.6
Merck and Company, Inc.	29.8	44.9	39.3
IBM	45.2	50.3	42.4
Union Carbide	20.6	31.9	34.6
Black & Decker Manufacturing Co.	57.6	55.4	40.3
The Coca Cola Company	58.0	43.6	32.9
Dow Chemical Company	33.4	44.6	28.2

Source: See the Appendix.

Note: NA = Not available.

*The data for the banks represent demand deposits.

1967, 187 U.S. corporations controlled 443 manufacturing corporations in Canada; 1,438 in Europe; and 950 in Latin America. By 1975, however, the numbers had increased to 594; 2,427; and 1,325. In addition, the number of U.S. parent corporations contained in the data base had shrunk from 187 in 1967 to only 180 in 1975, due to acquisitions and mergers. For example, during this period (1967 to 1975), Greyhound was acquired by Armour and Company; Esmark acquired Swift and Company. In gross numbers, U.S. corporations controlled approximately 60 percent more foreign-based manufacturing subsidiaries in 1975 than in 1967; the increase from 1939 to 1975 was a remarkable 807.7 percent.

Yet, even more remarkable are the figures indicating the amount of profit, sales, and assets accounted for by the foreign activities of U.S. corporations (see Table 32). For instance, in 1977 the percentage of total sales accounted for by foreign sales for Exxon was 73.5; for Mobil, 71.3; for Ford, 29.4; for Pfizer, 53.5; for IBM, 50.3; and for Coca-Cola, 43.6. Furthermore, the percentage of assets accounted for by foreign-based subsidiaries for Exxon was 68.3; for Mobil, 59.9; for Ford, 40.4; for Pfizer, 38.6; for IBM, 42.4; and for Coca-Cola, 32.9. In short, if either Ford or IBM were to somehow lose its foreign assets and sales, its size would be diminished by almost one-half.* In addition, as shown in Table 32, more than half of Citicorp's, Chase Manhattan's, and J. P. Morgan's demand deposits are accounted for by their foreign-based banking subsidiaries. Thus, as with Ford and IBM, were these banks to lose their foreign operations, their size would also show a dramatic reduction. Stated more succinctly, the size of many American-based corporations' *profits, sales, and assets* accounted for by foreign operations and/or foreign-based subsidiaries has grown so great that these operations are fast becoming as important (and, indeed, in some instances, even more important) to the business life of these corporations as their domestic operations and manufacturing facilities. One can clearly begin to see how an entrepreneur of an American-based corporation that actually manufactures and *sells* more products outside the United States than it manufactures and *sells* in the U.S. might begin to develop an anational perspective. In addition, it is also important to note that the corporations that are most active in terms of foreign-based operations, for the most part, are corporations within the economy's Centralized Private Sector Planning sphere. For example, all 15 of the corporations listed in Table 32 are part of the Central Planning Tableau. In short, the Central Planning Core is the focal point of the anational corporation movement.

While the above types of statistics may give one an initial inkling of the global nature of the modern corporation's worldwide production and marketing activities, they may not give one an existential feeling or understanding for the prodigious magnitude of these institutions in terms of sheer, absolute size. As depicted in Table 33, only 22 countries had Gross National Product (GNP), in 1977, larger than the annual total sales figures for Exxon and General Motors.† The data in this

---

*The percentage of profit, sales, and assets accounted for by foreign activities for each of the 138 corporations in this study, where available, is shown in the Central Planning Tableau.

†From a purely technical perspective, these two statistics—Gross National Product (GNP) and total sales—are not precisely comparable. The GNP purportedly measures the physical output of a country's goods and services, at the point of consumption, by consumers, while total sales represent the dollar value of all goods and services produced at *each* stage in the production process. Nevertheless, the comparison is quite useful in attempting to accurately portray the relative importance of many corporations vis-à-vis individual countries, as economic producing institutions in the world's economy.

Table 33

Comparative Economic Size of Corporations and Countries, by Total Annual Sales of Corporations and the GNP of Countries (1977, in billions of dollars)

1.	United States	1,900	56.	GULF OIL	18
2.	USSR	861	57.	Portugal	17
3.	Japan	737	58.	Libya	17
4.	Germany, Federal Republic of	529	59.	GENERAL ELECTRIC	17
5.	France	397	60.	CHRYSLER	17
6.	China, People's Republic of	373	61.	UNILEVER	16
7.	United Kingdom	254	62.	Pakistan	15
8.	Italy	199	63.	Kuwait	14
9.	Canada	194	64.	Israel	14
10.	Brazil	164	65.	New Zealand	14
11.	Spain	118	66.	ITT	13
12.	Poland	114	67.	PHILIPS GLOEILAMPEN-FABRIEKEN	13
13.	Netherlands	106	68.	STANDARD OIL OF INDIANA	13
14.	Australia	103	69.	Chile	13
15.	India	100	70.	Egypt, Arab Republic of	13
16.	Germany, Democratic Republic of	85	71.	Malaysia	12
17.	Belgium	82	72.	Hong Kong	12
18.	Sweden	77	73.	United Arab Emirates	11
19.	Mexico	73	74.	FRANÇOISE DES PÉTROLES	11
20.	Iran	72(E)	75.	SIEMENS	11
21.	Czechoslovakia	63	76.	Morocco	11
22.	Switzerland	70	77.	ATLANTIC RICHFIELD	11
23.	Saudi Arabia	55	78.	Korea, Democratic Republic of	11
24.	GENERAL MOTORS	55	79.	RENAULT	10
25.	EXXON	54	80.	HOECHST	10
26.	Austria	48	81.	ENI	10
27.	Argentina	48	82.	SHELL OIL (HOUSTON)	10
28.	Turkey	46	83.	VOLKSWAGENWERK	10
29.	Yugoslavia	46	84.	Ireland	10
30.	Denmark	46	85.	TOYOTA MOTORS	10

31.	Indonesia	43	86.	BASF	9
32.	Nigeria	40	87.	PETROLEOS DE VENEZUELA	9
33.	ROYAL DUTCH/SHELL GROUP	39	88.	U.S. STEEL	9
34.	South Africa	37	89.	BAYER	9
35.	FORD MOTOR COMPANY	37	90.	NIPPON STEEL	9
36.	Venezuela	35	91.	E. I. Du PONT DE NEMOURS	9
37.	Korea, Republic of	35	92.	CONTINENTAL OIL	9
38.	Norway	34	93.	DAIMLER BENZ	9
39.	Romania	33	94.	THYSSEN	8
40.	Hungary	33	95.	Puerto Rico	8
41.	MOBIL	32	96.	NESTLE	8
42.	Finland	29	97.	ELF-ACQUAITAINE	8
43.	TEXACO	28	98.	IMPERIAL CHEMICAL	8
44.	Greece	27	99.	PEUGOT-CITROEN	8
45.	Bulgaria	25	100.	PETROLAR	8
46.	NATIONAL IRANIAN OIL COMPANY	22	101.	HITACHI	8
47.	STANDARD OIL OF CALIFORNIA	21	102.	NISSAN MOTORS	8
48.	BRITISH PETROLEUM	21	103.	MITSUBISHI HEAVY INDUSTRY	8
49.	Philippines	20	104.	WESTERN ELECTRIC	8
50.	China, Republic of	20	105.	Cuba	8
51.	Colombia	19	106.	PROCTOR & GAMBLE	7
52.	Algeria	19	107.	TENNECO	7
53.	Iraq	18	108.	UNION CARBIDE	7
54.	Thailand	18	109.	GOODYEAR TIRE & RUBBER	7
55.	INTERNATIONAL BUSINESS MACHINES	18	110.	MATSUSHITA ELECTRIC INDUSTRIES	7

Sources: "The *Fortune* Directory of the 500 Largest U.S. Industrial Corporations," *Fortune*, 8 May 1978; "The *Fortune* Directory of the 500 Largest Industrial Corporations Outside the U.S.," *Fortune*, 14 August 1978; "1979 World Bank Atlas," *The World Bank*.

Notes: From a purely technical perspective, these two statistics (Gross National Product and total sales) are not precisely comparable. The GNP purportedly measures the physical output of a country's goods and services at the point of consumption by consumers while total sales represents the dollar value of all goods and services produced at *each* stage in the production process. Nevertheless, the comparison is quite useful in attempting to accurately portray the relative importance of many corporations vis-à-vis individual countries as economic producing institutions in the world's economy.

(E) = estimated.

table reveal that, if one uses the annual total sales of individual corporations and the GNP of individual countries as yardsticks, of the 110 largest economic entities in the world, 49 are corporations. Stated somewhat differently, in 1977 Proctor & Gamble's total sales (consisting primarily of soaps and detergents) were almost as large as Cuba's Gross National Product.

As astounding as these statistics may seem to the uninitiated, the philosophical vision of the anational corporation's proponents certainly matches the raw data. In the words of Samuel Pisar:

> I see the economic instincts of man—in the West and in the East—reaching out across artificially created political and ideological boundaries to join in a common cause: the promotion of peaceful commerce and industry. . . . It may be unprecedented but there is nothing inherently wrong when mature and intelligent men of diverse political and ideological persuasion seek to treat the world as one market . . . without regard to the arbitrary state barriers that have come into existence by accidents of history or force of arms. Their dynamism is generated by a simple principle: Optimum efficiency.
>
> *Like the ancient struggle between church and state the relationship between economic power,* which is becoming increasingly multinational, *and political power,* which is remaining stubbornly national, *is today an issue of universal significance.*
>
> . . . The challenge calls for a brand new mentality which is at once postnational and postideological.[5] (emphasis added)

In addition, the economic interdependence between nation states, created by the anational corporation's globalization of the production process, is also envisioned as being an instrument for forging world peace.

Again, in the words of Samuel Pisar:

> *This development has enormous potential for the welfare and well-being of all humanity. Once peoples and governments become inextricably tied to one another by economic self-interest, the specter of instability and war begins to recede.*
>
> Whatever its faults and abuses—and I do not wish to belittle them—the much maligned community of multinational corporations must be recognized as standing in the forefront of this process. Having helped to fuel a decade of prosperity across the national frontiers of the West, *it is now storming* across the ideological frontiers of the East.[6] (emphasis added)

G.M.'s past board chairman, Frederic Donner, also emphasizes the world peace theme:

> In short, the world-wide enterprise is potentially a most effective element in a world-wide desire for economic growth. Used well in an environment of freedom, it offers a potential unlimited today and in the years ahead. It provides an important element in the search for world peace. These are the objectives which constitute the ultimate challenge and the promise of world-wide industrial enterprise.[7]

In short, then, spokespersons for the anational corporation not only have a clearly stated economic goal—namely, the achievement of planetary production efficiency—but, in addition, have an equally clear-sighted vision concerning the political and social implications of the modern corporation's global activities—namely, the destruction of "arbitrary" political barriers and the establishment of world peace.

In attempting to capture the essential meaning of the term *anational corporation*, one may find the following definitions helpful:

> *International Firm*: One in which international operations are consolidated in a home office on the division level and which, as a matter of policy, is willing to consider all potential strategies for entering foreign markets, up to direct investment.
>
> *Multinational Firm*: One in which, both structurally and policy-wise, foreign operations are co-equal with domestic. . . . Decisions remain nationally based for ownership, and headquarters' management remains uni-national.
>
> *Trans-national Firm*: A multinational firm managed and owned by persons of different national origins.
>
> *Supra-national Firm*: A trans-national firm legally denationalized through allowing it the exclusive right to register with, be controlled by, and pay taxes to some international body.
>
> *Anational Corporation*: A trans-national firm totally free from control by any other institution—political, religious, or military.*

---

*The first four of these five definitions were taken from a book published by the National Asociation of Manufacturers (NAM), *The Role of the Multinational Corporation*. The NAM has never been considered a hotbed of radical Marxian thought. And, indeed, it is not. Yet, Marx also envisioned the downfall or demise of the nation state as an institutional reality, the difference being that business leaders see the demise of nation states as being brought about by the modern corporation, while old line Marxists believe that the demise of nation states will be brought about by an international workingmen's association.

Thus, the concept of the anational corporation may quite properly be viewed as the triumph of a laissez-faire economic philosophy on a global basis. It should be noted, however, that many scholars doing work in this area contend that the supranational corporation would undoubtedly be counterbalanced by a global political institution, such as the United Nations. For example, as noted by Harvard professor Raymond Vernon—

> . . . The multinational enterprise as a unit, though capable of wielding substantial economic power, is not accountable to any public authority that matches it in geographic reach and that represents the aggregate interest of all the countries the enterprise affects . . . [8]

And further:

> The basic asymmetry between multinational enterprises and national governments may be tolerable up to a point, but beyond that point there is a need to reestablish balance. When this occurs, the response is bound to have some of the elements of the world corporation concept: accountability to some body, charged with weighing the activities of the multinational enterprise against a set of social yardsticks that are multinational in scope.[9]

Yet, if the laissez-faire attitude prevailed, which is certainly what many in the corporate world intend, the creation of supposedly countervailing public institutions notwithstanding, the supranational corporation would be but a prelude to the total triumph of a corporate economic order in world affairs, or to the institutionalization of the anational corporation.

While all this may seem like an affront to one's common sense or like something one would expect to hear on a television program such as "Fantasy Island," a few brief quotes from the country's intellectual and corporate elite may instill a more sober attitude toward the corporate cosmology concept.

Quotations from the intellectual, political, and corporate elite

In 1972, New York University's Professor John Fayerweather, commenting on his belief in the immutability of the success of the transnational corporate institution, noted:

A century from now it seems quite likely that people will look back on the second half of the twentieth century as a . . . period of societal transition in which the nation-state and its supporting religion of nationalism readjusted to accommodate various new forms of international structure for the benefit of its peoples and society as a whole.[10]

John J. Powers, president of Pfizer, Inc., said that a true world economy

. . . is no idealistic pipe dream but a hard-headed prediction; it is a role into which we are being pushed by the imperatives of our own technology.[11]

In 1977, Pfizer's foreign operations accounted for 65.2 percent of the corporation's profits, 53.5 percent of its sales, and 38.6 percent of its assets.

Sidney E. Rolfe, commenting on the nation state's survival possibilities, stated:

international investment is a reflection of the development of technology, and if technology—internal in the corporations' discoveries and production adaptations and external in the case of travel, communication, and administrative control—is at the root of the movement, it is a movement certain to grow ever more important with time and to challenge every facet of the established order—financial, cultural, and political—in the course of that growth. Few human institutions in the past have withstood the march of technology, and those currently extant are no less likely to succeed. . . . In retrospect, the history of our time is likely to be recorded as the conflict between ethnocentric nationalism and geocentric technology.[12]

G. A. Costanzo, a member of Citicorp's board of directors, stated his position as follows:

My feeling is that there are very strong forces that are pushing the world toward internationalism, or a new era of the multinational firm. I look at it in the same way, I think, in which the Industrial Revolution made city states obsolete and forced people to adjust their thinking and move toward a national state, and thus created a great deal of backlash and political instability during the period. I think we're in a similar period now.[13]

In 1977, 65.6 percent of Citicorp's demand deposits were accounted for by foreign-based subsidiaries.

From the political community, George W. Ball, Undersecretary of State in both the Johnson and Kennedy administrations, set forth his thoughts on this subject rather bluntly:

> The Nation State is no longer an adequate or even a very relevant economic unit. Conflict will increase between the World Corporation, which is a modern concept evolved to meet the requirements of the modern age, and the nation state, which is still rooted in armchair concepts unsympathetic to the needs of our complex world.[14]

Finally, in an equally direct manner, Jacques G. Maisonrouge, chairman of the IBM World Trade Corporation, in an address to the American Foreign Service Association, stipulated that:

> [t]he world's political structures are completely obsolete. They have not changed in at least one hundred years and are woefully out of tune with technological progress. The critical issue of our time is the conceptual conflict between the search for global optimization of resources and the independence of nation states.[15]

In 1977, the foreign operations of IBM accounted for 45.2 percent of its profits, 50.3 percent of its sales, and 42.4 percent of its assets.

While many corporate leaders are seemingly unequivocal in their denunciation of the nation-state, they are even more straightforward and unequivocal in their advocacy of the anational corporation. The hallmark of an anational corporation, of course, is its lack of identity with, or allegiance to, any individual country, i.e., its nationlessness. A truly anational corporation would not be considered to be American, or British, or French—it would simply be a corporation. The following series of comments reveals vividly the psychological state of mind of many corporate leaders concerning the idea of nationless economic enterprises.

• Robert Stevens, Executive Vice-President, International Operations, Ford Motor Company:

> It is our goal to be in every single country there is, Iron Curtain countries, Russia, China. We at Ford Motor Company look at a world map without any boundaries. *We don't consider ourselves basically an American company.* We are a multinational company. And when we approach a

government that doesn't like the U.S., we always say, "Who do you like? Britain? Germany? We carry a lot of flags. We export from every country."[16] (emphasis added)

In 1977, the foreign operations accounted for 42.1 percent of Ford's profits, 29.4 percent of its sales, and 40.4 percent of its assets.

• W. J. Barnholdt, Vice-President, Caterpillar Tractor Company:

Caterpillar is owned by approximately 48,000 shareholders, and our stock is traded on exchanges in the United States, France, England, Scotland, West Germany, Switzerland, and Belgium. We have 65,000 employees, 22 percent of whom work abroad. We are a multinational company treating foreign operators as a co-equal with domestic in both structure and policy, willing to allocate resources without regard to national frontiers.

We will one day become a trans-national company—a multinational business managed and owned by people of different nationalities—through current programs aimed at developing top managers of different national origins and greater ownership by investors outside the U.S., our views as to transportation, markets and products are worldwide. For example, *there is no U.S.-made Caterpillar tractor. A Caterpillar product— wherever it is built—is just that—a Caterpillar product. . . .*[17] (emphasis added)

In 1977, foreign operations accounted for 50.7 percent of Caterpillar's sales. Similar figures for its profits and assets were not available.

• Dr. Antonie Knopper, President, Merck and Company, defines the modern corporation as:

. . . an enterprise that sees the world or a goodly portion of it as its market and acts to make the most of its opportunities on a supra-national basis.[18]

In 1977, foreign operations accounted for 29.8 percent of Merck and Company's profits, 44.9 percent of its sales, and 39.3 percent of its assets.

• Dr. Max Gloor, member of the Board of Directors of the Swiss-based firm, Nestle Alimentana:

We cannot be considered either as pure Swiss, or as purely multinational, i.e., belonging to the world at large, if such a thing does exist at all. We are probably something in between, a breed on our own. *In one word, we have the particular Nestle Citizenship.*[19] (emphasis added)

• The Chairman of Ronson Corporation's British subsidiary (1973) defined the duty of a corporate executive as follows:

> He must set aside any nationalistic attitude and appreciate that in the last resort his loyalty must be to the shareholders of the parent company and he must protect their interest even if it might appear that it is not perhaps in the national interest of the country in which he is operating. Apparent conflicts may occur in such matters as the transfer of funds at a period of national crisis, a transfer of production from one susidiary to another, or a transfer of export business.[20]

• A Union Carbide spokesman stated:

> It is not proper for an international corporation to put the welfare of any country in which it does business above that of any other.[21]

In 1977, foreign operations accounted for 20.6 percent of Union Carbide's profits, 31.9 percent of its sales, and 34.6 percent of its assets.

Clearly, then, many corporate leaders, both American and foreign and within and without of the American economy's Centralized Private Sector Planning sphere, are remarkably unequivocal, exact, and candid in setting forth the following propositions:

• The nation-state, as an institution, has become an anachronism and an impediment to worldwide economic progress.

• Corporate leaders must not consider their corporations as belonging to, being part of, or owing allegiance to the nation-state in which they are legally chartered, or to any other nation.

• The anational corporation is an institution whose star is in the ascendant.

• And, as always in human affairs, with the birth of a new social order and the demise of the old, anxiety, turmoil, and perhaps even open conflict are simply ingredients to be recognized and dealt with.

It would be a mistake and an oversimplification, however, to characterize the emergence of the anational economic enterprise simply in terms of a conflict between itself and the nation-state. To properly appreciate the totality of implications inherent in this struggle, one must also recognize its ideological dimensions.

The East-West conflict

Post–World War II: a brief historical perspective

Unfortunately, in attempting to win the hearts and minds of the world's people, the overwhelming majority of existing elites and would-be future elites *profess* to have pledged their lives and fortunes to the economic philosophies of either socialism or capitalism. In turn, the most powerful extant institution representing the socialist viewpoint is, unquestionably, Russia's Communist Party (RCP); its capitalist counterpart is, just as unquestionably, the Central Planning Core (CPC). Both institutions reign supreme over vast geographical areas. In addition, the CPC and the RCP quite often appear to base their claims of moral legitimacy on a purely materialist philosophy; that is, both institutions claim to possess superior organizational skills for producing and distributing goods and services. Each, in turn, claims to be more capable, therefore, not only of eliminating hunger in the world, but also of being able to sustain a rising standard of living for the world's people.

The struggle between these two institutions has been going on since the close of World War II. The initial battleground was Europe. Recent decades, however, have witnessed a shift to the less developed nations, often referred to as the Third World. Table 34 provides vivid testimony to the truly gargantuan nature of the task of raising the standard of living of the Third World's people to that which now exists in Europe, the USSR, Japan, and North America. For instance, the economic enterprises of Europe, the USSR, Japan, and North America account for approximately 80.9 percent of the world's GNP (excluding Oceania and Indonesia), but these same geographic areas account for only around 28.1 percent of the world's total population. Conversely, Third World countries account for 71.9 percent of the world's population but only 19.1 percent of the world's total GNP.*

---

*A word of caution about these statistics is in order, though. One cannot assume, for example, that the statistics in Table 34 can be interpreted as meaning that North America (Canada and the U.S.) represents 6.0 percent of the world's population and *consumes* 27.3 percent of the world's output of goods and services. This is primarily because of the limitations inherent in the statistical technique employed in making GNP comparisons. For example, the data in Table 34 were generated by using official international exchange rates to convert the national currencies of other

Table 34

Gross National Product (GNP), Gross National Product per Capita, and Population, for Selected Areas, (1977)

Region or country[1]	GNP		GNP per capita	Population	
	U.S. dollars (million)	Percentage of total		Mid-1977 (million)	Percentage of total
North America	2,091	27.3	8,710	240	6.0
Japan	737	9.6	6,510	113	2.8
Europe	2,504	32.7	4,810	521	12.9
USSR	861	11.3	3,330	259	6.4
Middle East	130	1.7	2,950	44	1.1
South America	308	4.0	1,360	227	5.6
Central America[2]	129	1.7	1,120	115	2.9
Africa	209	2.7	490	426	10.6
Asia	689	9.0	330	2,080	51.7
TOTAL	7,658	100.0		4,025	100.0

Source: The World Bank's 1979 World Bank Atlas.

[1]Excludes Oceania.

[2]Includes Mexico.

As mentioned above, both the socialists and the capitalists profess to have a more efficient and humane economic organizational system for dealing with the Third World's economic problems. The pros and cons of this worldwide (capitalist versus socialist) debate have traditionally been couched, as would be expected, in purely ideological terms. A brief review of some of the arguments set forth in this debate, especially since World War II, may prove instructive.

---

geographical areas into U.S. dollars. Yet, exchange rates are based only on the prices of internationally traded goods and services, and this presents problems. First, these prices may bear little resemblance to the prices of goods and services that are not involved in international trade. Second, the relative price differentials between prices in the agricultural and industrial sectors (wherein agricultural prices are always lower) are much more pronounced in the world's less developed areas than they are in the more industrialized regions. Third, agricultural products account for the bulk of the total output of many countries in the world's less developed areas. What this means in practical terms, then, is that using international exchange rates to convert the domestic currencies of other countries into U.S. dollars tends to exaggerate the real income differences between and among the nations of the world. Stated somewhat differently, this statistical procedure tends to undervalue the GNP statistics for the less developed countries. Nonetheless, these figures do represent a reasonably accurate picture of the vast differences in the standards of living between and among various geographical areas.

In the early 1950s, the Marxian socialist argument was that American corporations were interested only in obtaining the less developed world's raw materials for consumption in their American and European markets. The socialists claimed that, if corporations were genuinely interested in helping the people of the Third World, they would be earnestly attempting to industrialize these countries, rather than simply *exploiting* the Third World for its natural resources. By the 1960s, the number of manufacturing subsidiaries established by American corporations in the less developed countries had grown so rapidly that not even the most dogmatic ideologue could argue that American corporations were not contributing—certainly much more than the socialist camp—to the Third World's industrialization process. The socialist argument, of course, was still effective as an internal propaganda tool, but it was becoming much harder for Third World leaders to argue such a position with the leaders of the industrialized nations when both sides knew quite well that (1) the data proved conclusively otherwise, and (2) each side was aware of the data.

At this point, many of the Third World's leaders simply shifted the argument toward another Marxian socialist contention. The claim became that Third World workers were being savagely exploited by being paid extremely low wages. Once again, though, a quick glance at the wage scales in these countries revealed that, for the most part, workers in the American-owned facories enjoyed a much higher wage rate than that which prevailed in locally owned factories and, indeed, workers were experiencing a rise in their standard of living.

As if to prove the power of ideology over brute facts, the argument simply shifted ground once more. It was loudly proclaimed that the manipulative capitalist class was paying its workers higher wages so as to *buy out* the proletariat and, thereby, forestall the revolution.

By the mid 1960s, many of America's corporate and political leaders were quite conscious of the evolutionary aspects of the Marxian socialist arguments being used against them. Regardless of how their corporate institutions performed, they now understood that there would always be a readymade ideological counterpoint on which those who so desired, for whatever reason, could rely in attacking them and their institutions. In addition, they were also beginning to perceive an awareness among the Third World leaders that these ideological arguments were just that—ideological—and not very descriptive of their personal, or their country's, reality and experiences. In brief, in the middle 1960s, as an economic social philosophy, Marxian socialist ideas appealed to the hearts and minds of many Third World peoples just as the Divine Right of Kings and the suzerainty of the Pope had appeared compelling to European peoples in an earlier age. Furthermore, as long as this remained true, Marxian socialist ideas would be a powerful political force that could always be used to challenge the corporation's presence in the world's less developed countries. These types of experiences and considerations led many of the industrialized world's intellectual, political, and corporate leaders to begin formalizing an argument and building a consensus around the following key ideas:

1. The various elite groups in many Third World countries, while often relying on Marxian socialist concepts to attack "American corporate imperialism," were themselves *not* Marxian socialists.

2. The real source of tension between Third World elites and corporate elites was not because of ideological differences between capitalism and socialism but, rather, was because of—

a. the ideology of nationalism, and

b. the conflict between and among the various indigenous elite groups within the less developed countries which always accompanies the industrialization process (e.g., the conflict in Iran between the religious and political elites or the conflict in Afghanistan between the tribal chieftains and the central government's Marxian socialist political elites).

3. Eventually, most Third World elites (military, religious, capitalist, socialist, etc.) would be forced, however reluctantly, *to agree upon the necessity for industrialization*.

4. The nations of Western Europe and North America might, indeed, be entering a postindustrial era.

5. Therefore, the future growth and development of the corporate institution on a worldwide basis would depend on the CPC's ability to provide the leadership necessary to actually industrialize the Third World.

6. Finally, new types of economic institutions (i.e., supra- and transnational corporations), not identified with any particular nation-state, would be the most appropriate vehicles for, simultaneously—

a. industrializing the Third World, and

b. laying the foundations for the eventual triumph of the anational corporation.

While these ideas were being discussed and analyzed by a variety of groups in the United States, it was within the economy's CPSP sphere (or, more specifically, within the CPC) that a consensus was most nearly developed concerning the role to be played by corporations in the industrialization of the less developed countries of the world.

A new corporate and political strategy for the 1980s?

In the middle 1970s, based upon a recognition of the six principles mentioned above, many of the country's corporate and political leaders (with CPC members playing the key leadership role) developed a Third World economic strategy that might appropriately be called "aggressive benign neglect." The key to understanding the logic embedded in this strategy is to understand the interrelatedness of these six principles.

First, many of the country's political and corporate leaders became convinced that the industrialization process itself automatically generated tremendous anxiety and political turmoil, regardless of whether the process was guided by those who professed to be socialists or capitalists. Given this perspective, the causes of the present conflict in Afghanistan could quite logically be interpreted as an amalgamation of nationalistic beliefs, coupled with a desire to hold on to traditional values—values that seemingly were being eroded by the attempts of indigenous leaders to force rapid industrialization. Many of the "rebel" Afghan chieftains, for example, fiercely resented the attempts of the socialists in power in the central government to force women to learn to read and write, to collectivize agriculture, to introduce modern machinery, and to force nomadic tribesmen off their traditional tribal lands and into factories.

On the one hand, then, the conflict now occurring between the Russians and the Afghans probably has nothing to do with socialism, per se, but, rather, may be viewed as a fiercely independent people's resistance to industrialization. In short, the industrialization process necessarily sweeps away forever many of a people's values, life-styles, and institutions—values, life-styles, and institutions that people will oftimes fight and die to preserve.

On the other hand, it may be accurate to assume that, as the peoples of Third World countries become more conscious of and experienced with the socialist methods of achieving industrialization, socialist ideology will lose much of its appeal, its lustre, and its power as an idea. In other words, the elite socialist groups in countries such as Afghanistan will no longer be able to use socialism as an ideological organizing tool because the masses will equate and judge socialism on the basis of policies and actions of their socialist leaders. Thus, governmental policies and programs designed to encourage industrialization will, of necessity, also generate criticism and resentment toward the very idea of socialism itself.

Second, many of the country's political and corporate leaders also became convinced that the only viable method available for raising the standard of living in Third World countries was through massive industrialization.* Therefore:

• given the necessity for industrialization,

• the obvious strength of the Marxian socialists' ideology as an organizing tool in many of the less developed countries, and

• the social conflict seemingly inherent to the industrialization process,

it seemed logical to conclude that the most effective long-run strategy for combating the spread of Marxian socialism was not to continue to advocate and support armed intervention in these countries but, rather, to simply withdraw from the contest. *Withdrawal from the contest* was defined as a strong advocacy of a total cutoff of all types of technical and financial assistance from both the industrialized nations' political and their economic institutions. In other words, whenever socialists of either a left- or a right-wing persuasion become strong enough to force a revolutionary situation—as was the case recently, for instance, in Iran and in Nicaragua—the wise thing, in terms of the long run, is to withdraw from the contest in the short run.†

Stated somewhat differently, the logic of the aggressive benign neglect position becomes even clearer when one consciously compares America's experiences with China and Viet Nam. On the one hand, the Vietnamese were psychologically committed to nationalism and to

*It should be mentioned that environmentalists have raised serious questions about the necessity of the corporation's and/or the socialist's methods of massive industrialization. Indeed, many environmentalists see the use of *intermediate* and *soft path* technologies as being (a) less disruptive of traditional values, (b) inherently more decentralized and democratic, and (c) more environmentally sound. See, for example, Amory B. Lovins's *Soft Energy Paths: Toward a Durable Peace* (New York: Harper and Row, Publishers, 1977).

†In fact, the U.S. government did withdraw its support from both the Shah of Iran and Nicaragua's President Somoza, as the present political elites in both countries are aware. On the one hand, it should be added that, if the foreign policy actions of the Reagan administration match its foreign policy rhetoric, it would appear that the aggressive benign neglect strategy, at least on the part of the current government, is to be discarded. On the other hand, as has been the case with other presidents, President Reagan's rhetoric and symbolic acts may prove to be quite different from the administration's deeds. But more importantly, the evolution of the anational corporate institution is a long-run phenomena that should not be judged and/or evaluated solely on the basis of short-run tactics by a given administration.

Marxian socialism and proved willing to die by the tens of thousands. The socialists in China, on the other hand, are now asking the anational corporations to return to their country—after only thirty years. It would take a powerfully spellbinding performance to convince the Chinese people that Caterpillar Tractor's presence in China today reflects capitalistic imperialism. Nor would the Russian masses be easily convinced that the presence of Ford Motor Company, Pepsico, Inc., or the Chase Manhattan Bank in Mother Russia was the result of capitalistic enterprises' need for overseas markets. As all now know, both the USSR and China simply do not have the technological and administrative knowledge to create a standard of living for their people comparable to that in the West. In essence, then, if one is convinced that the methods of industrialization used by those who call themselves Marxian socialists will, in the long run, (a) fail and (b) generate worldwide resentment against Marxian socialist ideas, in the short run the best and perhaps only reasonable approach to both enhancing one's long-run profits and effectively defanging the Marxian socialist ideology as a worldwide political force is not to oppose (at least not to oppose with direct military intervention) those who prove capable of mobilizing the masses on the basis of Marxian socialist principles.

Finally, concerning the sixth principle cited above, if corporations are successful in creating an anational image, they will also have taken a significant step toward solving their "religion of nationalism" problem. In fact, though, an anational image may be harder to create than the reality. Indeed, from the point of view of the reality quotient, the actions of many American-based corporations can be explained only if one accepts that they *do not* believe themselves to be part of, or owe allegiance to, any particular geographical area. As has been stated repeatedly in this study, economic reality always changes much faster than our economic beliefs about and/or images of that reality. A brief glance at the worldwide production and investment activities of the automobile industry may prove instructive concerning this point.

The automobile industry: an anational institution in the process of being created?

In 1980, while the Big Three automobile companies were closing manufacturing facilities in the United States (some never to be reopened),*

---

*In early 1980, for example, Ford Motor Company permanently shut down manufacturing facilities in Mahway, New Jersey; Los Angeles, California; and Dearborn, Michigan.

they were simultaneously building facilities in Mexico. Specifically, GM, Ford, and Chrysler were constructing plants, located just outside of Mexico City, capable of producing 500,000; 400,000; and 200,000 automobile engines per year, respectively. In turn, Mexico's political and business leaders were perfectly aware of the fact that the Big Three automobile companies were simultaneously closing plants in the United States while building plants in Mexico, laying off workers in Mahway, New Jersey, while hiring workers in Mexico City. Between 1980 and 1985, the total investments of the automobile companies—just in Mexico—are expected to be around $1 billion.

On a worldwide basis, the auto industry estimates that it will invest approximately $80 billion from 1980 through 1990. This rather massive worldwide investment program is being undertaken in order for the auto companies to produce what they are calling the new "world car"—not a Japanese car, not a German car, not an American car, but a "world car." The component parts of this new world car will be manufactured in all parts of the planet. Ford's first such vehicles, known as the Mercury Lynx and the Ford Escort, will be assembled simultaneously in the United States, Britain, and West Germany from component parts manufactured in a dozen countries—engines from Mexico, rear brakes from Brazil, transaxles from Japan, cylinder heads from Italy, and so on.

The Ford Fiesta (Ford's initial experiment with the world car) was, and still is, assembled using engine blocks from England and Spain, body panels from West Germany, carburetors from Northern Ireland, wheels from Belgium, and gearboxes, transmissions, and axles from France. GM's version of the new world car—its "J" car—will have its engines manufactured simultaneously in Brazil, Australia, Japan, and West Germany. Ford Motor Company's board chairman, Philip Caldwell, characterized the world car as " . . . the most massive and profound industrial revolution in peacetime history. . . ." As per the sentiments expressed in a Textron Corporation's advertisement about their products, the world car may, in fact, be best described as "Made in the World by People."

The creation of an authentic "world car," a car manufactured and sold in all parts of the planet, is a significant step by American corporations in their attempt to create both the reality and the image of an economic institution viewed both domestically and internationally as an authentic anational enterprise.

The massive relocation of the auto industries' manufacturing facilities on a global scale (as well as those of many other industries) will—

especially in the short run—undoubtedly create resentment on the part of American workers. Indeed, it would appear that the ingredients for a populist-style political backlash are becoming more visible as American workers see more and more corporations creating job opportunities in other countries while simultaneously closing plants in America. Nonetheless, many of the country's corporate leaders seem convinced that:

• nothing short of this type of industrial revolution will allow their economic institutions to attain an anational image among the world's people;

• it is, perhaps, true that Americans are psychologically ready to begin deemphasizing material gain; and

• any criticism from American workers which began to take on serious political implications would probably tend to center on—

    a. the environment and/or zero economic growth movements, and

    b. on the government, of course.

The environmentalist argument is as follows. If those carrying the environmental and zero growth banners can convince Americans to conserve and do with less, or at least accept a lower growth rate in their living standards, the corporate enterprise will be freer to use its limited capital to expand in those areas of the world where people are not yet more concerned with the environment or with how they feel psychologically than with material comforts. GM's past board chairman, Thomas Murphy, stated the practical dimensions of these two issues: (1) the deemphasizing of material gain by Americans—perhaps even a zero growth American gross domestic product, and (2) the tremendous potential for economic growth for the automobile industry in the less developed countries, as follows:

> The ownership statistics show we have in the United States one car for about every 2.3 people, I believe it is. In some of these countries overseas it is one for every 200 and one for every 400, which gives you some idea of the dimension. So in these growing countries, developing countries, where population is so great, there would be a great opportunity for growth and we think that growth opportunity is there. It will take jobs, too, so that to that degree they are concerned about getting those jobs.[22]

Economist Irving Friedman, past senior vice-president for international relations at Citibank, stated the case in these terms:

> Look, if you tell a country where the per capita income is one-fifth that of the U.S., or even less, that it should tighten its belt, you'll lose credibility.

These countries know the history of the U.S. They know we did not grow by sustained poverty, that we grew by sustained prosperity. We had depressions and financial crises *but until recently the incentive was to produce efficiently and to produce abundantly.* The American people shared in that output and the developing countries want to do the same.[23] (emphasis added)

On the one hand, within limits, of course, and gradually over a period of time, GM, Ford, and Chrysler may be quite willing to cut back on or maintain the present levels of production and sales of motor vehicles in the American geographical area. On the other hand, they have *no* intention of cutting back on their global production and sales of motor vehicles. In planetary terms, the CPC views the automobile industry as one of its major growth institutions. It may surprise the reader to learn that, as early as 1970, 29.2 percent of the automobiles bought in Europe were manufactured by GM (11.1 percent), Ford (11.6 percent), and Chrysler (6.5 percent). Of course, these units were manufactured primarily in European-based subsidiaries by European workers. As of 1980, GM and Ford produced 7.1 and 4.3 million cars and trucks, respectively, with 2.1 and 2.3 million units, respectively, being produced in foreign countries. (See Table 35 for a more detailed geographic and country-by-country breakdown of GM's and Ford's foreign assembly production facilities as of 1981.)

Nonetheless, in the closing decades of this century, many corporate leaders envision their greatest potential for continued expansion and growth as residing within Third World countries. From their standpoint, the growth potential that would accompany the *actual industrialization* of Third World countries would by far—especially in the long run—offset any economic reversals they might experience because of a change in the traditional American attitudes " . . . to produce efficiently and to produce abundantly." In addition, as the living standards in these countries begin to rise and a middle class begins to emerge, political instability (especially that instigated by the Left and aimed primarily at corporations) may also become less of a problem. Thus, a zero growth economy in the United States, from the perspective of many corporate leaders, most certainly is *not* to be equated with a zero growth state of affairs for the anational corporations.

At this point, it should probably be stated explicitly that a natural resource base, capable of sustaining continued economic growth on a global basis, does exist. Corporate leaders know quite well that the world is *not even remotely* nearing resource exhaustion. Certainly,

Table 35

Ford and GM Assembly Plants (passenger cars, commercial vehicles, light trucks and buses) in Selected Foreign Countries and the Percentage of Total Production Accounted for (1981)

Geographic area/country	Production		Country total	Ford and GM as a percentage of total
	Ford	GM		
Europe				
Germany, West	486,917	816,648	3,897,007	33.5
Belgium	247,598	306,449	894,160	62.0
Great Britain	427,495	118,243	1,184,205	46.1
Spain	253,751	0	987,474	25.7
Turkey	8,486	0	72,659	11.7
Oceania				
Australia	124,000	111,000	274,000	85.8
New Zealand	0	0	0	0
Western hemisphere				
Argentina	75,566	0	172,350	43.8
Brazil	125,843	155,539	779,836	36.1
Canada	354,804	756,087	1,322,780	84.0
Chili	0	9,080	29,259	31.0
Mexico	111,695	67,236	597,118	30.0
Venezuela	44,486	69,053	154,471	73.5
SUBTOTAL	2,260,641	2,409,335	10,365,319	45.1
U.S. domestic production	1,937,572	4,079,291		

Source: World Motor Vehicle Data (Detroit: Motor Vehicle Manufacturer Association of the United States Inc., 1982), various pages.

petroleum spokesmen, for example, have never claimed that the world was running out of fossil fuels or that the technological ability for turning these raw materials into energy was lacking. Nonetheless, if the masses in the United States were to willingly adopt, or passively accept, the zero growth ethic, it would certainly make the global reallocation of manufacturing facilities much easier.*

On the other hand, if there is a serious political backlash against the "accept less" philosophy as automobile, steel, and mining facilities cut back production and/or shut down and the losses consequently cause dramatic changes in the life-styles of the American working class, most corporate leaders assume that their institutions will not be the primary foci of resentment because they themselves have frequently and force-fully spoken out in public against the zero growth position. Quite clearly, it has been the environmentalists—a group composed primarily of the children of the middle and upper-middle classes—who have taken the lead in criticizing Americans for their so-called selfish mate-rialism and for America's *supposed* monopolization of the world's ever scarcer resources. Therefore, in the judgment of the country's corpo-rate leaders, it is on the environmental movement, as well as on legisla-tors and government bureaucrats sympathetic to environmental issues, that the brunt of any political backlash on the part of the working class will be focused. In addition, the government, as an institution, will no doubt also be a focal point of resentment, as is usually the case when the country experiences economic adversity.

In essence, those who are striving mightily to create a new world order—a new world order wherein the anational corporation will be the dominant social institution—are also striving to continually modify old strategies and tactics (or completely change directions) when events so dictate, so as to maximize their chances of turning their opponents' ideas (e.g., Marxian-socialism, nationalism, zero economic growth, etc.) to their own benefit. Of course, if the country's business commu-nity (primarily under the leadership of the CPC) were to lose its will, technical ability, and/or raw power to manipulate—or at least to attempt to manipulate—its opponents and their ideas in this manner, the CPC would, at that point, simply cease to be *the* establishment.

Before concluding this chapter, we should state explicitly that the methods being followed by the anational corporations in establishing manufacturing facilities in Third World countries are not at all similar to the methods employed in industrializing the United States. For instance, an industrial base is *not* being created which would allow a country to nationalize the properties located on its soil of, say, the automobile industry, and then proceed to manufacture cars themselves.

---

*While it still may be too early to judge with any degree of accuracy, the results of the 1980, 1982, and 1984 general elections may be an indication that American workers do not intend to passively accept a zero growth economy.

As noted above, many of the component parts that make up an auto-mobile—engines, wheels, rear axles, carburetors, etc.—are each being manufactured in a different country. By employing this type of "decen-tralized development" in terms of siting manufacturing facilities, the anationals are simultaneously attempting—

• to create an economic interdependency between many different nation-states; that is, for example, if the world car is popular among the world's consumers, wages, employment, taxes, and so on in those countries that manufacture the various component parts will go up simultaneously as more of these cars are produced and sold;

• to insure that no one country can take control of the production of automobiles by nationalizing those manufacturing facilities located on its soil; and, therefore,

• to also insure that centralized control over the entire globalized production process remains in their hands.

Obviously, without being totally facile, it would be difficult to pre-dict whether the "divine right of capital" will eventually take its place in the sun among our species' other transcendent belief systems. It is quite possible that other institutional ideas and forces, such as national-ism and/or socialism, will prove indomitable. Perhaps the species will even evolve other new ideas and institutions. For instance, the growth and success of the European Economic Community (EEC) as an inte-grated economic and political institution may portend a world divided into a series of regional economic and political groupings. These re-gional groupings would transcend the nation-states as they now exist but would fall short of a truly worldwide social order as envisioned by proponents of the anational corporation. While predicting the future is always hazardous, of two things the species can be relatively certain. First, the struggle among the world's elites (religious, political, eco-nomic, etc.) for the hearts and minds of the nameless masses will not only continue but will grow increasingly more hazardous as the world becomes more and more interdependent. Second, neither the Afghan nomad, the Youngstown steelworker, nor the Argentinian gaucho will fully understand the social forces that are fiercely in pursuit of his soul.

In conclusion, let it be noted that much more has been left unsaid about the anational corporation than has been explicitly stated. None-theless, it is hoped—however abbreviated these few comments may be—that the reader's interest will have been heightened to the point where additional and more thorough studies will be undertaken. For, indeed, the triumph of a laissez-faire economic philosophy on a global basis, would most certainly be as profound an event for the human species and the planet upon which it lives as were the triumphs of Christianity, the nation-state, or the Industrial Revolution.

Notes

1. Norman O. Brown, *Life Against Death* (Middletown, Conn.: Wesleyan University Press, 1970), p. ix.

2. U. S. Congress, Senate, Hearings before the Subcommittee on International Trade of the Committee on Finance, *Multinational Corporations*, 93rd Congress, 1st Sess., 1973, p. 454.

3. Adolf A. Berle and Gardiner C. Means, *The Modern Corporation and Private Property*, revised ed. (New York: Harcourt, Brace and World, Inc., 1967), p. 313.

4. Adolf A. Berle, *The 20th Century Capitalist Revolution* (New York: Harcourt, Brace and Company, 1954), p. 144.

5. U.S. Congress, Senate, *Multinational Corporations*, pp. 225–227.

6. Ibid., p. 225.

7. Ibid., p. 115.

8. Ibid., p. 296.

9. Ibid.

10. C. L. Sulzberger, "New World of Business," *New York Times*, 1 November 1972, p. 45.

11. Richard J. Barnet, Ronald E. Muller, and Joseph Collins, "Global Corporations, Their Quest for Legitimacy," in *Exploring Contradictions*, ed. by Philip Brenner, Robert Borosage, and Bethany Weidner (New York: David McKay Company, Inc., 1974), p. 67.

12. Sidney E. Rolfe, "The International Corporation in Perspective," in *The Multinational Corporation in the World Economy*, ed. by Sidney E. Rolfe and Walter Damm (New York: Praeger Publishers, 1970), p. 32.

13. "U.S. Bankers Survey a Multinational Horizon," *New York Times*, 26 April 1970, p. 1.

14. U.S. Congress, Senate, *Multinational Corporations*, p. 450.

15. Jacques G. Maisonrouge, "Address to the American Foreign Service Association," Washington, D.C., 29 May 1969.

16. U.S. Congress, Senate, *Multinational Corporations*, p. 451.

17. Ibid.

18. Ibid., p. 450.

19. Ibid., p. 452.

20. Ibid.

21. Barnet, Muller, and Collins, "Global Corporations, Their Quest for Legitimacy," p. 58.

22. U.S. Congress, Senate, *Multinational Corporations*, p. 119.

23. Thomas C. O'Donnell, "A Worldwide Disaster," *Forbes*, 29 September 1980, p. 50.

Epilogue

What's To Be Done: The Starting Point

> *The persistence of a way of thinking which somehow fails to take account of what are proving to be the basic realities of modern economic life is itself one of the great economic mysteries of our civilization.*[1]
>
> C. E. Ayres

> *So Rome clung to its ancient political and religious forms long after they had lost their meaning, with a ritualistic reverence that disciplined and dignified its national life and that sapped its resourcefulness. While it cultivated the ideal of universal reason it remained devoted to a non-rational conservatism, which conserved irrational institutions.*[2]
>
> Herbert J. Muller

Quite frequently, authors (especially if their work has an iconoclastic bent) are reminded by their peers of the widely accepted belief in the author's responsibility to provide the community with possible solutions and/or courses of action for dealing with the problems and concerns addressed in the text. My rejoinder to this argument is contained in my remarks at the very beginning of this book:

> The simple fact is, though, that, given the dichotomy between our current beliefs and ideas about economics and power, and the realities of economics and power in our society, there is no viable solution to stagflation. Existing economic theories (neoclassical, Keynesian, Marxist, or the so-called and currently fashionable supply-side economics) concerning the causes of inflation, unemployment, pollution, a carcinogenic food supply, maldistribution of income, inadequate health care for the poor, retarded economic growth, and so on, are woefully devoid of adequate insight or understanding of the economy's dominant structural and functional characteristics. Of course, theories based on false assumptions, however rational and/or logical, cannot provide a foundation for effective and

responsible private or public policy decision making. Let there be no mistake. Orthodox economic theories and beliefs, whether of the left or of the right, have become part of the problem, rather than helping organize our thoughts and discussions so as to provide realistic and workable solutions to our problems.

If I am correct in asserting that the elimination of the dichotomy between our currently held economic beliefs and economic reality is a *necessary precondition* that must be met before viable solutions to our increasingly serious economic maladies can be found, then the starting point for developing such solutions is quite clear. In brief, it is long past time for the various leadership groups in our country to stop all the self-serving ideological prattling about the welfare state, socialism, and/or capitalism and, instead, take a long, hard look at the economy's dominant structural and functional characteristics. If this is not done, the nation's economic problems will, no doubt, become increasingly disruptive of society's basic social fabric. Fundamental reforms are now absolutely essential. Fundamental reforms that are not soundly based on the economy's structural and functional realities, however, no matter how well-intentioned the reformers may be, will simply not work.

Finally, it is the firm and unequivocal belief of this writer that three of the most fundamental lessons to be learned from history are—

• that evolutionary economic reform predicated on real world and/or concrete economic realities has in the past and can in the future lead to a better world for all;

• that reforms predicated on ideological world views inevitably lead to either a leftist or rightist totalitarian type of society; and

• that a society which clings to outmoded "political and religious forms" and/or also clings to a "non-rational conservatism" will not long endure as a vibrant and dynamic society.

Notes

1. C. E. Ayres, *The Theory of Economic Progress* (Chapel Hill: University of North Carolina Press, 1944), p. 7.

2. Herbert J. Muller, *The Uses of the Past* (New York: Oxford University Press, 1952), p. 222.

Appendix

Data Sources—
Central Planning Tableau

Banking:

The Chase Manhattan Bank, N.A.
Morgan Guaranty Trust Company of New York
Continental Illinois National Bank and Trust Company of Chicago
The First National Bank of Chicago
Citibank, New York

Trust Department stockholdings for the above banks were obtained from the respective banks' "Annual Report of Equity Holdings as of December 31, 1977," pursuant to Disclosure Report 9–102, Regulation 9. Until 1981, each federally chartered bank was required by Regulation 9 to submit an Annual Report on equity holdings to the Deputy Comptroller of the Currency for Trust, Administrator of National Banks, Washington, D.C. 20219. The individual bank reports for the institutions listed above were obtained directly from the office of the Deputy Comptroller of the Currency. As of this writing, reports on bank equity stock holding data are required by the Securities and Exchange Commission, pursuant to Section 13 (f) of the Securities Exchange Act of 1934 and Rules Thereunder. These latter reports are usually referred to as the 13 (f) equity reports and may be obtained directly from the Securities and Exchange Commission.

Chemical Bank—"1977 Report of the Trust and Investment Bank," prepared by Trust and Investors Bank, 277 Park Avenue, New York, New York 10017.

Manufacturers Hanover Trust Company—"Report of the Trust Division, 1977," prepared by Trust Division, 600 Fifth Avenue, New York, New York 10020.

Insurance:

Metropolitan Life Insurance Company—"Schedule of Investments, December 31, 1977," prepared by Metropolitan Life Insurance Company, 1 Madison Avenue, New York, New York, 10010.

New York Life—"Schedule of Investments, December 31, 1977," prepared by Investment Department, 51 Madison Avenue, New York, New York 10010.

Prudential—"Schedule of Securities, December 31, 1977," prepared by Investment Department, Prudential Plaza, Newark, New Jersey 07101.

The Equitable Life Assurance Society of the United States—"Portfolio of Investments 1977," prepared by Securities Operation Area, 1285 Avenue of the Americas, New York, New York 10019.

Diversified financial institution:

The Continental Corporation—"1977 Annual Report," prepared by the Continental Corporation, 80 Maiden Lane, New York, New York 10038.

Core families:

Official Summary of Security Transactions and Holdings, prepared quarterly by the United States Securities and Exchange Commission, Washington, D.C., various years 1970–1977.

"Rockefeller Details Securities Holdings Totaling over 168.8 Million at Hearings," *Wall Street Journal*, Tuesday, September 24, 1974, p. 16.

"Five Tables on Investments by Family," *New York Times*, December 4, 1974, p. 29.

DEBT HOLDINGS

Banking:

Bank debt holdings were not available except for the air transportation industry. Data for the air transport companies were taken from "Air Carrier Indebtedness (Long and Short Term Debt) by Major Holders as of December 31, 1977 ($000)," prepared by Financial Analysis and Cost Division, Bureau of Accounts and Statistics, Civil Aeronautics Board, Washington, D.C.

Insurance:

From same source as Equity Stock Holding data.

Diversified financial institution:

None available, except as noted in section on banking immediately above.

DIRECTORS, TRUSTEES, TRANSFER AGENTS, AND REGISTRARS

Banking:

Moody's Bank and Financial Manual, 1978.

Insurance:

Moody's Bank and Financial Manual, 1978.

Industrial:

Moody's Industrial Manual, 1978.

Transportation:

Moody's Transportation Manual, 1978.

Public utilities:

Moody's Public Utilities Manual, 1978.

TRUST ASSETS

Banking:

"Trust Assets of Insured Commercial Banks—1977," prepared by Federal Deposit Insurance Corporation, Washington, D.C. 20249.

SALES, ASSETS, EMPLOYEES, AND RANKINGS

Industrials:

"The Fortune Directory of the 500 Largest U.S. Industrial Corporations," *Fortune,* May 8, 1978, pp. 238–265.

Banking, insurance, transportation, retailing, utilities, and diversified financial company(ies):

"The Fortune Directory," *Fortune,* July 17, 1978, pp. 114–128.

FOREIGN SALES ASSETS AND PROFITS

Business International Weekly Report to Managers of World Wide Operation, published by Business International Corporation, One Dag Hammarskjold Plaza, New York, New York 10017. *Weekly Reports* dated August 4, 1978; August 11, 1978; August 25, 1978; September 8, 1978; September 13, 1978; and September 29, 1978.

Glossary

Glossary of frequently used acronyms and symbols as well as the various types of interlocking linkages between and among corporations:

Acronyms

BOD	Board of Directors
CPC	Central Planning Core
CPSP	Centralized Private Sector Planning
CPT	Central Planning Tableau
DPSP	Decentralized Private Sector Planning
II	Institutional Interlock
III	Indirect Institutional Interlock
IDI	Indirect Directorship Interlock

Interlocking linkages

Indirect BOD INTRAlock—non-CPC companies within the same industry that are linked through a third company. The third company may or may not be a CPC company:

Automobile industry

1. General Motors—"X" is a director on GM's BOD
2. Ford Motor Company—"Y" is a director on Ford's BOD
3. Exxon—Both "X" and "Y" are directors on Exxon's BOD

Therefore, GM and Ford have an Indirect BOD INTRAlock via Exxon.

Indirect BOD INTERlock—non-CPC companies in different industries that are linked through a third company. The third company may or may not be a CPC company.

Automobile and iron and steel industries

1. General Motors—"N" is a director on GM's BOD
2. United States Steel—"O" is a director on USS's BOD
3. Citicorp—"N" and "O" are both on Citicorp's BOD

Therefore, the automobile industry (GM) and the iron and steel industry (USS) have an Indirect BOD INTERlock via Citicorp.

Indirect Directorship Interlock (IDI)—In this study the IDI refers solely to linkages that involve one or more CPC corporations.

Example one

1. Citicorp—"A" and "B" are on citicorp's BOD
2. General Motors—"C" and "D" are on GM's BOD
3. Xerox—"A", "B", "C", and "D" are directors on Xerox's BOD

Therefore, GM and Citicorp have four IDI's via Xerox.

Example two

1. Citicorp—"S" and "T" are on Citicorp's BOD
2. Chemical Bank—"M" and "F" are on Chemical's BOD
3. General Motors—"S," "T," and "M," and "F" are on GM's BOD.

Therefore, Citicorp and Chemical have four IDI's via General Motors.

Indirect Institutional Interlock (III)—refers to the number of institutions in which two or more companies/corporations have established IDI's; e.g., in the illustration immediately above Citicorp and Chemical have established *one* III through General Motors.

Institutional Interlock (II)—refers *only* to CPC institutions that have personnel linkages that are *not* of the BOD type; e.g., an individual may be a BOD member for one CPC institution and also be on another CPC institution's International Advisory Committee.

Symbols

D	An interlock between and/or among the BOD's of various companies.
O	An interlock between and/or among the BOD's of various companies involving a senior officer(s) but not a chief executive officer(s).
*	An interlock between and/or among the BOD's of various companies involving a chief executive officer(s).
A	An interlock between and/or among various companies involving corporate officials who are not BOD members.
F	An interlock between and/or among various companies affected via relatives, e.g., a father sitting on the board of company A, while the son sits on the board of company B.
2A, 3F, or 3D	Signifies the actual number of whatever type of interlock is indicated

Index

225